The EU Constitution in Time of War

The EU Constitution in Time of War

Legal Responses to Russia's Aggression Against Ukraine

FEDERICO FABBRINI

Great Clarendon Street, Oxford, OX2 6DP,
United Kingdom

Oxford University Press is a department of the University of Oxford.
It furthers the University's objective of excellence in research, scholarship,
and education by publishing worldwide. Oxford is a registered trade mark of
Oxford University Press in the UK and in certain other countries

© Federico Fabbrini 2025

The moral rights of the author have been asserted

All rights reserved. No part of this publication may be reproduced, stored in a retrieval system, transmitted, used for text and data mining, or used for training artificial intelligence, in any form or by any means, without the prior permission in writing of Oxford University Press, or as expressly permitted by law, by licence or under terms agreed with the appropriate reprographics rights organization. Enquiries concerning reproduction outside the scope of the above should be sent to the Rights Department, Oxford University Press, at the address above.

You must not circulate this work in any other form
and you must impose this same condition on any acquirer

Public sector information reproduced under Open Government Licence v3.0
(https://www.nationalarchives.gov.uk/doc/open-government-licence)

Published in the United States of America by Oxford University Press
198 Madison Avenue, New York, NY 10016, United States of America

British Library Cataloguing in Publication Data
Data available

Library of Congress Control Number: 2024952163

ISBN 978-0-19-896348-6

DOI: 10.1093/oso/9780198963486.001.0001

Printed and bound by
CPI Group (UK) Ltd, Croydon, CR0 4YY

The manufacturer's authorised representative in the EU for product safety is Oxford University Press España S.A. of El Parque Empresarial San Fernando de Henares, Avenida de Castilla, 2 – 28830 Madrid (www.oup.es/en or product.safety@oup.com). OUP España S.A. also acts as importer into
Spain of products made by the manufacturer.

Ciao Seba!

Acknowledgements

I started conceiving and drafting this book in the academic year 2022/2023, when I was fortunate to spend a sabbatical at Princeton University School of Public & International Affairs and University Centre for Human Values as a Fellow in Law, Ethics, and Public Policy. In 2023 and 2024 I continued working on this manuscript from my Chair in Law at Dublin City University (DCU) School of Law & Government, while occasionally travelling to the European University Institute (EUI), first as a Fernand Braudel Fellow at its Law Department and then as a visiting fellow at the Robert Schuman Centre for Advanced Studies. I had the opportunity to present parts of this manuscript, or earlier drafts thereof, at several conferences and seminars hosted at a number of institutions, including among others the University of California Berkeley Law School, the College of Europe Legal Studies Department, Columbia Law School, the EUI School of Transnational Governance, Harvard University Center for European Studies, the Haute Ecole de Commerce in Paris, Humboldt University Berlin, Princeton University, and the University of Virginia Law School.

I also want to acknowledge that the book builds on several articles I previously published on the EU's responses to the war in Ukraine. In particular, parts of Chapter 2 appeared as 'European Defence Union ASAP: The Act in Support of Ammunitions Production and the development of EU Defence Capabilities in Response to the War in Ukraine' (2024) 29 *European Foreign Affairs Review* 67. Chapter 3 appeared in an earlier version as 'Funding the War in Ukraine' (2023) 11 *Politics and Governance* 52, and in a shorter version as 'From the Pandemic to the War: The EU Fiscal Response to Russia's Aggression of Ukraine, the Legacy of NGEU, and the Challenge "To Promote the General Welfare"' (2024) 118 *American Journal of International Law* 177. Furthermore, an earlier version of Chapter 4 is '"To Establish Justice": The EU Response to the War in Ukraine in the Field of Justice and Home Affairs' (2024) 49 *European Law Review* 359. A longer version of Chapter 5 appeared as 'The EU's Response to the War-Induced Energy Crisis: Legal and Budgetary Issues to "Insure Domestic Tranquility"' (2024) 51 *Legal Issues of Economic Integration* 349. Finally, some parts of Chapter 6 appeared as 'EU-UK Relations after the War in Ukraine: Options to Re-Engage Post-Brexit' (2024) 48 *West European Politics* 1.

I would like to thank Oxford University Press for agreeing to publish my 10th book with them in 10 years. I also wish to thank my team, including my doctoral students, at the DCU Brexit Institute—and now the recently established Dublin European Law Institute—for discussions and exchanges on the topics of this work.

Finally, I wish to thank my home institution for all the support, and especially the Faculty of Humanities and Social Science for funding through its 2024 book publication scheme.

* * *

This book is dedicated to the loving memory of my brother Sebastiano, who most dramatically and totally unexpectedly took his life in June 2024. Sebastiano was a beautiful, bright man, with a unique sensibility and kindness. He also had manifold intellectual interests—ranging from the history of architecture, on which he held a PhD from the University of California Los Angeles and an Assistant Professorship at IUAV University in Venice, to European integration, on which he had been carrying out some groundbreaking work, funded by the Jean Monnet programme, studying the physical architecture of the EU buildings. Sebastiano was my only brother, and we were incredibly close. In 34 years together we had done so many things—especially all sorts of sports, which was our common passion. So his self-inflicted death, worsened by the traumatic fact that it fell on me to find him lifeless, has left an infinite sorrow and profound grief ever since. This personal tragedy has also affected the writing of this book, which was nearing completion but still ongoing at the time of Sebastiano's death. While finishing this monograph has provided some solace from sadness, I am afraid my personal circumstances have impacted on the final outcome, which is certainly different from that which it would have been otherwise. Dedicating this book to my younger brother is the least I can do—but I am conscious it means very little.

Seba, life without you will never be the same. I will never know why you did it. But I love you, and I will forever miss you.

Contents

Table of Cases   xiii
List of Abbreviations   xv

1. Introduction   1
   1. Introduction   1
   2. The book's rationale   5
   3. The book's analytical frame   8
   4. The book's argument and structure   12
   5. Conclusion   20

2. To 'provide for the common defense': Developments in foreign affairs and defence   21
   1. Introduction   21
   2. The core measures   24
      - 2.1 Strategic posturing   24
      - 2.2 Military assistance and security commitments   25
      - 2.3 Defence production   28
   3. The consequences   33
   4. The challenges   39
      - 4.1 Decision-making   39
      - 4.2 Military capabilities   41
      - 4.3 Industrial capacity   43
   5. Conclusions   46

3. To 'promote the general welfare': Developments in fiscal and economic policy   48
   1. Introduction   48
   2. The core measures   51
      - 2.1 The European Peace Facility   51
      - 2.2 The macro-financial assistance instrument   54
      - 2.3 The Ukraine Facility   56
   3. The consequences   61
   4. The challenges   64
      - 4.1 Funding   64
      - 4.2 Decision-making   66
      - 4.3 Rule of law   69
   5. Conclusion   72

CONTENTS

4. To 'establish justice': Developments in justice and home affairs — 73
   1. Introduction — 73
   2. The core measures — 76
      2.1 Solidarity — 76
      2.2 Sanctions — 78
      2.3 Criminal investigations and compensation — 80
   3. The consequences — 84
   4. The challenges — 86
      4.1 Decision-making — 86
      4.2 Domestic legality — 88
      4.3 International legality — 92
   5. Conclusion — 97

5. To 'insure domestic tranquility': Developments in energy and industrial policy — 99
   1. Introduction — 99
   2. The core measures — 101
      2.1 Interventions in the energy market — 101
      2.2 Promotion of the green transition — 108
      2.3 Development of an industrial policy — 110
   3. The consequences — 113
   4. The challenges — 116
      4.1 Domestic legality — 116
      4.2 Level playing field — 119
      4.3 Funding — 121
   5. Conclusions — 123

6. To 'secure the blessings of liberty': Developments in enlargement and reforms — 125
   1. Introduction — 125
   2. The core measures — 127
      2.1 The relaunch of the enlargement process — 127
      2.2 The establishment of the European Political Community — 129
      2.3 The renewal of partnerships with the Council of Europe, NATO, and the United Kingdom — 131
   3. The consequences — 134
   4. The challenges — 137
      4.1 Candidate countries' preparation — 138
      4.2 EU preparation — 140
      4.3 The stagnation of constitutional reforms — 143
   5. Conclusion — 147

7. Conclusion 149
  1 Introduction 149
  2 The flexible constitution 149
  3 The inadequate constitution 155
  4 To 'form a more perfect union' 159
  5 Conclusion 163

Bibliography 165

Table of Cases

COUNCIL OF EUROPE—EUROPEAN CONVENTION ON HUMAN RIGHTS

European Court of Human Rights

Ukraine v Russia (re Crimea), Applications nos 20958/14 and 38334/18,
    Judgment of 25 June 2024 (GC) 1–2, 73–74

EUROPEAN UNION

General Court

Case T-306/01 *Ahmed Ali Yusuf and Al Barakaat International Foundation v Council of the EU and Commission*, ECLI:EU:T:2005:331...................... 89
Case T-315/01 *Yassin Abdullah Kadi v Council of the EU and Commission*, ECLI:EU:T:2005:332... 89
Case T-253/02 *Ayadi v Council of the EU*, ECLI:EU:T:2006:200.................... 89–90
Case T-85/09 *Kadi v European Commission (Kadi II)*, ECLI:EU:T:2010:418......... 89–90
Case T-883/16 *Poland v Commission* ECLI:EU:T:2019:567......................... 115
Case T-125/22 *RT France v Council of the EU*, ECLI:EU:T:2022:483... 14–15, 90–91, 92, 156
Case T-212/22 *Prigozhina v Council of the EU*, ECLI:EU:T:2023:104.................. 90
Case T-313/22 *Abramovich v Council of the EU*, ECLI:EU:T:2023:830 .... 10, 90
Case T-743/22 *Mazepin v Council of the EU*, ECLI:EU:T:2024:180 .... 10, 90, 156
Case T-759/22 *Electrawinds Shabla South v Council*, pending..................... 116–17
Case T-797/22, *Ordre néerlandais des avocats du barreau de Bruxelles v Council*, ECLI:EU:T:2024:670.. 91, 92, 156
Case T-802/22 *ExxonMobil Producing Netherlands v Council*, pending.. 15–16, 116–17, 156–57
Case T-803/22 *Petrogas E&P Netherlands v Council*, pending 15–16, 116–17, 156–57

Court of Justice

Case 26/62, *NV Algemene Transport- en Expeditie Onderneming van Gend & Loos*, ECLI:EU:C:1963:1... 6
Case 6/64, *Costa v Enel*, ECLI:EU:C:1964:66. 6
Case 294/83, *Parti écologiste "Les Verts" v European Parliament*, ECLI:EU:C:1986:166. 6
Opinion 2/94, *Accession to the ECHR*, ECLI:EU:C:1996:140....................... 132
Case C-414/97 *Commission v Spain* ECLI:EU:C:1999:417........................ 28
Case C-337/05 *Commission v Italy* ECLI:EU:C:2008:203.......................... 35
Joined Cases C-402/05 P and C-415/05 P *Yassin Abdullah. Kadi and Al Barakaat International Foundation v Council of the EU and Commission*, ECLI:EU:C:2008:461 89
Case C-157/06 *Commission v Italy* ECLI:EU:C:2008:530.......................... 35
Case C-584/10 P, *European Commission v Kadi (Kadi II)*, ECLI:EU:C:2013:518........ 89
Case C-370/12 *Pringle*, ECLI:EU:C:2012:756................................... 113–14
Opinion 2/13 *Accession to the ECHR*, ECLI:EU:C:2014:2454................ 96–97, 132
Case C-589/15 P, *Anagnostakis v Commission*, ECLI:EU:C:2017:663 113–14

xiv   TABLE OF CASES

Case C-5/16 *Poland v Parliament and Council*, ECLI:EU:C:2018:483. 118
Case C-64/16 *Associação Sindical dos Juízes Portugueses*, ECLI:EU:C:2018:117 69–70
Case C-216/18 PPU, *LM*, ECLI:EU:C:2018:586 69–70
Case C-848/19 P *Germany v Poland*, ECLI:EU:C:2021:958. 115
Case C-791/19 *Commission v Poland*, ECLI:EU:C:2021:596 69–70
Case C-896/19 *Repubblika v Il-Prim Ministru*, ECLI:EU:C:2021:311 69–70
Case C-124/20 *Bank Melli Iran*, ECLI:EU:C:2021:1035 85–86
Case C-156/21 *Hungary v Parliament and Council*, ECLI:EU:C:2022:97 69–70
Case C-157/21 *Poland v Parliament and Council*, ECLI:EU:C:2022:98. 69–70
Case C-204/21 *Commission v Poland*, ECLI:EU:C:2023:442 69–70
Case C-563/21 PPU *Openbaar Ministerie* ECLI:EU:C:2022:100. 69–70
Case C-620/22 P, *RT France v Council of the EU*, ECLI:EU:C:2023:615. 90–91
Case C-675/22 *Poland v Council*, pending. 117, 118

GERMANY

Bundesverfassungsgericht (Federal Constitutional Court)
BVerfG 2 BvR 547/21, 2 BvR 798/21, Final Judgment of 6 December 2022. .... 64–65, 118–19
BVerfG 2 BvF 1/22, Judgment of 15 November 2023. 122–23

ITALY

Corte Costituzionale (Constitutional Court)
Sentenza no 111/2024 117–18

UNITED NATIONS

International Court of Justice
Jurisdictional Immunity of the State (Germany v Italy, Greece intervening),
    judgment of 3 February 2012. 94
Ukraine v Russia, order of 16 March 2022 and judgment of 2 February 2024,
    No. 2024/10. 1–2
Certain Iranian Assets (Islamic Republic of Iran v United States of America),
    judgment of 30 March 2023... 94

UNITED STATES

Supreme Court
Schenck v United States, 249 US 47 (1919). 92
Dennis v United States, 341 US 494 (1951). 92
Youngstown Sheet & Tube Co. v Sawyer, 343 US 579 (1952)........................ 44–45
Brandenburg v Ohio, 395 US 444 (1969).. 92
Yaser Hamdi v Donald Rumsfeld, 542 US 507 (2004). 89–90
Salim Hamdan v Donald Rumsfeld, 548 US 557 (2006)............................ 89–90
Lakhdar Boumediene v George W. Bush, 553 US 723 (2008)....................... 89–90

Abbreviations

ACER	Agency for the Cooperation of Energy Regulators
ASAP	Act in Support of Ammunition Production
BVerfG	Bundesverfassungsgericht
CARD	Coordinated Annual Review on Defence
CBAM	Carbon Border Adjustment Mechanism
CFR	Charter of Fundamental Rights
CFSP	Common Foreign and Security Policy
CoE	Council of Europe
CSDP	Common Security and Defence Policy
CSDs	central securities depositories
CVM	Cooperation and Verification Mechanism
DPA	Defense Production Act (US)
ECB	European Central Bank
ECHR	European Convention on Human Rights
ECJ	European Court of Justice
ECtHR	European Court of Human Rights
EDA	European Defence Agency
EDIDP	European Defence Industrial Development Programme
EDIP	European Defence Industry Programme
EDIRPA	European defence industry reinforcement through common Procurement Act
EDIS	European Defence Industrial Strategy
EDTIB	EU's Defence Technological and Industrial Base
EFSM	European Financial Stabilisation Mechanism
EPC	European Political Community
EPF	European Peace Facility
ERA	extraordinary revenue acceleration
ESMA	European Securities and Market Authority
ETS	Emission Trading Scheme
EU	European Union
EUMC	EU Military Committee
EURI	EU Recovery Instrument
FAST	defence supply chain transformations
GBER	General Block Exemption Regulation
GNI	Gross National Income
ICC	International Criminal Court
ICJ	International Court of Justice
ICPA	Centre for the Prosecution of the Crime of Aggression Against Ukraine
INSTEX	Instrument in Support of Trade Exchanges
IRA	Inflation Reduction Act

JIT	joint investigation team
LNG	liquefied natural gas
MCM	market correction mechanism
MFA+	Macro-Financial Assistance Instrument for Ukraine
MFF	Multi-annual Financial Framework
NATO	North Atlantic Treaty Organization
NGEU	Next Generation EU
NRRPs	national recovery and resilience plans
NZIA	Net-Zero Industry Act
OECD	Organisation for Economic Cooperation and Development
ORD	Own Resource Decision
PESCO	permanent structured cooperation
QMV	qualified majority voting
R&D	research and development
RCB	Russian Central Bank
RRF	Recovery and Resilience Facility
SMEs	small and medium-sized enterprises
STEP	Strategic Technologies for Europe Platform
SWIFT	Society for Worldwide Interbank Financial Telecommunication
TCA	Trade and Cooperation Agreement
TCF	temporary crisis framework
TCTF	temporary crisis and transition framework
TEEC	Treaty establishing the European Economic Communities
TFEU	Treaty on the Functioning of the European Union
TPD	temporary protection directive
TTF	Title Transfer Facility
UAF	Ukraine Assistance Fund
UF	Ukraine Facility
UK	United Kingdom
ULCM	Ukraine Loan Cooperation Mechanism
UN	United Nations
UNHCR	UN High Commissioner for the Refugees
US	United States
WA	Withdrawal Agreement

1
Introduction

1 Introduction

The war in Ukraine resulting from Russia's aggression has been a watershed moment for the European Union (EU). The return of land warfare on the European continent was a profound shock as it shattered the illusion of perpetual peace that had historically surrounded the path of European integration. Needless to say, while the EU as a peace project had been successful at ending war among its Member States, since the end of the Second World War military conflicts had never ceased to occur elsewhere around the world. As historian Margaret McMillan pointed out, 'there has been no year since 1945 when there has not been fighting in one part of the world or another'.[1] In fact, Russia had already invaded Ukraine in 2014, and illegally annexed the Crimean Peninsula. Yet, the impact of these other conflicts on the EU's mindset and action had been limited. Even the bloody wars stemming from the dissolution of the former Yugoslavia in the EU's backyard, during the 1990s, had not caused existential questions in the EU. War was seen as a distant thing, in the confidence that the United States (US) as the post-Cold War hegemonic superpower would take care of solving it.[2]

February 2022 constitutes a turning point. Russia's large-scale invasion of Ukraine awoke the EU to the reality of hard power, and brought back the problem of war on the EU's horizon. In fact, it is hard to deny that the war in Ukraine has impacted the EU much more dramatically than any other conflict at play elsewhere around the globe. Even the new devastating conflict which started in the Middle East in October 2023 has not elicited strong responses by the EU—as demonstrated by the European Council's difficulties in taking a position on the matter for almost six months.[3] The war in Ukraine, instead, has been different. From an international law viewpoint, Russia's invasion of Ukraine clearly constitutes an unlawful

---

[1] Margaret McMillan, *War: How Conflict Shaped Us* (Profile Books 2020) 2.
[2] See G John Ikenberry, *After Victory: Institutions, Strategic Restraint and the Rebuilding of Order after Major Wars* (Princeton University Press 2001) (discussing the US's hegemonic role after the end of the Cold War).
[3] See Statement by the Members of the European Council, 15 October 2023, statement 750/23. See European Council conclusions, 15 December 2023, EUCO 20/23, para 12 (simply stating 'The European Council held an in-depth strategic debate on the Middle East'—without adding anything to this single line). For a first substantive position on the situation in the Middle East see European Council conclusions, 21–22 March 2024, EUCO 7/24, paras 20–28 (calling among other things for an immediate humanitarian pause).

The EU Constitution in Time of War. Federico Fabbrini, Oxford University Press. © Federico Fabbrini 2025.
DOI: 10.1093/oso/9780198963486.003.0001

aggression, in breach of the principles of the United Nations (UN) Charter[4]—as well as of the 1975 Helsinki Accords[5] and the 1994 Budapest Memorandum.[6] Indeed, the UN General Assembly acknowledged as much[7]—although as a permanent member of the UN Security Council, Russia thwarted any global response. Furthermore, the International Court of Justice (ICJ) denied that Russia had any legal justification for attacking Ukraine,[8] and the European Court of Human Rights (ECtHR) ruled that the annexation of Crimea had resulted in systemic human rights abuses.[9] Nevertheless, as is well known, the war in Ukraine is by no means the only contemporary conflict to occur in breach of international and human rights law, or to escape a multilateral response in the framework of the UN Charter Chapter VII provisions regarding breaches of the peace and acts of aggression.

So legal reasons alone do not explain why the EU responded to the war in Ukraine in ways in which it had not to other conflicts. Geography, history, and politics matter more. To begin with, Ukraine is geographically close to the EU, bordering four EU Member States, and the war altered not just the perception of the risk, but also the reality thereof, as evidenced by the occasional inadvertent fall of Russian missiles in EU territory. Moreover, the war in Ukraine marked a departure from 21st century trends in warfare, which had recently been characterized primarily by intra-state conflicts and counter-insurgencies, as opposed to large-scale, multi-year, inter-state wars:[10] Russia's massive ground invasion of Ukraine rather evoked dark memories of the 20th century, calling for a firm response. Finally, Russia's unprovoked aggression against Ukraine was also construed differently by the EU institutions. As political scientist Vivien Schmidt explained, institutions shape policies through ideas and public discourse.[11] In 2014, a number of Central

---

[4] UN Charter, art 2 (stating that 'All Members shall refrain in their international relations from the threat or use of force against the territorial integrity or political independence of any state').

[5] Conference on Security and Cooperation in Europe Final Act, art II (binding parties, including Russia, to 'refraining from the threat or use of force').

[6] Memorandum on Security Reassurances, art 2 (binding parties, including Russia 'to refrain from the threat or use of force against the territorial integrity and political independence of Ukraine').

[7] UN General Assembly resolution ES-11/1, 'Aggression against Ukraine', 2 March 2022.

[8] ICJ, *Ukraine v Russia*, order of 16 March 2022 (holding that Ukraine has a plausible right not to be subjected to military operations) and judgment of 2 February 2024, No 2024/10 (rejecting Russia's argument—repeatedly used in the national propaganda to justify the aggression against Ukraine—that Ukraine was committing genocide against Russian minorities in eastern Ukraine).

[9] ECtHR, *Ukraine v Russia (re Crimea)*, Applications nos 20958/14 and 38334/18, Judgment of 25 June 2024 (GC).

[10] See Anne-Marie Slaughter, 'War and Law in the 21st Century: Adapting to the Changing Face of Conflict' [2011] Europe's World 32 (stating that the post-9/11 wars 'are likely to be the last examples of 20th century-style warfare: large-scale, multi-year conflicts involving the ground invasion of one country by another [...] In the 21st century] conflicts are much more likely to take place within states than between them').

[11] See Vivien Schmidt, 'Discursive Institutionalism: The Explanatory Power of Ideas and Discourse' (2008) 11 Annual Review of Political Science 303 (arguing that ideas and discourse shape institutional change, and thus providing a theory to integrate historical institutionalism with constructivism to understand policy change).

and Eastern EU Member States had cried foul and seen a major threat from Russia's illegal occupation of Crimea. Yet, this feeling was not widely shared across the EU. In fact, large Member States such as Germany and France continued to engage, and trade, with Russia, as if nothing had happened.[12]

On 24 February 2022, instead, when Russian tanks rolled into the sovereign territory of Ukraine, the EU institutions and the Member States forcefully responded in unison. On that same day, the European Council convened with unusual speed to condemn the Russian aggression as a threat to the European security architecture and vowed to respond;[13] Ursula von der Leyen, the President of the European Commission—an office that according to the EU treaties has only limited foreign policy and security competences—vocally embraced the cause of Ukraine and promised EU support;[14] Olaf Scholz, the Chancellor of Germany—a country that for two decades had seen Russia as a partner, rather than a threat, building severe energy dependencies on it—proclaimed the invasion of Ukraine a *'Zeitenwende'*, a turn in history;[15] and EU heads of state and governments collectively announced that 'Russia's war of aggression constitutes a tectonic shift in European history'.[16]

The united EU institutional response to Russia's large-scale aggression against Ukraine[17] combined with widespread popular outrage for this blunt act of aggression.[18] In April 2022, the Eurobarometer survey revealed that 89% of respondents felt sympathy for Ukraine and showed a large consensus among EU citizens in all EU Member States in favour of the EU's response to Russia's invasion of Ukraine.[19] And in May 2022, the Conference on the Future of Europe—an innovative bottom-up process launched in 2021 to involve European citizens in a reflection on the future of the EU—concluded its work with a strong plea in favour of strengthening the EU's ability to defend itself, on the understanding that 'the invasion of Ukraine by Russia ... changed the face of the EU'.[20]

---

[12] See Rajan Menon and Eugene Rumer, *Conflict in Ukraine: The Unwinding of the Post-Cold War Order* (MIT Press 2015).
[13] See European Council conclusions, 24 February 2022, EUCO 18/22.
[14] See European Commission President Ursula von der Leyen, Press statement on Russia's aggression against Ukraine, 24 February 2022.
[15] German Chancellor Olaf Scholz, Policy Statement in the German Parliament, 27 February 2022, available in English at https://www.bundesregierung.de/breg-en/news/policy-statement-by-olaf-scholz-chancellor-of-the-federal-republic-of-germany-and-member-of-the-german-bundestag-27-february-2022-in-berlin-2008378.
[16] Informal meeting of the Heads of State and Government, Versailles Declaration, 10–11 March 2022, para 6.
[17] See also Council of the EU, 'Ukraine: press statement from the EU Ministers for Finance, European Commission and the European Central Bank', 25 February 2022, 174/22; High Representative/Vice-President Josep Borrell press statement, 'Further measures to respond to the Russian Invasion of Ukraine', 27 February 2022; and European Parliament resolution of 1 March 2022 on the Russian aggression against Ukraine, P9_TA(2922) 0052.
[18] See also Nils Steiner et al, 'Rallying around the EU Flag: Russia's Invasion of Ukraine and Attitudes towards European Integration' (2022) 61 Journal of Common Market Studies 283.
[19] Eurobarometer, May 2022, https://europa.eu/eurobarometer/surveys/detail/2772.
[20] Conference on the Future of Europe, Report on the Final Outcome, 9 May 2022, 53.

Furthermore, in the now 32 months since Russia's large-scale invasion of Ukraine,[21] the EU institutions have maintained their united position.[22] The European Council has regularly expressed its unwavering support for Ukraine and called on Russia to end its illegal military action.[23] In fact, support for Ukraine in a stronger Europe has been enshrined as a cornerstone of the new European Council 2024–2029 Strategic Agenda, approved in June 2024.[24] The Commission championed solidarity towards Ukraine,[25] with its President Ursula von der Leyen, who had been elected in 2019 to lead a 'geopolitical' body,[26] emerging during the war as a key player in shaping a strong international response against Russia.[27] In fact, her re-election in July 2024 was largely based on steadfast support for Ukraine's fight for freedom and democracy.[28] Finally, the European Parliament condemned Russia's escalation of the war,[29] even declared it a state sponsor of terrorism,[30] and forcefully called the EU to support Ukraine's right of self-defence against Russia's illegal, unprovoked, and unjustified aggression.[31] In fact, the European Parliament kept pushing for continued military and financial support for Ukraine,[32] including calling on Member States to lift restrictions on the use of weapons against legitimate military targets on Russian territory.[33]

Certainly, the EU's response to the war in Ukraine has not been faultless, as will be discussed in this book—and fractures in the EU's united reaction against Russia's aggression have emerged. Most remarkably, shortly after Hungary took over the six-month rotating Presidency of the Council of the EU on 1 July 2024, its Prime Minister Viktor Orban made an unplanned visit to Moscow to meet Russian President Vladimir Putin and negotiate a possible truce. However, his action quickly sparked negative responses from the other EU institutions, which

---

[21] This book has been completed on, and therefore is updated to, 15 October 2024, just ahead of the US Presidential elections of 5 November 2024.
[22] Joint statement by the President of the European Council, the President of the European Commission, and the President of the European Parliament, 23 February 2024, Doc 154/24.
[23] See eg Statement by the Members of the European Council, 23 February 2023, statement 119/2023.
[24] See European Council conclusions, 27 June 2024, EUCO 15/24, Annex: 'Strategic Agenda 2024-2029'.
[25] See Joint Statement by President Biden and President Von der Leyen, 10 March 2023.
[26] See European Commission President-elect Ursula von der Leyen, 'A Union that Strives for More: My Agenda for Europe', Political Guidelines for the Next European Commission 2019-2024, 16 July 2019.
[27] See European Commission President Ursula von der Leyen, Keynote speech at EDA Annual Conference, 30 November 2023.
[28] See European Commission President-elect Ursula von der Leyen, 'Europe's Choices', Political Guidelines for the Next European Commission 2024-2029, 18 July 2024.
[29] European Parliament resolution of 6 October 2022 on Russia's escalation of its war of aggression against Ukraine, P9_TA(2022) 0353.
[30] European Parliament resolution of 23 November 2022 on recognising the Russian Federation as a state sponsor of terrorism, P9_TA(2022) 0405.
[31] See eg European Parliament resolution of 16 February 2023 on one year of Russia's invasion and war of aggression against Ukraine, P9_TA(2023) 0056.
[32] European Parliament resolution of 19 September 2024 on continued financial and military support to Ukraine by EU Member States, P10-TA(2024) 0012.
[33] Ibid para 8.

clarified that Hungary had no legal mandate to represent the EU abroad.[34] The heads of state or government of other Member States—not just at Europe's Eastern periphery but at its core too—have clearly maintained the view that a Russian victory in Ukraine would imperil the EU.[35] Moreover, surveys in May 2024 revealed that the war still represented for European citizens the most important issue facing the EU,[36] and the European Parliament election outcome in June 2024 confirmed ongoing political support for Ukraine.[37] The very first resolution approved by the new European Parliament in July 2024 concerned the need for the EU's continuous support for Ukraine,[38] and by a wide majority it strongly condemned 'the recent visit of Hungarian Prime Minister Viktor Orban to [Russia … as] a blatant violation of the EU's Treaties and common foreign policy, including the principle of sincere cooperation'.[39]

Yet, the EU not only was, and remained, united in condemning Russia's aggression against Ukraine—it also repurposed its machinery of government to address something new for it: the challenge of war. Hence the purpose of this book.

2 The book's rationale

Since Russia's aggression against Ukraine, the EU has faced—practically for the first time since its existence—the question of war. It is hence urgent to reflect from an EU law perspective how the EU's constitution has operated under the circumstances, analysing *de lege lata* the EU's responses to the war in Ukraine, and its shortcomings, and considering *de lege ferenda* how to fix them. In doing so, this book seeks to fill a gap in the law literature. As is well known, extensive comparative constitutional law scholarship exists on how democracies address questions of war and peace.[40] Unsurprisingly, this is particularly the case in the US, the country that has come to play the most defining role in global security—and voluminous literature on this matter was recently produced during the so-called war on terror.[41] So

---

[34] High Representative/Vice-President Josep Borrell, Statement, 5 July 2024.
[35] See eg French President Emmanuel Macron, Speech at GLOBSEC Conference, 31 May 2023; and German Chancellor Olaf Scholz, 'A Russian Victory in Ukraine Would Imperil Us All', Op-Ed, *The Wall Street Journal* (7 February 2024).
[36] Eurobarometer, May 2024, https://europa.eu/eurobarometer/surveys/detail/3216.
[37] See also European Council conclusions, 27 June 2024, EUCO 15/24, s VI.
[38] European Parliament resolution of 17 July 2024 on the need for the EU's continuous support for Ukraine, P10_TA(2024) 0003.
[39] Ibid para 4.
[40] See eg Giuseppe de Vergottini, *Guerra e costituzione* (Il Mulino 2004); Elisabeth Zoller, 'The War Powers in French Constitutional Law' (1996) 90 Proceedings of the Annual Meeting (American Society of International Law) 46; Russel Miller, 'Germany's Basic Law and the Use of Force' (2010) 17 Indiana Journal of Global Legal Studies 197. See also Arianna Vedaschi, *À la guerre comme à la guerre? La disciplina della guerra nel diritto costituzionale comparato* (Giappichelli 2007).
[41] See from very different perspectives eg David Cole and James Dempsey, *Terrorism and the Constitution* (The New Press 2002); John Yoo, *The Powers of War and Peace: The Constitution and Foreign Affairs after 9/11* (University of Chicago Press 2005); Bruce Ackerman, *Before the Next*

far, however, no comprehensive study has focused on the *EU* constitution in time of war. Of course, a rich body of legal scholarship exists on EU foreign relations law,[42] but this does not address specifically the issue of war. This is mainly because, as mentioned above, the EU had largely insulated itself, and seen itself as immune, from the reality of hard power. The war in Ukraine, however, proved that this is an illusion, and this book seeks to explore how the EU fared as a wartime, rather than a peacetime, organization.

From its very title, this book starts from the assumption that the EU has a constitution—with a small c.[43] In a formal sense, the EU is constituted by several international treaties, last modified by the Treaty of Lisbon—the Treaty on the EU (TEU), the Treaty on the Functioning of the EU (TFEU), and the Charter of Fundamental Rights (CFR).[44] Member states have sovereignly ratified these EU treaties as subjects of international law.[45] Few would question, however, that the EU treaties are exceptional—not least due to the commitments enshrined in both the TEU and the TFEU preambles to creating 'an ever closer union'. In a material sense, the EU treaties establish a sophisticated system of government with significant delegated competences, a separation of powers, and the protection of fundamental rights—the essence of what a constitution is.[46] In fact, despite the failure of the EU Constitution—with the capital c—in the early 2000s,[47] for more than 50 years the EU Court of Justice (ECJ) has claimed that the EU treaties constitute the basic constitutional charter of the EU,[48] endowed with direct effect in the legal systems of the Member States,[49] and supremacy over conflicting national laws.[50] This implies, as an extensive number of scholars have argued, that the EU treaties can legally be examined as the constitutional law of the EU.[51]

Attack: Preserving Civil Liberties in an Age of Terrorism (Yale University Press 2006); Louis Fisher, *The Constitution and 9/11: Recurring Threats to America's Freedoms* (University of Kansas Press 2008).

[42] See eg Geert De Baere, *Constitutional Principles of EU External Relations Law* (OUP 2008); Piet Eeckhout, *EU External Relations Law* (OUP 2012); Robert Schütze, *Foreign Affairs and the EU Constitution: Selected Essays* (OUP 2014).

[43] See Neil Walker, 'Big "C" or Small "c"?' (2006) 12 European Law Journal 12.

[44] See Paul Craig, *The Lisbon Treaty: Law, Politics and Treaty Reform* (OUP 2010).

[45] See also Bruno de Witte, 'The European Union as an international legal experiment' in Gráinne de Búrca and J H H Weiler (eds), *The Worlds of European Constitutionalism* (CUP 2012) 19.

[46] See also 1789 French Declaration of the Right of Men, art 16 (stating that 'Toute société dans laquelle la garantie des droits n'est pas assurée, ni la séparation des pouvoirs déterminée, n'a point de constitution' ['All societies in which the protection of right is not guaranteed, nor the separation of powers determined, has no constitution'], my translation).

[47] See Nick Barber et al (eds), *The Rise and Fall of the European Constitution* (Hart Publishing 2019).

[48] Case 294/83 *Parti écologiste 'Les Verts' v European Parliament* ECLI:EU:C:1986:166, para 23.

[49] Case 26/62 *NV Algemene Transport- en Expeditie Onderneming van Gend & Loos* ECLI:EU:C:1963:1.

[50] Case 6/64 *Costa v Enel* ECLI:EU:C:1964:66.

[51] See Koen Lenaerts and Piet Van Nuffel, *Constitutional Law of the European Union* (Sweet & Maxwell 1999); Robert Schütze, *European Constitutional Law* (OUP 2012); Allan Rosas and Lorna Armati, *EU Constitutional Law: An Introduction* (Hart Publishing 2012); Roberto Bin, Paolo Caretti and Giovanni Pitruzzella, *Profili costituzionali dell'Unione europea* (Il Mulino 2015); Edouard Dubout, *Droit constitutionnel de l'Union europeénne* (Bruylant 2023).

Moreover, this legal view is supported by the political practice of the EU institutions and the Member States, which over the years have increasingly seen the EU as the inevitable framework in which they operate—a pattern that has been strengthened, rather than weakened, by Brexit.[52] Indeed, since the United Kingdom (UK)'s decision to leave the EU in 2016, and its eventual withdrawal in 2020, no other Member State has sought a formal exemption from the commitment to 'ever closer union'[53]—much less seriously questioned its EU membership. Rather, populist governments have deployed multiple strategies to influence the EU short of exit— including criticism, extortion, and obstruction.[54] In fact, EU Member States clash on what they wish the EU to be—with alternative visions of polity, market, and autocracy increasingly competing between themselves.[55]

Yet, national go-it-alone action seems increasingly off the table in the EU, and as political scientist Chris Bickerton put it, nation states have become Member States.[56] Needless to say, this does not mean that Member States have been losing any importance in the functioning of the EU. On the contrary, national governments have actually increased their influence on the EU decision-making machinery through the Council and the European Council: in fact, intergovernmentalism has recently overshadowed opposite trends towards parliamentarism in the EU, arguably resulting in a weakening of the EU supranational institutions.[57] Yet, the institutional developments within the EU have contributed to cement the EU treaties, which according to Article 53 TEU are concluded for an unlimited period, as the constitutional framework in which Member States unite and operate.

If therefore the EU can plausibly be regarded as having a constitution, the consequential question is how to assess the EU constitution's operation in time of war. This is new because so far the EU never had to address the problem of war seriously. As the Schuman Declaration had hoped,[58] thanks to almost 75 years of integration, intra-EU war had become not only unthinkable but impossible.[59] Yet, the EU somehow projected its internal experience to the outer world: as a 'global actor',[60] it leveraged its regulatory prowess[61] and economic might to promote international commerce and 'transformation through trade' (*'Wandel durch Handel'*).[62] The

[52] See Federico Fabbrini (ed), *The Law & Politics of Brexit* (OUP 2017).
[53] See also European Council conclusions, 18–19 February 2016, EUCO 1/16, Annex I 'New Settlement for the UK in the EU', s C1 (exempting the UK from the commitment to 'ever closer union').
[54] See Agnese Pacciardi, Kilian Spandler, and Friederik Soderbaum, 'Beyond Exit: How Populist Governments Disengage from International Institutions' (2024) 100 International Affairs 2025.
[55] See Federico Fabbrini, *Brexit & the Future of the European Union* (OUP 2020) 75.
[56] Chris Bickerton, *European Integration: From Nation States to Member States* (OUP 2012).
[57] See Sergio Fabbrini, *Which European Union? Europe after the Euro Crisis* (CUP 2015).
[58] See Schuman Declaration, 9 May 1950.
[59] See Mette Eilstrup-Sangiovanni and Daniel Verdier, 'European Integration as a Solution to War' (2005) 11 European Journal of International Relations 99.
[60] See Marise Cremona, 'The EU as a Global Actor: Roles, Models and Identity' (2004) 41 Common Market Law Review 553.
[61] See Anu Bradford, *The Brussels Effect: How the European Union Rules the World* (OUP 2020).
[62] See Bernhard Blumenau, 'Breaking with Convention? *Zeitenwende* and the Traditional Pillars of German Foreign Policy' (2022) 98 International Affairs 1895.

EU instead largely shied away from engaging in militarily-related world affairs—a stance much criticized by US foreign policy realists in the aftermath of 9/11.[63] The war in Ukraine, however, was a 'wake-up call'.[64] The return of large-scale conventional warfare on the EU's doorstep forced the EU to shelve the assumption of the 'end of history',[65] and to face the growing threats to the international liberal order on which its security and prosperity rested.[66] This makes compelling an examination of the EU's constitution in time of war. As the EU for the first time faces the reality of war, how has its constitutional structure of government responded to the threat of hard power?

3 The book's analytical frame

This book endeavours to study whether the EU constitution has empowered the EU to address the unprecedented challenges of war, but also whether in responding to Russia's aggression against Ukraine the EU has complied with its constitution. The task of a constitution in a liberal democratic regime is both to enable power and to constrain it.[67] In fact, the EU is a law organization: according to the treaties, the EU has limited powers, based on conferred competences.[68] Moreover, in its action the EU must respect fundamental rights, as enshrined especially in the CFR;[69] it must comply with the principle of proportionality;[70] and abide by the rule of law, including international law.[71] By examining the EU's response to the war in Ukraine from a legal perspective—as opposed to a public policy,[72] economics,[73] or an international relations one[74]—the book explores how the EU treaties' legal bases have been construed in a novel form to authorize war-related action by the EU. At the same time, the book evaluates the legality of several EU responses to the

---

[63] See famously Robert Kagan, *Of Paradise and Power: America and Europe in the New World Order* (Knopf 2003) (describing Americans as coming from Mars, and Europeans as coming from Venus).

[64] See also UK House of Lords International Relations and Defence Committee report 'Ukraine: a wake-up call', HL Paper 10, 26 September 2024 (explaining how Russia's aggression against Ukraine challenged the strategic assumptions that have shaped Western defence policies, including in the UK, for decades).

[65] See famously Francis Fukuyama, *The End of History and the Last Man* (Free Press 1992).

[66] See Serhii Plokhy, *The Russo-Ukranian War: The Return of History* (Norton 2023).

[67] See Augusto Barbera (ed), *Le basi filosofiche del costituzionalismo* (Laterza 1997).

[68] TEU, art 5.

[69] Ibid art 6.

[70] Ibid art 5(4).

[71] Ibid art 3(5).

[72] For a political science and public policy perspective on the EU response to the war in Ukraine see eg Mitchel A Orenstein (guest ed), 'Special Issue: Transformation of Europe after Russia's Attack on Ukraine' (2023) 45 Journal of European Integration 333.

[73] For an economic and legal assessment of the EU and international sanctions imposed on Russia in response to the war in Ukraine see eg Christine Abely, *The Russia Sanctions: The Economic Response to Russia's Invasion of Ukraine* (CUP 2024).

[74] See Gwendolyn Sasse, *Russia's War Against Ukraine* (Polity 2023).

war in Ukraine in light of the limits that its constitution introduces to EU action, and reflects on the longer-term constitutional dynamics that the war generated in the EU system of governance.

To approach this topic as comprehensively as possible, the book uses a framework of analysis inspired by the wording of the preamble to the US Constitution. In words that are world famous, this proclaims that the US Constitution was ordained and established 'in Order to form a more perfect Union, establish Justice, insure domestic Tranquility, provide for the common defence, promote the general Welfare, and secure the Blessings of Liberty to ourselves and our Posterity'. As comparative constitutional law scholarship has emphasized, constitutional preambles serve an important symbolic function.[75] And the US Constitution's preamble is emblematic in this respect.[76] As is well known, the US Constitution was drafted by the Philadelphia Convention in 1787 with the purpose of replacing the dysfunctional 1781 Articles of Confederation and to strengthen the bonds between the 13 American states, which had emerged as victorious in the war of independence against Great Britain.[77] Yet, the words of the US Constitution's preamble have somehow become the summary *par excellence* of the functions of a constitutional government.[78]

Borrowing from the words and concepts of the US Constitution's preamble, therefore, the book explores whether, and how, in response to the war in Ukraine, the EU constitution has: (1) provided for the common defence; (2) promoted the general welfare; (3) established justice; (4) insured domestic tranquillity; and (5) secured the blessing of liberty. By focusing *ad litteram* on these five conventional policy functions of a constitutional government, the book takes first and foremost a *substantive* approach to the EU constitution in wartime, analysing several major war-related legal developments in core EU fields of competences. Specifically, the book considers: (1) foreign and defence policy, known technically as Common Foreign and Security Policy (CFSP) and Common Security and Defence Policy (CSDP); (2) fiscal and economic policy; (3) justice and home affairs; (4) energy and industrial policy; and (5) enlargement policy and treaty reforms. In each of these five domains, the book maps the core measures taken by the EU in response to Russia's aggression against Ukraine, examines their consequences, and discusses their challenges—thus pursuing a systematic overview of the operation of the EU constitution in wartime.

---

[75] See Justin Frosini, 'Constitutional Preambles: More than Just a Narration of History' (2017) 2 University of Illinois Law Review 603.
[76] See Akhil Reed Amar, *The Words that Made Us: America's Constitutional Conversation, 1760-1840* (Basic Books 2021).
[77] See Gordon Wood, *The Creation of the American Republic, 1776-1787* (University of North Carolina Press 1969).
[78] See Max Edling, *A Revolution in Favor of Government: Origins of the U.S. Constitution and the Making of the American State* (OUP 2003).

Nevertheless, in mapping how the EU substantive constitution has been deployed to address the challenges posed by the war in Ukraine, and whether and how it constrained it, the book also assesses the decision-making and oversight role of the EU institutions. As Bruno de Witte has pointed out, research in the field of EU law 'should not be narrowly limited to the study and exposition of written legal norms, but should include the study of institutional practices that are not, or only partially, based on legal norms'.[79] As such, the book considers the evolving role of the EU executive, legislative, and judicial branches of government in times of war, including the growing case law of the ECJ on this matter.[80] Moreover, it highlights how the EU system of government—and especially the dominant role of intergovernmentalism in EU decision-making—profoundly shapes and hampers the ability of the EU to rise to the challenges of a military conflict. From this point of view, therefore, the primary analysis of the EU substantive constitution is interwoven with that of the EU *institutional* constitution, in the effort to assess how the EU responded to the war in Ukraine in providing for the common defence, promoting the general welfare, establishing justice, insuring domestic tranquillity, and securing the blessings of liberty.

Of course, the analytical framework followed by this book lends itself to some possible criticisms. On the one hand, it may be questioned whether the US Constitution's preamble provides a useful prism at all to assess the performance of a constitutional government. In fact, there is even an intense debate among US constitutional law scholars on whether US practice itself lives up to the ambitious promises set out in the Constitution's preamble: Louis Seidman, in particular, has used the same analytical frame of the US Constitution's preamble to criticize the fitness of the US Constitution today,[81] and other scholars have emphasized how the Constitution is to blame for many of the US's current problems.[82] Yet, this view is contested, as other scholars have praised the open-ended, principled nature of the US Constitution, as a roadmap for a continuing democratic work-in-progress.[83] And in any case this debate is beyond the point here. On the other hand, it may be questioned whether the US Constitution's preamble can be a good benchmark to

---

[79] Bruno de Witte, 'Legal Methods for the Study of EU Institutional Practice' (2022) 18 European Constitutional Law Review 637, 638

[80] See eg Case T-743/22 *Mazepin v Council* ECLI:EU:T:2024:180 (striking down a restrictive measure). But see Case T-313/22 *Abramovich v Council of the EU* ECLI:EU:T:2023:830 (upholding an individual sanction).

[81] See especially Louis Seidman, *From Parchment to Dust: The Case for Constitutional Skepticism* (Beacon 2021) (dedicating a titled chapter to each of the preamble's goals of 'establishing justice', 'promoting the general welfare', 'securing the blessings of liberty', 'establishing a more perfect union', and 'insuring domestic tranquility'—and criticizing the performance of the US Constitution under each of these headings).

[82] See recently Erwin Chemerinsky, *No Democracy Lasts Forever: How the Constitution Threatens the United States* (Liverlight 2024).

[83] See Akhil Reed Amar, *America's Constitution: A Biography* (Random House 2005).

assess the *EU* constitution. After all, is not the nature of the EU still disputed?[84] Yet, I want to suggest that the wording of the US Constitution's preamble can help illuminate the EU's contemporary state of affairs—for both rhetorical and conceptual reasons.

To begin with, the EU treaties lay out constitutional objectives which largely correspond, in essence, to those listed in the US Constitution's preamble. Typically, the EU treaties do so in a much more legalistic and verbose way. For example, the preamble to the TEU proclaims that the EU aspires, inter alia, 'to promote economic and social progress', 'to facilitate the free movement of persons, while ensuring the safety and security of their peoples', and 'to promote peace, security and progress in Europe and the world'. The preamble to the TFEU proclaims the EU's commitment to 'pooling their resources to preserve and strengthen peace and liberty, and calling upon the other peoples of Europe who share their ideal to join in their efforts', and—as mentioned above—both preambles enshrine a commitment to 'an ever closer union'. Moreover, additional goals and ambitious aspirations are specifically indicated in Articles 3 and 21 TEU,[85] as well as in Part I, Title I of the TFEU.[86] From these sources, it clearly emerges that the EU aspires to pursue normative goals related to freedom, democracy, and prosperity, and is consequently tasked with powers and responsibilities, which are precisely connected to the fields of CFSP/CSDP, justice and home affairs, economic and financial affairs, energy and industry, enlargement, etc. Ultimately, these appear akin to the constitutional objectives listed in the US Constitution's preamble, which has just the advantage of being shorter and clearer.

Furthermore, the US Constitution is—like it or not[87]—the global benchmark of constitutionalism. Therefore, it makes sense for the EU as a union of states founded on representative democracy to measure itself to that standard.[88] In fact, starting with the *Integration through Law* project developed at the European University Institute in the 1980s,[89] the US experience has been regarded as the standard

---

[84] See for different disciplinary views Signe Rehling Larsen, *The Constitutional Theory of the Federation and the European Union* (OUP 2021) (arguing that the EU is an example of constitutional federalism); Jospeh H H Weiler, 'Federalism without a Constitution' in Kalypso Nicolaïdis and Robert Howse (eds), *The Federal Vision* (OUP 2002) (arguing that the EU is a special case); Sabino Cassese, 'Che tipo di potere pubblico è l'Unione Europea?' [2002] Quaderni fiorentini per la storia del pensiero giuridico 109 (arguing that the EU has features of multinational empires); Pavlos Eleftheriadis, *A Union of Peoples* (OUP 2020) (arguing that the EU is an international organization of peoples).

[85] See also Joris Larik, *Foreign Policy Objectives in European Constitutional Law* (OUP 2016).

[86] TFEU, arts 2–6.

[87] Compare Bruce Ackerman, 'The Rise of World Constitutionalism' (1997) 83 Virginia Law Review 771 with Martin Laughlin, *Against Constitutionalism* (Harvard University Press 2023).

[88] See also Koen Lenaerts, 'Constitutionalism and the Many Faces of Federalism' (1990) 38 American Journal of Comparative Law 205; Giuseppe Federico Mancini, *Democrazia e costituzionalismo nell'Unione europea* (Il Mulino 2004) and Walter van Gerven, *The European Union: A Polity of States and People* (Hart Publishing 2005).

[89] Mauro Cappelletti, Monica Seccombe and Joseph H.H. Weiler (eds), *Integration Through Law: Europe and the American Federal Experience. Volume 1, Book 1* (de Gruyter 1986).

comparative model to examine the EU's integration process. An extensive scholarship in law, political science, and political economy has analysed many aspects of the EU institutions and policies in light of the US federal experience,[90] and along those lines in my prior work I have recurrently compared the EU with the US federal constitutional system, both in the field of fundamental rights protection and in that of economic governance and fiscal capacity.[91] Hence, the globally renowned words of the US Constitution can provide a helpful lens to look at the state of the EU's constitution, and assess its prospects, in wartime.

At the same time, this comparison is all the more fitting as the EU is now accelerating the debate about its constitutional outlook.[92] In the aftermath of Brexit, the Covid-19 pandemic, and the war in Ukraine, the Conference on the Future of Europe advanced a number of recommendations to improve the EU's effectiveness and legitimacy.[93] Crucially, the Conference pleaded for 'reopening the discussion about the [EU] constitution'[94] on the understanding that: '[a] constitution may help to be more precise as well as involve citizens and agree on the rules of the decision-making process.'[95] As the EU reflects on how to improve its constitutional set-up, then it is worth assessing how the current EU constitution (small c) has fared when measured by the ordinary aims of a Constitution (capital C). And these are *grosso modo* to provide for the common defence, to promote the general welfare, to establish justice, to insure domestic tranquillity, and to secure the blessings of liberty.

4 The book's argument and structure

The book advances a threefold argument. First, it claims that the EU constitution has proved flexible enough to allow the EU institutions and Member States to act in wartime. As evidence of this, the book examines a number of groundbreaking

---

[90] See eg Miguel Maduro, *We the Court: the European Court of Justice and the European Economic Constitution* (Hart Publishing 1998); Kalypso Nicolaïdis and Robert Howse (eds), *The Federal Vision: Legitimacy and Levels of Governance in the United States and the European Union* (OUP 2001); Sergio Fabbrini, *Compound Democracies: Why the United States and Europe Are Becoming Similar* (OUP 2008); Robert Schütze, *From Dual to Cooperative Federalism: The Changing Structure of European Law* (OUP 2009); Aida Torres Pérez, *Conflicts of Rights in the European Union* (OUP 2009); Daniel Kelemen, *Eurolegalism* (Harvard University Press 2011); Tomasz Woźniakowski, *Fiscal Unions: Economic Integration in Europe and the United States* (OUP 2022). See also Thomas Sargent, 'Nobel Lecture: United States Then, Europe Now' (2012) 120 Journal of Political Economy 1.

[91] See Federico Fabbrini, *Fundamental Rights in Europe: Challenges and Transformations in Comparative Perspective* (OUP 2014): Federico Fabbrini, *Economic Governance in Europe: Paradoxes and Challenges in Comparative Perspective* (OUP 2016); Federico Fabbrini, *EU Fiscal Capacity: Legal Integration after Covid-19 and the War in Ukraine* (OUP 2022).

[92] See further Matej Avbelj (ed), *The Future of EU Constitutionalism* (Hart Publishing 2023).

[93] See Federico Fabbrini, 'The Conference on the Future of Europe: Process and Prospects' (2020) 26 European Law Journal 401.

[94] Final report (n 20), Proposal 39, recommendation 7.

[95] Ibid.

EU legal acts in the fields of foreign affairs and defence, economic and fiscal policy, justice and home affairs, energy and industrial policy, as well as enlargement, which were adopted in response to Russia's aggression against Ukraine. Secondly, however, the book also maintains that the return of conventional warfare in Europe exposed the limits of the EU constitution. On the one hand, structural constraints and governance shortcomings weakened the ability of the EU to act with resolve. On the other hand, the EU constitution also proved at times too weak to constrain action by the EU institutions and Member States properly—especially when respect for fundamental rights and the rule of law were at stake. As a result, thirdly, the book posits that the EU wartime constitution must be improved, and identifies ways to do so. The book develops its argument in five chapters, which use the framework of analysis outlined in the previous section, and inspired by the US Constitution's preamble.

Chapter 2 analyses developments in the field of CFSP/CSDP, examining whether the EU constitution provided for the common defence. The chapter maps the core diplomatic, military, and defence production measures adopted by the EU in response to the war. The EU clarified its foreign policy strategy by adopting a Strategic Compass;[96] it strengthened its military action by delivering lethal weapons to the Ukrainian army, launching a military assistance mission to support it,[97] and offering security guarantees to Ukraine;[98] and it boosted its defence production, especially through the Act in Support of Ammunition Production.[99] The chapter discusses the consequences of these measures, highlighting how the war led to an acceleration of EU integration in CFSP/CSDP, also through the use of constructive abstention in the Council.[100] In particular, the chapter emphasizes how the EU has exploited its so-far underused competences in the field of industrial policy[101] to develop a defence production strategy, including by funding for the first time the procurement and production of ammunition—thus contributing to the development of EU military capabilities. Nevertheless, the chapter also highlights how EU action in CFSP/CSDP was hampered by governance rules which require unanimity in the Council, and limited budgetary resources for defence production. In fact, the EU failed to reach its self-proclaimed goal to deliver

---

[96] Council of the EU, 'A strategic compass for security and defence: For a EU that protects its citizens, values and interests and contributes to international peace and security', 21 March 2022, Doc 7371/22.

[97] Council Decision (CFSP) 2022/2245 of 14 November 2022 on an assistance measure under the European Peace Facility to support the Ukrainian Armed Forces trained by the European Union Military Assistance Mission in support of Ukraine with military equipment, and platforms, designed to deliver lethal force [2022] OJ L294/25.

[98] Joint Security Commitments between the European Union and Ukraine, 27 June 2024.

[99] Regulation (EU) 2023/1525 of the European Parliament and of the Council of 20 July 2023 on supporting ammunition production (ASAP) [2023] OJ L185/7.

[100] TEU, art 31(1)(2).

[101] TFEU, art 173.

at least 1 million rounds of ammunition in a year to Ukraine.[102] And despite the adoption of EU security guarantees, given the lack of any credible EU hard power, the war strengthened the role of the North Atlantic Treaty Organization (NATO) as the leading organization for European security—a pattern proven by Finland and Sweden's accession to NATO in 2023 and 2024, respectively.

Chapter 3 analyses developments in the field of economic and fiscal policy, examining whether the EU constitution promoted the general welfare. The chapter maps the core financial instruments that the EU put in place to help the Ukrainian government face the fiscal problems resulting from Russia's aggression. Specifically, the EU deployed brand new common funding mechanisms, including a European Peace Facility, initially worth €5.6 billion and later increased to €17 billion,[103] a 2023 Macro-Financial Assistance Instrument for Ukraine (MFA+), worth €18 billion,[104] and ultimately a Ukraine Facility (UF) for 2024–2027, worth €50 billion.[105] The chapter discusses the consequences of these measures, highlighting how the war swiftly led the EU to reproduce the legal and policy model used to address the socio-economic damages of the Covid-19 pandemic, with the establishment of the Next Generation EU (NGEU). In particular, both the MFA+ and the UF empower the Commission to raise resources on the financial market through the issuance of common debt, and to transfer these to Ukraine for its reconstruction—thus contributing to the consolidation of an EU fiscal capacity. Nevertheless, the chapter also highlights how EU action in fiscal and economic policy was constrained by decision-making rules that grant every Member State a veto on revisions to the Multiannual Financial Framework (MFF) and the authorization to issue common debt[106]—a privilege which Hungary repeatedly abused to obtain concessions on unrelated matters, and which delayed the approval of both the MFA+ and the UF.[107]

Chapter 4 analyses developments in the field of justice and home affairs, examining whether the EU constitution established justice. The chapter maps the core solidarity, sanctions, and investigation and compensation measures that the EU put in place to support Ukraine and make Russia pay for its illegal aggression. In

---

[102] See Council of the EU, Doc 7632/23, Annex: Speeding up the delivery and joint procurement of ammunition for Ukraine, 20 March 2023 and High Representative/Vice-President Josep Borrell press remarks, 31 January 2024.
[103] Council Decision (CFSP) 2021/509 of 22 March 2021 establishing a European Peace Facility and repealing Decision (CFSP) 2015/528 [2021] OJ L102/14.
[104] Regulation (EU) 2022/2463 of the European Parliament and the Council of 14 December 2022 establishing an instrument for providing support to Ukraine for 2023 (macro-financial assistance +) [2022] OJ L322/1.
[105] Regulation (EU) 2024/792 of the European Parliament and the Council of 29 February 2024 establishing the Ukraine Facility [2024] OJ L1.
[106] TFEU, art 312.
[107] European Council meeting, 14–15 December 2023, Multiannual Financial Framework 2021–2027 Negotiating Box, EUCO 23/23 (indicating that 26 heads of state and government agreed to amend the MFF—including funding for the UF—but that Hungary had vetoed the package).

response to the war, for the first time ever the EU triggered the temporary protection directive to welcome a major wave of war refugees;[108] it rolled out 14 rounds of wide-ranging sanctions, also making the violation of restrictive measures a new EU crime;[109] it set up joint investigative team to prosecute Russian war crimes, and ultimately enacted laws to seize the extraordinary profits resulting from the frozen assets of the Russian Central Bank (RCB).[110] The chapter discusses the consequences of these measures, including the addition of a new 'EU crime' to the list of Article 83 TFEU, and the adoption for the first time of EU secondary sanctions. Nevertheless, the chapter underlines how governance inefficiencies weakened EU solidarity. Moreover, it highlights how EU action in this field—while motivated by the desire to remedy the injustice of the war—raised legal challenges in terms of compliance with human rights and international law. In particular, the chapter overviews the EU General Court case law reviewing sanctions, highlighting how this was deferential towards the Council;[111] and discusses whether the seizure of the extraordinary profits resulting from RCB's immobilized assets is compatible with international rules on foreign sovereign immunity—suggesting that the need to fight a war led to silencing some of the EU constitutions' fundamental values.

Chapter 5 analyses developments in the field of energy and industrial policy, examining whether the EU constitution insured domestic tranquillity. The chapter explains how Russia's weaponization of oil and gas caused an energy crisis for the EU, which threatened its support for Ukraine. As such, it maps the core measures that the EU enacted to mitigate the skyrocketing prices of energy, to speed up the green transition, and repower the EU with renewable energies; and to develop a new industrial policy for the net-zero age. The chapter discusses the consequences of these measures, emphasizing in particular how the EU exploited the emergency powers provided under the treaties,[112] for instance to introduce a

---

[108] Council Implementing Decision (EU) 2022/382 of 4 March 2022 establishing the existence of a mass influx of displaced persons from Ukraine within the meaning of Article 5 of Directive 2001/55/EC, and having the effect of introducing temporary protection [2022] OJ L71/1.

[109] Council Decision (EU) 2022/2332 of 28 November 2022 on identifying the violation of Union restrictive measures as an area of crime that meets the criteria specified in Article 83(1) of the Treaty on the Functioning of the European Union [2022] OJ L308/18.

[110] Council Decision (CFSP) 2024/577 of 12 February 2024 amending Decision 2014/512/CFSP concerning restrictive measures in view of Russia's actions destabilising the situation in Ukraine [2024] OJ L577; and Council Regulation (EU) 2024/576 of 12 February 2024 amending Regulation (EU) No 833/2014 concerning restrictive measures in view of Russia's actions destabilising the situation in Ukraine [2024] OJ L576. Council Decision (CFSP) 2024/1470 of 21 May 2024 amending Decision 2014/512/CFSP concerning restrictive measures in view of Russia's actions destabilising the situation in Ukraine [2024] OJ L; and Council Regulation (EU) 2024/1469 of 21 May 2024 amending Regulation (EU) No 833/2014 concerning restrictive measures in view of Russia's actions destabilising the situation in Ukraine [2024] OJ L.

[111] See eg Case T-125/22 *RT France v Council* ECLI:EU:T:2022:483 (upholding the EU ban of several Russian media channels).

[112] TFEU, art 122.

market correction mechanism for the price of gas.[113] At the same time, in reaction to the war, the EU strengthened its economic security,[114] developing an industrial strategy among others on critical raw materials and advanced technologies such as chips. Nevertheless, the chapter also underlines how measures adopted to tackle the energy crisis have raised domestic legal questions, especially on the adoption of a windfall tax on the extraordinary profits of energy companies,[115] and reflects on the threats to the level playing field at the heart of the EU internal market posed by the relaxation of EU state aid law. Finally, the chapter also highlights how EU measures to facilitate the decarbonization of industry have been funded by resources which are very limited when compared to those deployed by other global players, and how this puts the competitiveness of the EU economy at stake.

Chapter 6 examines whether the EU constitution secured the blessings of liberty, mapping the core measures that the EU adopted to enlarge and reform. Under the pressure of war, the EU promised membership to Ukraine,[116] as well as to Moldova, Georgia, and Bosnia Herzegovina, while also reviving its enlargement process towards five other countries of the Western Balkans (Albania, Kosovo, Montenegro, North Macedonia, and Serbia), which together with Turkey had already been on the waiting list to join the EU. Moreover, the EU promoted the creation of a new European Political Community (EPC), bringing together 47 countries of the wider Europe; and started to reflect more properly on constitutional reforms. The chapter discusses the consequences of these developments, emphasizing how the war relaunched the enlargement process after a decade of stalemate—opening the prospect for a future EU of 35 Member States or more. Nevertheless, the chapter underlines how, given the existence of the unanimity rule on treaty changes, the EU has been unable to start preparations for enlargement by adjusting its institutional set-up. While calls for treaty reforms designed to strengthen the EU's substantive powers and increase the efficiency of its decision-making systems were made by the Conference on the Future of Europe, the European Parliament,[117] and several Member States,[118] opposition by other countries—mostly from northern, central, and eastern Europe[119]—have so far hampered any step towards EU treaty

---

[113] Council Regulation (EU) 2022/2578 of 22 December 2022 establishing a market correction mechanism to protect Union citizens and the economy against excessively high prices [2022] OJ L335/45.

[114] European Commission and High Representative, Joint communication on European economic security strategy, 20 June 2023, JOIN(2023) 20 final.

[115] See Case T-803/22 *Petrogas E&P Netherlands v Council*, pending; Case T-802/22 *ExxonMobil Producing Netherlands v Council*, pending.

[116] European Council conclusions, 23–24 June 2022, EUCO 24/22.

[117] See European Parliament resolution of 9 June 2022 on the call for a Convention for the revision of the Treaties, P9_TA(2022) 0244, and European Parliament resolution of 22 November 2023 on proposals for the European Parliament for the amendment of the Treaties, P9_TA(2023) 0427.

[118] Report of the Franco-German Working Group on EU Institutional Reforms, 'Sailing on High Seas: Reforming and Enlarging the EU for the 21st Century', 18 September 2023.

[119] Government of Sweden press release, 9 May 2022 (indicating that the governments of Bulgaria, Croatia, the Czech Republic, Denmark, Estonia, Finland, Latvia, Lithuania, Malta, Poland, Romania,

amendment. This has so far left the EU unprepared to face the prospects of a prolonged war and an enlarged union.

In sum, the book argues that the EU constitution was interpreted constructively to deal with the reality of war. Nevertheless, the book maintains that the EU's response to the war in Ukraine has also revealed a number of weaknesses, which are largely due to structural and governance constraints of the EU constitution itself. Granted, several of these weaknesses predate Russia's aggression against Ukraine. In particular, the rule of law crisis has been a long-standing defect in the EU constitutional system.[120] However, the war has made it even more problematic.[121] In fact, democratic backsliding and outright defiance of EU rules by several Member States, notably Hungary and Poland, have delayed and complicated EU attempts to help Ukraine. For instance, Hungary repeatedly wielded its veto on sanctions, financial assistance for Ukraine, and enlargement in order to secure payouts on its NGEU funding, which was suspended under the rule of law conditionality regulation: thus, in December 2023 the European Council could agree to open accession negotiations with Ukraine[122] only after Hungary's Prime Minister Viktor Orban left the meeting room.[123] And while in an expression of solidarity the EU decided to waive custom duties on Ukraine's grain exports to facilitate its access to international markets, and connectedly to allow Ukrainian truckers to operate within the EU, Poland, Hungary, Romania, and Slovakia unilaterally blocked the border and boycotted Ukrainian produce, in complete breach of EU law, leading Ukraine to start dispute settlement proceedings before the World Trade Organization.[124]

Yet, the war in Ukraine has also revealed new shortcomings in the EU constitution, which could not be properly appreciated in peacetime. On the one hand, some provisions of the EU constitution—for example, that prohibiting the use of the EU budget for military purposes[125] or requiring unanimity to develop EU operational capabilities[126]—prevented the EU from adequately responding to Russian aggression. On the other hand, the EU constitution was too weak to restrain several of the

---

Slovenia, and Sweden did 'not support unconsidered and premature attempts to launch a process towards Treaty change').

[120] See Wojciech Sadurski, *Poland's Constitutional Breakdown* (OUP 2019); and Andras Sajo, *Ruling by Cheating: Governance in Illiberal Democracy* (CUP 2021).
[121] See Petra Bard and Dimitry Kochenov, 'War as a Pretext to Wave the Rule of Law Goodbye? The Case for an EU Constitutional Awakening' (2021) 27 European Law Journal 39; and Benedetta Lobina, 'Between a Rock and a Hard Place: The Impact of the Rule of Law Backsliding on the EU's Response to the Russo-Ukrainian War' (2023) 8 European Papers 1143.
[122] European Council conclusions, 14–15 December 2023, EUCO 20/23, para 15.
[123] See Philippe Jacqué et al, 'Accession Talks with Ukraine: How the EU Managed to Avoid a Hungarian Veto', *Le Monde* (15 December 2023).
[124] See World Trade Organization, 'Ukraine initiates WTO dispute complaints against Hungary, Poland, and Slovak Republic', 21 September 2023, https://www.wto.org/english/news_e/news23_e/ds619_620_621rfc_21sep23_e.htm.
[125] TEU, art 41(2).
[126] Ibid art 42(2).

EU's responses to the war. As a result, as has often been the case in constitutional democracies in times of emergency, the EU reaction to the war was occasionally shrouded in secrecy, and led to problematic consequences in terms of the protection of fundamental rights and the rule of law, including international law. Yet, a constitution should neither be a suicide pact[127] nor remain silent in times of war.[128] As the instrument of government for its 27 Member States, the EU treaties must enable the institutions they constituted to take effective and legitimate action when the EU faces existential security challenges. At the same time, as the basic charter of a polity founded on values of democracy, human rights, and the rule of law, the EU treaties should also continue to speak in wartime. In light of this, the book concludes by outlining several changes to the EU constitution that would be required, both to increase the EU institutions' capacity to act, and to constrain it properly through democratic mechanisms of checks and balances and fundamental rights protection.

From this perspective, the book advances both positive and normative arguments. On the positive side, it analyses *de jure condito* the developments that have occurred since the beginning of the war in the fields of CFSP/CSDP, economic and fiscal policy, justice and home affairs, energy and industrial policy, enlargement, and reforms. Here, the book claims that the EU constitution proved to be a 'living document',[129] which enabled the adoption of groundbreaking initiatives to deal with a war. However, the book also sheds light on how the EU constitution limited the EU's ability fully to address the challenges posed by the return of large-scale warfare on the European continent, due to several structural shortcomings in the current EU constitutional set-up—including most notably an ineffective governance, limited fiscal capacity, and the lack of military capabilities. At the same time, the book emphasizes how the EU constitution was occasionally too weak to constrain EU action in wartime. Hence, on the normative side, the book seeks to identify *de jure condendo* revisions to the EU constitution which would increase the EU capacity to provide for the common defence, promote the general welfare, establish justice, insure domestic tranquility, and secure the blessings of liberty—in other words changes that would 'form a more perfect Union'.

In this respect, the book also offers some thoughts on how the EU should adjust to Ukraine's enlargement, preparing its constitutional framework for this scenario. As mentioned above, in December 2023 the European Council opened accession talks with Ukraine, in June 2024 enlargement negotiations formally

---

[127] The statement that 'the Constitution is not a suicide pact' is usually attributed to US President Abraham Lincoln. For a more recent reappraisal see Richard Posner, *Not a Suicide Pact: The Constitution in a Time of National Emergency* (OUP 2006).

[128] The statement that 'the laws are silent in times of war' is originally by Cicero, Pro Milone, 11 ('*silent enim leges inter arma*'). For a more recent reappraisal see William Renquist, *All the Laws But One: Civil Liberties in Wartime* (Random House 1998).

[129] Alberto de Gregorio Merino, 'The EU Treaties as a Living Constitution of the Union in Times of Crisis' (2024) 118 American Journal of International Law 162.

INTRODUCTION 19

begun,[130] and in August 2023 European Council President Charles Michel indicated that he expects Ukraine to join the EU by 2030.[131] This book does not take a position on whether this timeline is realistic. In fact, according to some observers it is not even clear whether Ukraine will ultimately join the EU—not only due to uncertainties regarding the outcome of the war, but also to silent opposition against this in various quarters.[132] Yet, if there are strong geo-political pressures pushing for Ukraine's EU accession, it is essential that the EU at best prepares for it, and this implies introducing all the necessary adjustment to its constitutional set-up. With a pre-war population of approximately 41 million people, a per capita GDP of approximately US$4,500,[133] Ukraine would become the fifth most populous EU Member State, the primary beneficiary of EU structural and agriculture funds, and a major game-changer for the functioning of the EU. So, in this respect, the prospect of enlargement interplays with the EU's response to the war in Ukraine, and has to be assessed concurrently.

With that said, it is important to clarify what this book is *not* about. This volume does not examine the ongoing war in Ukraine and its day-to-day development per se. It is neither an historical study of the conflict's causes and continuation[134] nor an international relations analysis of the scenarios for its resolution, either on the battlefield or in the negotiating room. Similarly, this volume is not a public policy or international law work specifically focusing on the prospects of Ukraine's accession to the EU[135]—or to NATO, for that matter—particularly as a country at war, with one-fifth of its territory currently under enemy occupation.[136] Excellent research already exists on some of these questions, although of course nobody can know if, when, and how Ukraine will become a member of the EU—and indeed when and how the war will end. As reported by *The New York Times*, in Spring 2022 Ukrainian and Russian negotiators were apparently close to reaching a ceasefire and settling the conflict.[137] Eventually, however, diplomatic talks collapsed

---

[130] Council of the EU press release, 'EU opens accession negotiations with Ukraine', 25 June 2024, 577/24.
[131] European Council President Charles Michel, Speech at Bled Strategic Forum, 28 August 2023.
[132] See eg Göran von Sydow and Valentin Kreilinger (eds), *Fit for 35? Reforming the Politics and Institutions of the EU for an Enlarged Union* (Swedish Institute for European Political Studies 2023); and Laszlo Bruszt and Erik Jones, 'Ukraine's Perilous Path to EU Membership: How to Expand Europe without Destabilizing It', Foreign Affairs (30 May 2024).
[133] World Bank, 'GDP per capita (current US$): Ukraine', https://data.worldbank.org/indicator/NY.GDP.PCAP.CD?locations=UA.
[134] See eg Timothy Snyder, *The Road to Unfreedom: Russia, Europe, America* (Crown Publishing 2018) (historically explaining Russia's aggression against Ukraine—at the time of the publication of that book, related primarily to the illegal occupation of Crimea—through the prism of imperialism).
[135] See eg Roman Petrov and Christoph Hillion, '"Accession through War": Ukraine's Road to the EU' (2022) 59 Common Market Law Review 1289.
[136] See eg Federica Favuzza, 'How Does Belligerent Occupation End? Some Reflections on the Future of the Territories Occupied in the Russia-Ukraine Conflict' (2023) 8 European Papers 803.
[137] See Anton Troianovski et al, 'Ukraine-Russia Peace Is as Elusive as Ever: But in 2022 They Were Talking', *The New York Times* (15 June 2024) (disclosing draft negotiating documents for a peace agreement).

over security guarantees, and since then international initiatives have failed to achieve their objective,[138] given the continuing unbelievable brutality of Russia's illegal aggression, uncertainty on the US commitments,[139] and disagreements on the peace formula.[140] This book steers away from these issues, which are important but ultimately irrelevant for the purposes of this research. As mentioned above, this book's goal is to examine the EU constitution in time of war—a topic which is surely relevant, and that can safely be approached now, without sliding into a questionable prediction business.

5 Conclusion

As the writing of this book came to an end, it is now 32 months—1,000 days—since Russia launched a massive invasion of its sovereign neighbour. Thus, it is time to provide a comprehensive assessment of how the EU constitution has fared in the face of the first war of its history. How did the EU provide for the common defence? How did the EU promote general welfare? How did it establish justice? How did it insure domestic tranquillity? And how did it secure the 'Blessings of Liberty'? The book is structured according to this analytical grid, with the next five chapters each critically assessing the core war-related legal developments in key domains of EU law, their consequences, and their challenges. Needless to say, some of the topics addressed in one chapter overlap with those examined in another—but this is inevitable, as government action can never be squeezed into fully separate silos. The book's structure is primarily designed to facilitate the exposition, and guide the reader, who can zoom in only on the topics which are of interest. Yet, the book is a comprehensive whole, as will also become apparent from the conclusion, which sums up the overall theses of this volume and finally advances possible avenues to form a more perfect EU for both times of war and peace.

---

[138] See also Switzerland Department of Foreign Affairs, Summit on Peace in Ukraine, 15–16 June 2024.
[139] See also Camille Grand, 'Defending Europe with Less America', European Council on Foreign Relations Policy Brief, 3 July 2024.
[140] See also Tracey German and Andriy Tyushka, 'Ukraine's 10-point peace plan and the Kyiv Security Compact: An assessment', study commissioned by the European Parliament Foreign Affairs and Trade Committee, January 2024.

2
To 'provide for the common defense'
Developments in foreign affairs and defence

1 Introduction

Wars are violent. But the war in Ukraine has been particularly brutal in scale and duration, turning into the most high-intensity military conflict in the European continent since the end of the Second World War. As stated by the Secretary General of the North Atlantic Treaty Organization (NATO) Jens Stoltenberg, when Russia launched its large-scale invasion of Ukraine in February 2022, it attacked with coordinated air and missile bombing, and ground and special forces from multiple directions.[1] In early March 2022, the media reported that Russian military convoys directed towards Kyiv, the capital of Ukraine, stretched for 40 miles.[2] The Ukrainian army, however, fought back fiercely, and repelled the invading forces. With Russia still occupying approximately one-fifth of Ukraine's territory, however, since summer 2022 the fighting has turned into a furious war of attrition stretching over a 600-mile front line, in which the average number of shells fired by the Ukrainian army exceeds 120,000 rounds every month.[3] This has resulted in staggering civilian and military casualties. In fact, by August 2023 the United States (US) Department of Defense estimated that the number of Ukrainian and Russian troops killed or wounded surpassed 500,000;[4] by February 2024, the United Kingdom (UK) Ministry of Defence estimated over 350,000 Russian deaths, and the destruction of at least 2,600 tanks and 4,900 armoured vehicles;[5] and by September 2024, the number of Russian and Ukrainian dead and injured reached almost 1 million.[6]

---

[1] NATO Secretary General Jens Stoltenberg press briefing, 24 February 2022, https://www.nato.int/cps/en/natohq/opinions_192408.htm.
[2] See Peter Beaumont, 'Vast Russian military convoy may be harbinger of a siege of Kyiv', *The Guardian* (1 March 2022).
[3] See Steven Erlanger, 'Ukraine Needs Shells, and Arms Makers Want Money. Enter the E.U.', *The New York Times* (8 March 2023)
[4] See Helene Cooper et al, 'Troop Deaths and Injuries in Ukraine War Near 500,000, U.S. Officials Say', *The New York Times* (18 August 2023).
[5] See George Allison, 'UK Estimates 350,000 Russian Troops, 2600 Tanks Lost in Ukraine', *UK Defence Journal* (1 February 2024).
[6] See Bojan Pancevski, 'One Million Are Now Dead or Injured in the Russia-Ukraine War', *The Wall Street Journal* (17 September 2024).

The purpose of this chapter is to examine from an European Union (EU) law and policy perspective the key measures that the EU deployed from 2022 to 2024 to respond to Russia's aggression against Ukraine in the fields of foreign affairs and defence—Common Foreign and Security Policy (CFSP) and Common Security and Defense Policy (CSDP). Needless to say, important defence measures to assist Ukraine were taken by EU Member States individually, primarily in the NATO framework, and in coordination with the US.[7] In fact, the US has been by far the largest provider of military support to Ukraine.[8] Nevertheless, this chapter focuses specifically on the EU itself, mapping the significant diplomatic, military assistance, and defence production measures that it has taken since the start of the war. In particular, the chapter examines the security guarantees adopted by the EU towards Ukraine, and analyses the Act in Support of Ammunition Production (ASAP),[9] a groundbreaking EU regulation adopted by the European Parliament and the Council in 2023 with the aim of ramping up the production capabilities of the EU defence industry, and providing weapons to Ukraine. A particular urgency surrounded this new EU defence production effort: hence the acronym of the regulation, which reveals the EU's ambition to replenish Ukrainian stockpiles—as soon as possible.

As the chapter argues, the EU constitution enabled the EU to take steps to 'provide for the common defense',[10] and the EU's response to the war in Ukraine in the field of CFSP/CSDP has been wide-ranging. The EU clarified its foreign policy strategy and provided direct military support to Ukraine, procuring lethal weapons and setting up a military assistance mission for its armed forces. Moreover, in line with the goal set by EU leaders in the March 2022 Versailles Declaration to 'take more responsibility for our security and take further more decisive steps towards building our European sovereignty [...by] (a) bolstering our defence capabilities',[11] the EU strengthened its defence industrial capacity. In particular, through the ASAP, the instrument for the reinforcement of the European defence industry through common Procurement Act (EDIRPA),[12]

---

[7] See Claire Mills, 'Military Assistance to Ukraine since the Russian Invasion', House of Commons Library research briefing, 30 March 2023, now updated as Claire Mills, 'Military Assistance to Ukraine since the Russian Invasion', House of Commons Library research briefing, 24 September 2024.

[8] See US Government Accountability Office, 'Ukraine: Status and Use of Supplemental US Funding, as of First Quarter, Fiscal Year 2024', 30 May 2024, https://www.gao.gov/products/gao-24-107 232 (estimating over US$113 billion of federal funding provided for US agencies as of 31 December 2023 to provide arms to Ukraine, aid civilians, impose sanctions, and more).

[9] Regulation (EU) 2023/1525 of the European Parliament and of the Council of 20 July 2023 on supporting ammunition production (ASAP) [2023] OJ L185/7.

[10] US Const, preamble..

[11] Informal meeting of the heads of state or government, Versailles Declaration, 10–11 March 2022, para 7.

[12] Regulation (EU) 2023/2418 of the European Parliament and of the Council of 18 October 2023 on establishing an instrument for the reinforcement of the European defence industry through common procurement (EDIRPA) [2023] OJ L1.

and other initiatives, the EU ventured into the field of industrial defence production and fostered greater common investment in defence. Specifically, with the ASAP the EU accelerated the procurement and delivery of ground-to-ground and artillery munitions, as well as missiles, which are needed by Ukraine on the battlefield, and funded for the first time ever with EU money ammunitions' production and procurement. These acts move the EU in the direction of establishing a European defence union, seen both as a combination of military capability and industrial capacity.

Nevertheless, as this chapter maintains, structural limitations in the EU constitution in the fields of CFSP and CSDP have weakened the EU's ability to respond properly to the challenge of the war in Ukraine. In fact, Russia's aggression has reinvigorated the leading role of NATO as the centrepiece of European security—a pattern visible in the recent decisions of Finland and Sweden to join the transatlantic defence alliance.[13] Moreover, due to funding and governance problems, EU investment in defence industrial production proved underwhelming, and failed to reach the self-imposed goal to provide at least 1 million rounds of ammunition to the Ukrainian army within a year.[14] In fact, the limits of the ASAP become evident when this measure is compared with the gold standard in the field, namely the US Defense Production Act (DPA).[15] To begin with, the funding for the ASAP charged on the EU budget is remarkably limited—only €500 million for two years. Moreover, the final ASAP regulation dropped some of the ambitions of the original Commission proposal, including the power to compel private companies to produce specific defence equipment as a priority—a hallmark of the DPA. As a consequence, it appears that if the EU wants to be serious about its defence, given the ongoing conflict and the uncertainties about future US commitment, new and more ambitious EU initiatives will be needed.

As such, this chapter is structured as follows. Section 2 examines the core strategic, military assistance, and defence production measures adopted by the EU in response to the war in Ukraine. Section 3 discusses the consequences of war-related developments in CFSP/CSDP, assessing among others the novel use of EU legal bases in the field of industrial policy and its significance for the role of the EU in defence production. Section 4, however, critically considers a number of weaknesses in CFSP/CSDP developments during the war in Ukraine, and highlights the unsettled status of the EU defence union. Section 5, finally, concludes.

---

[13] See Carl Bildt, 'NATO's Nordic Expansion', Foreign Affairs (26 April 2022).
[14] High Representative/Vice-President Josep Borrell press remarks, 31 January 2024.
[15] Defense Production Act of 1950, Pub L No 81–774.

2 The core measures

2.1 Strategic posturing

The outbreak of the war in Ukraine led the EU to clarify its foreign policy strategy. In 2016, the EU High Representative for Foreign Affairs and Security Policy—which since the entry into force of the Lisbon Treaty is also *ex officio* Vice President of the European Commission and the head of the European External Action Service—had laid out an EU global strategy to deal with CFSP.[16] But as EU heads of state and government pointed out in the March 2022 Versailles Declaration, Russia's aggression against Ukraine required a profound rethink of the EU's geo-strategic role and position. As a result, under the aegis of the High Representative in March 2022 the Council adopted in accordance with the provisions of Title V TEU a new strategic compass for security and defence[17]—an official document designed to outline the EU's CFSP/CSDP stance. The strategic compass had been long in the making, and had largely been hampered by Member States' diverging external relations interests. In response to Russia's aggression against Ukraine, however, the strategic compass was decisively revised, and quickly approved by the Council on the understanding that 'Russia's war of aggression constitutes a tectonic shift in European history'.[18]

Specifically, the strategic compass identified the threat posed by Russia, acknowledged more explicitly the geo-strategic challenges arising from China, and called for 'a quantum leap forward'[19] in CFSP/CSDP. To this end, it identified four strands of action. First—under the heading 'Act'—the strategic compass called for stepping up efforts to prepare for crises, and in this framework planned to develop 'by 2025, an EU Rapid Deployment Capacity, allowing the swift deployment of a modular force of up to 5,000 troops in a non-permissive environment'.[20] Secondly—under the heading 'Secure'—the strategic compass stressed the need to enhance the EU's ability to anticipate threats, including through greater intelligence sharing. Thirdly—under the heading 'Invest'—the strategic compass set the goal 'to resolutely invest more and better in defence capabilities and innovative technologies'.[21] Finally—under the heading 'Partner'—the strategic compass underlined the need for the EU to reinforce its multilateral, regional, and bilateral

---

[16] See High Representative of the EU for Foreign Affairs and Security Policy, 'Shared Vision, Common Action: A Stronger Europe, A Global Strategy for the EU Foreign and Security Policy, June 2016.
[17] See Council of the EU, 'A strategic compass for security and defence: For a European Union that protects its citizens, values and interests and contributes to international peace and security', 21 March 2022, Doc 7371/22.
[18] Ibid 5.
[19] Ibid 6.
[20] Ibid 19.
[21] Ibid 30.

partnerships. In particular, in view of the 'competition of governance system' between democracy and autocracy,[22] the strategic compass highlighted the importance of cooperation with the US and NATO, a development that will be further examined in detail in Chapter 6.

The strategic compass also called for an intensification of permanent structured cooperation (PESCO) in defence.[23] As is well known, Article 42(6) TEU allows those Member States 'whose military capabilities fulfil higher criteria and which have made more binding commitments to one another' to deepen their cooperation, in accordance with the more detailed rules of Protocol 10, attached to the TEU and the TFEU. In fact, in 2017 Member States had launched PESCO,[24] and subsequently authorized a number of operational projects.[25] Following the approval of the strategic compass, PESCO efforts were increased, with for instance initiatives to facilitate intra-EU military mobility.[26] Furthermore, the strategic compass acknowledged the need for greater force generation by the EU for military missions and operations.[27] The EU had previously attempted to create a rapid reaction force through multinational battlegroups or the like,[28] and in 2017 it had set up a military command and control structure for CSDP missions.[29] The strategic compass, however, called for a more robust development in this domain, by envisioning the creation of a rapid reaction force capable of operating in conflict zones. In fact, the EU response to the war in Ukraine did not remain confined to the strategic and diplomatic arena.

2.2 Military assistance and security commitments

In the immediate aftermath of Russia's large-scale invasion of Ukraine, Denmark decided to reconsider the opt-out it had enjoyed for 30 years—since the 1992 Treaty of Maastricht—on CSDP, pursuant to Article 5, Protocol 22 on the position of Denmark, attached to the TEU and the TFEU. Following a referendum held on 1 June 2022, therefore, Denmark joined the CSDP, including the European

---

[22] Ibid 5.
[23] Ibid 33.
[24] See Council Decision (CFSP) 2017/2315 of 11 December 2017 establishing permanent structured cooperation (PESCO) and determining the list of participating Member States [2017] OJ L331/57.
[25] See Council Decision (CFSP) 2018/340 of 6 March 2018 establishing the list of projects to be developed under PESCO [2018] OJ L65/24.
[26] See European Commission and High Representative Joint Communication Action Plan on Military Mobility 2.0, 10 November 2022, JOIN(2022) 48 final.
[27] Council of the EU (n 17) 17.
[28] See Christoph O Meyer, Ton Van Osch, and Y F Reykers, 'From EU Battlegroups to Rapid Deployment Capacity: Learning the Right Lessons?' (2024) 100 International Affairs 181.
[29] See Council of the EU conclusions, 'On Progress in Implementing the EU Global Strategy in the Area of Security and Defence, Annex: Concept Note: Operational Planning and Conduct Capabilities for CSDP Missions and Operations', 6 March 2017, Doc 110/117.

Defence Agency (EDA).[30] This ensured that all 27 EU Member States were now participating in CSDP policies and institutions, albeit with the proviso, enshrined in the second paragraph of Article 42(2) TEU, that this 'shall not prejudice the specific character of the security and defence policy of certain Member States'. This is, as is well known, a nod to the fact that some EU countries abide by a principle of neutrality. Yet, with the accession to NATO in 2023 and 2024 of Finland and Sweden—two traditionally non-aligned EU countries—the number of neutral EU Member States has now been reduced to just four small Member States, namely Austria, Cyprus, Ireland, and Malta. In any event, the neutrality of these four Member States did not prevent the EU from embracing a strong military response to Russia's brutal aggression against Ukraine.

In particular, for the first time ever the EU mobilized the European Peace Facility (EPF)[31]—a novel financial instrument established in connection with the new EU Multi-annual Financial Framework (MFF), which will be examined in greater detail in Chapter 3. In February 2022, the EU decided to use the EPF to support the Ukrainian military directly, providing funding for the purchase of lethal weapons.[32] Moreover, also through the EPF, the EU activated a military assistance mission, code named EUMAM Ukraine, to train Ukrainian soldiers to use the advanced weapons provided by European countries.[33] While Article 42(1) TEU foresees that the EU may carry out missions 'for peace-keeping, conflict prevention and strengthening international security in accordance with the principles of the United Nations Charter'—and the EU had done so before[34]—EUMAM Ukraine constituted a significant upscaling of EU involvement in CSDP,[35] as this military assistance mission provided large-scale training to an ever growing number of soldiers of the Ukrainian army—over 55,000 by summer 2024.[36] At the same time, the EU also incentivized Member States to donate weapons and advanced military technology available in their arsenals

---

[30] See also High Representative/Vice-President Josep Borrell, statement on the outcome of the referendum on the opt-out in defence matters, 1 June 2022.

[31] Council Decision (CFSP) 2021/509 of 22 March 2021 establishing a European Peace Facility and repealing Decision (CFSP) 2015/528 [2021] OJ L102/14.

[32] Council Decision (CFSP) 2022/338 of 28 February 2022 on an assistance measure under the European Peace Facility for the supply to the Ukrainian Armed Forces of military equipment, and platforms, designed to deliver lethal force [2022] OJ L60/1.

[33] Council Decision (CFSP) 2022/2245 of 14 November 2022 on an assistance measure under the European Peace Facility to support the Ukrainian Armed Forces trained by the European Union Military Assistance Mission in support of Ukraine with military equipment, and platforms, designed to deliver lethal force [2022] OJ L294/25.

[34] See eg Council Decision (CFSP) 2021/1143 of 12 July 2021 on a European Union Military Training Mission in Mozambique (EUTM Mozambique) [2021] OJ L247/93.

[35] See Ulrich Krotz and Katerina Wright, 'CSDP military operations' in Hugo Meijer and Marco Wyss (eds), *The Handbook of European Defence Policies and Armed Forces* (OUP 2018) 870.

[36] See Council of the EU press release, 'European Peace Facility: Council greenlights further funding for training of the Ukrainian Armed Forces under EUMAM Ukraine', 28 November 2023, 943/23; and European Parliament resolution of 17 July 2024 on the need for the EU's continuous support for Ukraine, P10_TA(2024) 0003, para C.

to Ukraine, opening the possibility in April 2023 of obtaining a reimbursement from the EPF.[37]

Furthermore, on 27 November 2023 the Council of the EU endorsed a framework of security commitments to Ukraine.[38] While this was initially not made public, following bilateral security cooperation agreements with Ukraine concluded by the UK,[39] several EU Member States,[40] and especially the US,[41] on 27 June 2024 the EU officially adopted joint security commitments with Ukraine.[42] These commitments, laid out in a 12-page document released at the margin of a European Council meeting, aimed at providing 'predictable, long-term and sustainable support for Ukraine's security and defence'[43] but considered these 'in a holistic manner'.[44] As such, the joint security commitments covered several defence-specific matters,[45] including long-term provision of military equipment, military training, cooperation between the EU and Ukrainian defence industry, cyber and hybrid threats, demining, law enforcement, and intelligence sharing. However, the arrangements also included 'wider security commitments',[46] including support for Ukraine's accession path, diplomatic outreach, financial support, gradual integration in the EU single market, temporary protection for Ukrainian refugees, sanctions, the use of extraordinary revenues resulting from Russia's immobilized assets, and support for accountability. The commitments also included a consultation mechanism,[47] whereby 'in the event of a future aggression, the [EU] and Ukraine, at the request of either side, will consult within 24 hours on Ukraine needs ... and determine appropriate next steps'.[48] Finally, the commitments envisioned a review no later than 10 years from the date of signature,[49] subjected the validity of the deal to Ukraine's compliance with the values of Article 2 TEU, and clarified that the EU's security commitments 'are complementary and

---

[37] Council Decision (CFSP) 2023/810 of 13 April 2023 amending Decision (CFSP) 2022/338 on an assistance measure under the European Peace Facility for the supply to the Ukrainian Armed Forces of military equipment, and platforms, designed to deliver lethal force [2023] OJ L101/64.
[38] See Alberto Nardelli and Natalia Drozdiak, 'EU Prepares Plan to Give Ukraine Lasting Security Commitments', *Bloomberg* (21 November 2023) https://www.bloomberg.com/news/articles/2023-11-21/eu-prepares-plan-to-give-ukraine-lasting-security-commitments (reporting about a framework of the EU's Security Commitments to Ukraine, endorsed by the Council on 27 November 2023).
[39] Agreement on Security Cooperation between the United Kingdom of Great Britain and Northern Ireland and Ukraine, 12 January 2024.
[40] See eg Agreement on security cooperation between France and Ukraine, 16 February 2024; Agreement on Security Cooperation and Long Term Support between the Federal Republic of Germany and Ukraine, 16 February 2024; Agreement on Security Cooperation between Italy and Ukraine, 24 February 2024.
[41] Bilateral Security Agreement between the United States of America and Ukraine, 13 June 2024.
[42] Joint Security Commitments between the European Union and Ukraine, 27 June 2024.
[43] Ibid 2.
[44] Ibid.
[45] Ibid s I.
[46] Ibid s II.
[47] Ibid s III.
[48] Ibid 11.
[49] Ibid s IV.

mutually reinforc[e]'[50] the bilateral commitments provided by several EU Member States.

Finally, in July 2024 the EU also signed the Ukraine compact[51] concluded at the margin of the NATO 75th anniversary summit held in Washington DC.[52] This document— also endorsed by the US, the UK, Japan, Canada, Norway, and 17 EU Member States, as well as by Ukraine—was designed to provide security reassurances to Ukraine on its path towards NATO membership.[53] To this end, the compact reaffirmed the signatories' commitment to 'support Ukraine's immediate defence and security need, including through the continued provision of security assistance and training, modern military equipment, and defence industrial and necessary economic support'.[54] Moreover, the compact contained a commitment to 'accelerate efforts to build a Ukrainian future force that maintains a credible defence and deterrence capability',[55] and 'in the event of a future Russian armed attack against Ukraine [... to] convene swiftly and collectively at the most senior levels to determine appropriate next steps in supporting Ukraine as it exercises its right of self-defence'.[56]

2.3 Defence production

The war in Ukraine quickly exposed the limited military capabilities and dwindling arsenals of the EU Member States—a process caused by two interrelated factors. On the one hand, under the post-Cold War peace dividend, Member States had consistently reduced their defence spending, shifting expenditures towards the welfare state. In fact, this had long been a matter of complaint by US administrations, both Democratic and Republicans: while in 2014, following Russia's illegal invasion and annexation of Crimea, NATO had set a target of 2% of national GDP spending on defence,[57] European countries had largely failed to abide by this rule.[58] On the other hand, uncoordinated national military expenditure had led to fragmentation, duplication, and waste—a dynamic often called the cost of non-Europe in defence.[59] To address this daunting state of affairs, the Versailles

---

[50] Ibid 12.
[51] European Commission statement: 'Ukraine Compact', 11 July 2024.
[52] NATO Washington Summit Declaration, 10 July 2024, para 16.
[53] See also Louisa Brooke-Holland, 'NATO enlargement: Ukraine', House of Commons Library research briefing, 20 July 2023.
[54] Ukraine Compact (n 51) s 1.
[55] Ibid s 2.
[56] Ibid s 3.
[57] See Summit Declaration Issued by the Heads of State and Government Participating in the Meeting of the North Atlantic Council in Wales, 5 September 2014, para 14.
[58] See Federico Fabbrini, 'Do NATO Obligations Trump European Budgetary Constraints?' (2018) 9 Harvard National Security Journal 121.
[59] See Blanca Ballester, 'The Cost of Non-Europe in Common Security and Defence Policy', European Parliament Research Service, December 2013.

Declaration explicitly called on the European Commission to analyse the EU's 'defence investment gaps … and to propose any further initiative necessary to strengthen the European defence industrial and technological base'.[60]

In response to this request, in May 2022 the European Commission and High Representative published a joint communication on the defence investment gap and the way forward, where they outlined options to incentivize joint procurement of military equipment.[61] Building on this policy document, in July 2022 the Commission put forward a legislative proposal for an EDIRPA:[62] this short-term instrument, which had its legal basis in Article 173 TFEU on industrial policy, was specifically designed to incentivize the EU Member States to procure defence products jointly, addressing the EU's most urgent and critical defence capability gaps and developing the EU's Defence Technological and Industrial Base (EDTIB). To this end, the Commission proposed for EDIRPA a dedicated financial envelope of €500 million, to be drawn down from the EU budget. The EDIRPA regulation was ultimately approved by the European Parliament and the Council in October 2023, but with a smaller budget of €300 million for the period until 31 December 2025.

As the war increasingly turned into a high-intensity conflict of attrition, however, a specific need emerged to supply the Ukrainian army with ammunition on the battlefield. On 20 March 2023, therefore, the Council unanimously approved a three-step plan to secure the delivery and joint procurement of ammunition for Ukraine.[63] First, the 'Council call[ed] on Member States to urgently deliver ground-to-ground and artillery ammunition to Ukraine and, if requested, missiles'[64] Secondly, the "Council further call[ed] on Member States to jointly procure 155mm ammunition and, if requested, missiles for Ukraine in the fastest way possible before 30 September 2023".[65] Thirdly, the 'Council invite[d] the Commission to present concrete proposals to urgently support the ramp-up of manufacturing capacities of the European defence industry, secure supply chains, facilitate efficient procurement procedures, address shortfalls in production capacities and promote investments, including, where appropriate, mobilising the Union budget'.[66] On this basis, in May 2023 the Commission put forward a proposal for an ASAP regulation,[67] as a complement to the EDIRPA. The ASAP—which has

---

[60] Versailles Declaration (n 11) para 11.
[61] See European Commission and High Representative Joint Communication on Defence Investment Gap Analysis and Way Forward, 18 May 2022, JOIN(2022) 24 final, 9–10.
[62] See European Commission proposal for a Regulation of the European Parliament and of the Council on establishing the European defence industry Reinforcement through common procurement Act, 19 July 2022, COM(2022) 349 final.
[63] Council of the EU, Doc 7632/23, Annex: Speeding up the delivery and joint procurement of ammunition for Ukraine, 20 March 2023.
[64] Ibid para 2.
[65] Ibid para 3.
[66] Ibid para 4.
[67] European Commission proposal for a Regulation of the European Parliament and of the Council on establishing the Act in Support of Ammunition Production, 3 May 2023, COM(2023) 237 final.

as its legal bases Article 173 TFEU on industrial policy, together with Article 114 TFEU on internal market—was approved by the co-legislators at record speed, indeed much faster than the EDIRPA, and entered into force in July 2023, with an envelope of €500 million, funded from the EU budget, for the period from 25 July 2023 until 30 June 2025.[68]

The ASAP regulation is a relatively lean piece of EU legislation, comprising 24 articles, structured in five chapters. The preamble to the regulation recalls the historical setting in which the ASAP was put forward, including the outbreak of the war in Ukraine and the consequential decision taken by heads of state and government in the Versailles summit of 11 March 2022 to 'take further decisive steps towards building European sovereignty'.[69] The preamble also explains the rationale for the adoption of the ASAP, namely Ukraine's pressing defence need of ground-to-ground and artillery munitions and missiles and the urgency of increasing production to replenish rapidly depleting national stocks.[70] The regulation furthermore highlights 'the specificities of the defence industry, where demand comes almost exclusively from Member States',[71] clarifying that 'the functioning of the defence industry sector does not follow the conventional rules and business models that govern more traditional markets'.[72] As such, the ASAP emphasizes how 'additional [EU] industrial policy measures are necessary to ensure a rapid ramp-up of manufacturing capacities'[73] and stresses that EU 'defence industry is a crucial contribution to the resilience and the security of the [EU]'.[74]

Article 1 of the regulation states that the purpose of the ASAP is to 'establish[] a set of measures and lay[] down a budget aimed at urgently strengthening the responsiveness and ability of the [EDTIB] to ensure the timely availability and supply of ... relevant defence products'. This overall purpose if further teased out in Article 4, which clarifies that: 'The objective of the Instrument is to foster the efficiency and competitiveness of the [EDTIB] to support the ramp-up of the production capacity and timely delivery of relevant defence products through industrial reinforcement.' To this end, Article 5 sets aside a budget of €500 million in current prices, 'for the period 25 July 2023 to 30 June 2025'. Indeed, as indicated in Article 24(2), '[t]his Regulation shall apply until 30 June 2025'—hence with a sunset clause. Nevertheless, pursuant to Articles 1(2) and 23, '[b]y 30 June 2024, the Commission shall draw up a report evaluating the implementation of the measures set out in this Regulation and their results, as well as the opportunity to extend their applicability and provide for their funding'[75]—and the Commission

---

[68] Regulation (EU) 2023/1525 (n 9).
[69] Ibid recital 2.
[70] Ibid recital 4.
[71] Ibid recital 20.
[72] Ibid.
[73] Ibid recital 6.
[74] Ibid recital 34.
[75] Ibid art 23(1).

has recently assessed the implementation of the programme in positive terms.[76] Moreover, as stated in Article 6, ASAP funding 'shall be implemented in synergy with other [EU] programmes', with the consequence that an action receiving funding under this regulation may also receive support from other EU funding schemes, provided alternative contributions do not cover the same costs.

The substantive core of the ASAP is enshrined in Article 8. This provision clarifies the eligible actions to be funded, and states that '[t]he Instrument shall provide financial support for actions addressing identified bottlenecks in production capacities and supply chains with a view to securing and accelerating the production of relevant defence products in order to ensure their effective supply and timely availability'.[77] The provision, in particular, lists a number of defence production activities, including the optimization, expansion, modernization, upgrading, or repurposing of existing, or the establishment of new, production capacities, in relation to relevant defence products; the establishment of cross-border industrial partnerships; the testing and reconditioning of defence products; and the training, reskilling, or upskilling of personnel. At the same time, Article 8(4) prohibits the use of ASAP funding for 'actions related to the production of goods or delivery of services which are prohibited by applicable international law; [and] actions related to the production of lethal autonomous weapons'. From this point of view, for example, the ASAP could not be used to produce cluster munitions, which the US controversially decided to provide to Ukraine at its request,[78] but which are banned by an international convention.[79]

From a management viewpoint, Article 12 of the regulation empowers the Commission to lay out a work programme, and directly award ASAP funding to relevant defence industries, based on their applications. According to Article 11(2), the 'Commission shall, by means of implementing acts, award the funding under this Regulation'. Pursuant to Article 10(1), eligible entities include 'public or privately owned [companies], which are established and have their executive management structures in the [EU] or in an associated country'. In fact, as stated in Article 3, the ASAP is open also to members of the European Economic Area. As clarified in Article 11, the award of funding depends on several criteria, including: increase in production capacity in the EU; reduction of lead production time; elimination of sourcing and production bottlenecks; and resilience through cross-border cooperation. As stated in Article 9, the financing rate offered by the EU can fund 'up to 35% of the eligible costs of an eligible action related to the

---

[76] See European Commission report on the implementation of the of Regulation (EU) 2023/1525 of the European Parliament and of the Council of 20 July 2023 on supporting ammunition production (ASAP), 8 July 2024, COM(2024) 296 final.

[77] Regulation (EU) 2023/1525 (n 9) art 8(2).

[78] 'Pourquoi la livraison d'armes à sous-munitions à l'Ukraine annoncée par Washington est controversée', *Le Monde* (7 July 2023).

[79] Convention on Cluster Munitions (CCM).

production capacities of relevant defence products, and up to 40% of the eligible costs of an eligible action related to the production capacities of components and raw materials insofar as they are intended or used wholly for the production of relevant defence products'. However, this percentage can increase further 'where applicants demonstrate a contribution to the creation of new cross-border cooperation' or 'where applicants commit to prioritising, for the duration of the action, orders stemming from ... the common procurement of relevant defence products by at least three Member States; [or] the procurement of relevant defence products [... for] Ukraine'.[80]

Moreover, the regulation introduces further special provision to secure the security of supply. To ensure the timely availability of relevant defence products, Member States are encouraged to accelerate the permit granting process related to the planning, construction, and operation of production facilities, and transfer of inputs within the EU, as well as qualification and certification of end products.[81] To facilitate common procurement during the ammunition supply crisis, Article 14 of the regulation introduces a derogation to Directive 2009/81/EC on defence procurement,[82] allowing at least two EU Member States to modify existing framework agreements to increase production. At the same time, 'to leverage, de-risk and speed-up investments needed to increase manufacturing capacities' Article 15 authorizes the establishment of a ramp-up fund, which the Commission will manage.[83] The regulation then introduces final provisions on security of information,[84] confidentiality,[85] data protection,[86] and publicity,[87] while also foreseeing standard audit mechanisms to protect the financial interests of the EU.[88]

The Commission allocated the full €500 million of funding under the ASAP, and the €300 million under EDIRPA, by March 2024.[89] At the same time—building on these instruments' experience and considering their limited life-spans—in March 2024 the Commission jointly with the High Representative also advanced a new European Defence Industrial Strategy (EDIS), designed to increase EU military readiness through a responsive and resilient European defence industry.[90] As

---

[80] Regulation (EU) 2023/1525 (n 9) art 9(2).
[81] Ibid art 13.
[82] Directive 2009/81/EC of the European Parliament and of the Council of 13 July 2009 on the coordination of procedures for the award of certain works contracts, supply contracts and service contracts by contracting authorities or entities in the fields of defence and security, and amending Directives 2004/17/EC and 2004/18/EC [2009] OJ L216/76.
[83] Regulation (EU) 2023/1525 (n 9) art 7(1).
[84] Ibid art 17.
[85] Ibid art 18.
[86] Ibid art 19.
[87] Ibid art 22.
[88] Ibid arts 20 and 21.
[89] European Commission press release, 'The Commission allocates €500 million to ramp up ammunition production, out of a total of €2 billion to strengthen EU's defence industry', 15 March 2024.
[90] European Commission and High Representative Joint Communication, 'A new European Defence Industrial Strategy: Achieving EU readiness through a responsive and resilient European Defence Industry', 5 March 2024, JOIN(2024) 10 final.

a core part of the EDIS, the Commission proposed a European Parliament and the Council regulation—based among others on Article 173 TFEU on industry, and Article 114 TFEU on internal market—establishing the European Defence Industry Programme (EDIP) and a framework of measures to ensure the timely availability and supply of defence products.[91] The EDIP, which would be allocated a budget of €1.5 billion—funded from the EU budget until 31 December 2027—would include a fund to accelerate defence supply chain transformations (FAST),[92] as well as a Structure for European Armament Programme, supporting common procurement of defence products.[93] Moreover, the EDIP would also establish a Defence Industrial Readiness Board,[94] and empower the Commission to exercise authoritative power in cases of security of supply challenges.[95]

In March 2024, the European Council 'invite[d] the Council to take forward without delay [... the] EDIP'.[96] The issue of strengthening the EU defence industry market was also at the core of two high level reports on the deepening of the internal market and the future of EU economic competitiveness written by former Italian Prime Ministers Enrico Letta[97] and Mario Draghi,[98] released respectively in April 2024 and September 2024. In fact, the Strategic Agenda 2024–2029 approved by the European Council in June 2024 indicated the plan '[g]oing forward... [to] invest substantially more and better together, ... scale up our capacities and strengthen the European defence technological and industrial base'.[99] Moreover, the political guidelines presented before the European Parliament by European Commission President von der Leyen in July 2024 confirmed her forthcoming plan 'to invest more in [EU] defence industry ... and reinforce the [EDIP] to incentivize common procurement'.[100] Hence, further action is to be awaited in this space.

3 The consequences

The measures adopted by the EU to respond to Russia's aggression against Ukraine in the field of foreign affairs and defence are significant, and reveal the potential of

---

[91] European Commission proposal for a regulation of the European Parliament and of the Council establishing the European Defence Industry Programme and a framework of measures to ensure the timely availability and supply of defence products, 5 March 2024, COM(2024) 150 final.
[92] Ibid art 19.
[93] Ibid art 22.
[94] Ibid art 57.
[95] Ibid art 50.
[96] European Council conclusions, 21–22 March 2024, EUCO 7/24, para 16.
[97] See Enrico Letta, 'Much More than a Market: Speed, Security, Solidarity', 17 April 2024.
[98] See Mario Draghi, 'The Future of European Competitiveness. Part A. A Competitiveness Strategy for Europe', 9 September 2024.
[99] European Council conclusions, 27 June 2024, EUCO 15/24, Annex: Strategic Agenda 2024–2029, 16.
[100] European Commission President-elect Ursula von der Leyen, 'Europe's Choice: Political Guidelines for the next European Commission 2024-2029', 18 July 2024, 14.

the EU constitution in times of war. As Steven Blockmans has argued, European integration in the fields of CFSP and CSDP has advanced more in the three years since 2022 than it had during the previous three decades.[101] Facing the return of war in Europe, and in view of the brutal violence of Russia's aggression against Ukraine, the EU responded forcefully. In particular, the EU adjusted its strategic posturing, provided military assistance and security commitments to Ukraine, and developed a domestic defence production programme to strengthen the EDTIB and its ability to provide arms. The EU's unwavering response to Russia's invasion was facilitated by the leadership of European Commission President Ursula von der Leyen, who during the war emerged as a staunch defender of Ukraine and a key player in the building of an international coalition to repel Russia[102]—in line with a growing presidentialization of the European Commission.[103] At the same time, EU action in CFSP was also strongly backed by the European Parliament.[104]

Yet, because pursuant to Article 24 TEU both the Commission and the European Parliament have very limited formal powers in CFSP/CSDP, from an institutional perspective it is really the Council—especially the Foreign Affairs Council, ex Article 27 TEU under the permanent chairmanship of the High Representative—which has served as the motor of EU legal action. Moreover, the adoption of groundbreaking measures, such as the activation of the EUMAM Ukraine, and the delivery of lethal weapons to the Ukrainian army, were made possible by the mechanism of constructive abstention in the Council, foreseen by the second paragraph of Article 31(1) TEU. While decisions in CFSP/CSDP have to be taken by the Council unanimously, constructive abstention pragmatically allows a Member State to abstain from a vote and not apply a specific measure, while accepting that it still commits the EU. As underlined by Ramses Wessel and Viktor Szép, constructive abstention had been used in the Council only once before the start of the war in Ukraine. However, this mechanism has been triggered more frequently since 2022—first by Ireland, Austria, and Malta with regard to the Council decision of military assistance to Ukraine via the EPF, and then by Hungary in relation to the set-up of EUMAM Ukraine.[105]

Be that as it may, the constitutional consequences of the EU's response to the war in Ukraine in CFSP/CSDP are very significant. In particular, the provision of military assistance and weapons for the Ukrainian armed forces can been

---

[101] See Steven Blockmans, 'Editorial: The Birth of a Geopolitical EU' (2022) 27 European Foreign Affairs Review 155.
[102] See also Matina Stevis-Gridneff, 'Top E.U. Official Is Becoming an Unexpected Wartime Leader', *The New York Times* (14 September 2022).
[103] See Maria Patrin, *Collegiality in the European Commission: Legal Substance and Institutional Practice* (OUP 2023) 115.
[104] See European Parliament resolution of 1 March 2022 on the Russian aggression against Ukraine, P9_TA(2922) 0052; and European Parliament resolution of 19 September 2024 on continued financial and military support to Ukraine by EU Member States, P10-TA(2024) 0012.
[105] Ramses Wessel and Viktor Szép, 'The Implementation of Article 31 of the Treaty on European Union and the use of Qualified Majority Voting', study commission by the European Parliament Constitutional Affairs Committee, November 2022, 60–63.

attributed from an international law viewpoint entirely to the EU, rather than to its Member States,[106] and consequently can be regarded as 'the first case of the European Union, an entity without its own armed forces, exercising collective self-defence'.[107] Furthermore, the conclusion of joint security commitments with Ukraine, and of the Ukraine compact, introduces—albeit in political, rather than strictly legal terms—a mutual defence pledge between the EU and Ukraine, which is currently a third country but one to which the EU has promised membership, as will be discussed in detail in Chapter 6. This also has implications for Article 42(7) TEU, which states that 'if a Member State is the victim of armed aggression on its territory, the other Member States shall have towards it an obligation of aid and assistance by all the means in their power'. Article 42(7) TEU formally calls for support by the other Member States, but in the case of Ukraine, the assistance is coming from the EU itself.

Moreover, from a substantive EU law perspective the EU measures to enhance defence production, such as the ASAP, also appear groundbreaking. As Panos Koutrakos explained, the EU institutions, and especially the Commission, had long emphasized the structural and economic problems of the EU defence industries and endeavoured to enhance the capacity of the European defence technological and industrial base—but 'for a long time, defence industries were considered to be entirely beyond the reach of EU law'.[108] In fact, a provision of the treaties dating back to the early stages of European integration, now Article 346(1)(b) TFEU, seemed to exclude a role for the EU in this domain by stating that 'any Member State may take such measures as it considers necessary for the protection of the essential interests of its security which are connected with the production of or trade in arms, munitions and war material'. However, through several important rulings, the European Court of Justice (ECJ) eventually interpreted this provision strictly.[109] This opened the door for greater EU involvement in the field of defence procurement, although legal commitments in the area of industrial integration proved difficult.[110]

At the time of the Constitutional Treaty in 2004, EU Member States agreed to set up an EU agency for coordinating their defence industrial policy and military procurement—the EDA—going beyond purely international mechanisms such as the Organisation for Joint Armament Cooperation (OCCAR), established by a specific convention.[111] Nevertheless, Member States did so in an intergovernmental

---

[106] See Aurora Rasi, 'Providing Weapons to Ukraine: The First Exercise of Collective Self-Defence by the European Union?' (2024) 9 European Papers 397.
[107] Ibid 421.
[108] Panos Koutrakos, *The EU Common Security and Defence Policy* (OUP 2013) 252.
[109] Case C-414/97 *Commission v Spain* ECLI:EU:C:1999:417; Case C-337/05 *Commission v Italy* ECLI:EU:C:2008:203; Case C-157/06 *Commission v Italy* ECLI:EU:C:2008:530.
[110] Steven Blockmans, 'The EU's Modular Approach to Defence Integration: An Inclusive, Ambitious and Legally Binding PESCO?' (2018) 55 Common Market Law Review 1785.
[111] Convention on the Establishment of the Organisation for Joint Armament Cooperation.

fashion.[112] As such, the EDA—which was initially established through a Council joint action[113] and then institutionalized by the Lisbon Treaty—is an intergovernmental body. According to Article 45 TEU, the EDA shall have as its task among others to 'contribute to identifying the Member States military capability objectives, [... to] support defence technology research [... and to] strengthening the industrial and technological base of the defence sector'. The EDA, in particular, launched in 2017 a process known as the Coordinated Annual Review on Defence (CARD), which allows Member States to gain a better view of national investment in defence, to coordinate defence procurement, and develop opportunities for cooperation.

With the explosion of the war in Ukraine, however, the European Commission has taken a much more influential role in the area of defence industry—also through a more expansive use of the supranational legal bases available in the treaties. The legal bases of the ASAP are in fact Articles 114 and 173(3) TFEU, which is also the sole legal basis of EDIRPA. While the former is the well-known EU internal market legal basis, the latter is a provision dedicated to industrial policy. Specifically, Article 173(1) TFEU states that 'The Union and the Member States shall ensure that the conditions necessary for the competitiveness of the Union's industry exist' and clarifies that 'in accordance with a system of open and competitive markets' they shall inter alia 'speed[...] up the adjustment of industry to structural changes; encourag[e] an environment favourable to initiative and to the development of undertakings [... and] foster[...] better exploitation of the industrial potential of policies of innovation, research and technological development'. According to Article 173(3) TFEU, then, 'The Union shall contribute to the achievement of the objectives set out in paragraph 1 through the policies and activities it pursues under other provisions of the Treaties.' Nevertheless, pursuant to the same provision, the European Parliament and the Council, acting in accordance with the ordinary legislative procedure, 'may decide on specific measures in support of action taken in the Member States to achieve the objectives set out in paragraph 1'.

Traditionally, Article 173 TFEU—which is the only provision of Title XVII of Part III of the TFEU, named 'Industry'—had been regarded as a marginal legal basis for EU action. In fact, while the clause, which was originally introduced by the Treaty of Maastricht, brought industrial policy under EU competences, it clearly left the dominant role in this field to the Member States. According to Article 173(2) TFEU: 'The Member States shall consult each other in liaison with the Commission and, where necessary, shall coordinate their action.' The Commission can establish guidelines and organize the exchange of best practices

---

[112] Martin Trybus, 'The New European Defence Agency: A Contribution to a Common European Security and Defence Policy or a Challenge to the Community *Acquis*?" (2006) 43 Common Market Law Review 667.

[113] Council Joint Action 2004/551/CFSP of 12 July 2004 on the establishment of the European Defence Agency [2004] OJ L245/17.

in line with the open method of coordination. However, Article 6 point (b) TFEU explicitly indicates 'industry' as a policy area where the EU 'shall have competence to carry out actions to support, coordinate or supplement the action of the Member States'. This means, pursuant to Article 2(5) TFEU, that the EU shall thereby not 'supersed[e]' the Member States' competence in this area. Moreover, Article 173(3) TFEU specifically 'exclude[s] any harmonisation of the laws and regulations of the Member States'. Finally, pursuant to the final paragraph of Article 173(3) TFEU, '[t]his Title shall not provide a basis for the introduction by the Union of any measure which could lead to a distortion of competition or contains tax provisions or provisions relating to the rights and interests of employed persons'.

Article 173(3) TFEU had been used by the EU, together with Article 175 TFEU on cohesion policy, as the legal basis for the adoption of several economic stimulus programmes, such as the 2015 European Fund for Strategic Investment,[114] and the 2021 InvestEU programme.[115] In the field of defence industrial development, Article 173 TFEU had also been used before the war in Ukraine for some early common initiatives—but these were essentially designed to fund defence-related research and development (R&D). In particular, Article 173(3) TFEU was the sole legal basis for the approval in 2018 of a regulation establishing the European Defence Industrial Development Programme (EDIDP) aiming at supporting the competitiveness and innovation capacity of the Union's defence industry with a two-year budget of €500 million for R&D.[116] Moreover, Article 173(3) TFEU was, jointly with other legal bases on research and technological development, the foundation for the 2021 regulation establishing the European Defence Fund (EDF),[117] as part of the EU Multi-annual Financial Framework (MFF) 2021–2027. The EDF repealed the EDIDP and set aside a seven-year budget of €7.9 billion to 'support collaborative research that could significantly boost the performance of future capabilities throughout the Union'.[118]

Nevertheless, since the beginning of the war in Ukraine, Article 173(3) TFEU has arguably been used more frequently and more aggressively. This provision is a legal basis for the ASAP, for EDIRPA, and the Commission has proposed grounding EDIP on Article 173 TFEU, together with Articles 114, 212, and 322

---

[114] Regulation (EU) 2015/1017 of the European Parliament and of the Council of 25 June 2015 on the European Fund for Strategic Investments, the European Investment Advisory Hub and the European Investment Project Portal and amending Regulations (EU) No 1291/2013 and (EU) No 1316/2013: the European Fund for Strategic Investments [2015] OJ L169/1.

[115] Regulation (EU) 2021/523 of the European Parliament and of the Council of 24 March 2021 establishing the InvestEU Programme and amending Regulation (EU) 2015/1017 [2021] OJ L107/30.

[116] Regulation (EU) 2018/1092 of the European Parliament and of the Council of 18 July 2018 establishing the European Defence Industrial Development Programme aiming at supporting the competitiveness and innovation capacity of the Union's defence industry [2020] OJ L200/30.

[117] Regulation (EU) 2021/697 of the European Parliament and of the Council of 29 April 2021 establishing the European Defence Fund and repealing Regulation (EU) 2018/1092 [2021] OJ L170/149.

[118] Ibid art 3(2)(a).

TFEU. Moreover, this legal basis has also been used for other important EU acts adopted since 2022 to increase economic competitiveness, which will be discussed in Chapter 5. At the same time, in the ASAP this legal basis is pushed in a clear defence-related direction. While the EDF only funded R&D, the ASAP goes beyond that by specifically funding ammunitions' production and procurement with EU money. This development mirrors to some extent what happened in the response to the pandemic: as Bruno de Witte has pointed out, legal bases that 'had originally (after their inclusion in the Treaty text) been dormant [... were] rediscovered' to tackle the socio-economic consequences of Covid-19 and legally engineer an economic policy shift like the establishment of the Next Generation EU (NGEU).[119] Moreover, this confirms that the system of competences in the TFEU is less clear-cut than may prima facie emerge from reading Article 2 TFEU, which categorizes EU competences as either exclusive, shared, coordinating, supporting, or supplementing.[120] In fact, the TFEU system of allocation of competences is very complex, particularly in the economic domain.[121] While Article 114 TFEU—the EU internal market competence—has conventionally been constructed as a flexible legal basis,[122] if one considers the entirety of the Treaties' provisions one can find support for the view that the EU has significant powers to take legislative action in the field of economic policy *lato sensu*.[123] As a result, the EU lawmaking institutions have the ability—subject to the principles of subsidiarity and proportionality[124]—to adjust to changing circumstances and act when necessary.

From a substantive point of view, therefore, the adoption of the ASAP aligns with the EU effort to enhance its strategic autonomy—a process which, as will be further discussed in Chapter 5, began before the war in Ukraine but was accelerated by it. As Frank Hoffmeister has pointed out, strategic autonomy has driven the development of a number of new EU policy tools in the field of external relations, including trade and CFSP[125]—and arguably the ASAP further advances that trend in CSDP. Needless to say, there is much academic and policy debate about the significance and success of the push towards EU strategic autonomy. As political scientists have claimed, the goal to increase EU strategic autonomy is in tension with the EU's attempt to deepen transatlantic relations in a more threatening geostrategic environment, and ultimately 'the war underline[d] the dependence on

---

[119] Bruno de Witte, 'The European Union's Covid-19 Recovery Plan: The Legal Engineering of an Economic Policy Shift' (2021) 58 Common Market Law Review 635, 653.

[120] See Takis Tridimas, 'Competence after Lisbon: the elusive search for bright lines' in Diamond Ashiagbor et al (eds), *The European Union after the Lisbon Treaty* (CUP 2012) 47.

[121] See Monica Claes and Bruno de Witte, 'Competences' in Steven Blockmans and Adam Lazowski (eds), *Research Handbook of EU Institutional Law* (Edward Elgar Publishing 2016) 9.

[122] See Niamh Nic Shuibhne, *Regulating the Internal Market* (Edward Elgar Publishing 2006).

[123] See Roland Bieber, 'The Allocation of Economic Policy Competences in the European Union' in Loïc Azoulai (ed), *The Question of Competence in the European Union* (OUP 2015) 86.

[124] See TFEU, art 5.

[125] Frank Hoffmeister, 'Strategic Autonomy in the European Union's External Relations Law' (2023) 60 Common Market Law Review 667.

US security guarantees'.[126] Yet, measures taken in response to the war in Ukraine reveal the EU's effort to enhance its autonomous capabilities to act.[127]

In fact, the adoption of the ASAP is all the more significant because, as is well known, Article 41(2) TEU states that 'expenditure arising from operations having military or defence implications' cannot be charged to the EU budget. To be clear, the ASAP does not conflict with Article 41(2) TEU, since this instrument is focused on defence production, which entails the development of the capabilities, not defence operations, which rather concerns the deployment of these capabilities. However, through its internal market and industrial policy competences the EU has ended a budgetary taboo and taken an inroad into financing EU defence and military capabilities,[128] which so far remained essentially a purview of the Member States, either separately or jointly. The ASAP goes beyond the purely intergovernmental mechanisms experimented with in the framework of the EDA by providing a truly supranational solution to the defence industrial challenges posed by the war in Ukraine.[129] Moreover, while the ASAP regulation, in line with Article 42(2) TEU, proclaims that the instrument 'should apply without prejudice to the specific character of the security and defence policy of certain Member States',[130] by leveraging the EU budget to procure weapons it effectively positions the EU *as a whole* in the conflict. As such, the ASAP contributes to strengthen the EU's role in building common defence capabilities, and can be seen as a positive step towards developing a real EU defence union, as envisaged by Article 42(2) TEU.

4 The challenges

4.1 Decision-making

While the EU leveraged the potentials of the EU constitution in the field of foreign affairs and defence, the war in Ukraine also exposed structural limitations on the EU's ability to act in CFSP/CSDP. In particular, institutional shortcomings in the EU constitution have undermined the cohesion and effectiveness of the EU response to Russia's aggression. Such dynamics are not new, and follow from the 'intergovernmental constitution'[131] of CFSP and CSDP—a policy area that

---

[126] Niklas Helwig, 'EU Strategic Autonomy after the Russian Invasion of Ukraine: Europe's Capacity to Act in Times of War' (2023) 61 Journal of Common Market Studies 1.
[127] See also Editorial Comments, 'Keeping Europeanism at Bay? Strategic Autonomy as a Constitutional Problem' (2022) 59 Common Market Law Review 313.
[128] See Stéphane Rodrigues, 'Financing European Defence: The End of Budgetary Taboos' (2023) 8 European Papers 1155.
[129] See also Roberto Caranta, 'The EU's Role in Ammunition Procurement' (2023) 8 European Papers 1047.
[130] Regulation (EU) 2023/1525 (n 9) recital 44.
[131] See Daniel Thym, 'The Intergovernmental Constitution of the EU's Foreign, Security and Defence Executive' (2011) 7 European Constitutional Law Review 466.

traditionally falls in the remit of 'core state powers'.[132] On the one hand, scholars have pointed out how the institutional complexities of the CFSP—with external representation roles for, among others, the European Council President, the High Representative, and the rotating presidency of the Council—creates confusion about who speaks for Europe.[133] On the other hand, academics have also repeatedly emphasized how the governance requirement to take decisions unanimously in the field of CFSP/CSDP waters down the ambition of the EU, and often paralyses it.[134] In fact, both problems have visibly emerged during the war in Ukraine.

On the one hand, the coherence of the EU's foreign policy posture has been challenged by Member States' unilateral actions. According to Article 26 TEU, 'the European Council shall identify the [EU]'s strategic interests' and '[t]he Council shall frame the [CFSP] and take the decisions necessary for defining and implementing it', while Article 24(3) TEU states that Member States 'shall refrain from any action which is contrary to the interests of the [EU] or likely to impair its effectiveness as a cohesive force in international relations'. Yet, this did not prevent the Prime Minister of Hungary Viktor Orban from making an unannounced travel to Moscow to meet Russian President Vladimir Putin just days after Hungary had taken over the rotating presidency of the Council of the EU on 1 July 2024. The visit, which broke with the EU approach to insulate the Russian leadership for its war of aggression against Ukraine, led to a profound rebuttal by other EU institutions, which claimed that the rotating presidency of the Council could not speak for the whole EU.[135] However, it also exposed structural shortcomings in the EU's institutional representation in CFSP/CSDP, and the ongoing challenges of projecting a unified EU voice to the rest of the world in matters of foreign affairs and security.

On the other hand, the unanimity requirement for CFSP/CSDP decisions set out in Articles 24 and 31 TEU—save for the above-mentioned possibility of the constructive abstention—and the attribution to each EU Member States of a veto right delayed and diluted the outcome of the decision-making process. This is evidenced by the strategic compass: not only its objectives appear underwhelming when seen in light of the return of war in the European continent, but two years

---

[132] See Philipp Genschel and Markus Jachtenfuchs (eds), *Beyond the Regulatory Polity? The European Integration of Core State Powers* (OUP 2014).

[133] See Hylke Dijkstra and Peter van Elsuwege, 'Representing the EU in the area of CFSP: legal and political dynamics' in Steven Blockmans and Panos Koutrakos (eds), *Research Handbook on the EU's Common Foreign and Security Policy* (Edward Elgar Publishing 2018) 44; and Sophie Meunier and Kalypso Nicolaïdis, 'Who Speaks for Europe? The Delegation of Trade Authority in the EU' (1999) 37 Journal of Common Market Studies 477.

[134] Sergio Fabbrini, 'Intergovernmentalism and Its Limits' (2013) 46 Comparative Political Studies 1003.

[135] See High Representative/Vice-President Josep Borrell, Statement, 5 July 2024; European Parliament resolution of 17 July 2024 on the need for the EU's continuous support for Ukraine, P10_TA(2024) 0003, para 4.

after its approval its implementation is advancing slowly.[136] In particular, the goal of establishing an EU Rapid Reaction Force, capable of deployment in hostile environments, of 5,000 men by 2025[137] seems very unambitious especially considering that in the early 2000s the EU had already envisaged the creation of EU Battlegroups, with larger amount of troops, although these were never operationalized.[138] Furthermore, at the time of writing, the Rapid Reaction Force has not yet been made operational, and it is unclear if the steer for this may come from the new head of the EU Military Committee (EUMC)—a body which until May 2025 will be led by an Austrian general, and subsequently by an Irish one,[139] ie officials from two neutral EU Member States. The ambiguities of the strategic compass reflect the reluctance by some EU Member States to deepen to their fullest extent their cooperation in the field of defence, with NATO being perceived by most as the real defence union for Europe.

4.2 Military capabilities

If EU institutional constraints weakened the ability of the EU to act autonomously in foreign affairs, substantive constraints hampered its role in CFSP/CSDP too. This is most evident in the EU's approval in June 2024 of joint security commitments to Ukraine, which appeared fairly vague and non-committal. Admittedly, the bilateral security agreements also concluded by the US, the UK, and other Member States enshrine mostly obligations of best efforts to support Ukraine in case of armed aggression. Yet, these commitments are still laid down in legal agreements, and—at least in the case of the US—included a number of detailed arrangements to bolster defence cooperation in air and missile defences, ground manoeuvres, cyber security, command and control, and sustainment.[140] The EU's security commitments to Ukraine, instead, are effectively framed as a declaration, with no real legal value, and lack meaningful deterrence against Russia, focusing primarily on non-defence-related matters. This is ultimately the consequence of the fact that the EU does not have military capabilities of its own to deploy: not only because according to Article 42(1) TEU the EU shall carry out CSDP tasks 'using capabilities provided by the Member States'—but also because European security has been effectively delegated since the mid-1950s to NATO.

---

[136] See also EEAS, Annual Progress Report on the Implementation of the Strategic Compass for Security and Defence, March 2024.
[137] Council of the EU (n 17) 14.
[138] See Domenico Moro, *Verso la difesa europea* (Il Mulino 2018).
[139] See Carl O'Brien, 'Head of Defence Forces elected first Irish chair of the EU's highest military body', *The Irish Times* (15 May 2024).
[140] See Bilateral security agreement between the United States of America and Ukraine, 13 June 2024, Annex.

In fact, so far NATO has been strengthened by the war in Ukraine as the preeminent organization for the security of Europe—also thanks to the supporting stance in the US of the Biden administration, in office from 2021 to 2024. From an international relations perspective, the decision by Finland and Sweden to abandon their military neutrality and join NATO, in 2023 and 2024 respectively, dwarfed in importance the decision by Denmark to renounce its output and join CSDP. NATO is backed by the US military commitment, which makes the mutual defence clause of Article V NATO Treaty credible.[141] After all, notwithstanding recent efforts to revitalize European militaries,[142] their war readiness is very limited.[143] US military might is therefore essential for the credibility of the transatlantic alliance. At the moment, however, no similar credibility underpins the EU's mutual defence clause, Article 42(7) TEU. On the one hand, this clause foresees that if a Member State is victim of armed aggression, the other Member States—rather than the EU—should have an obligation of aid and assistance. On the other hand, even if the EU were legally bound to intervene, it would lack the capabilities to deter foreign adversaries.

This state of affairs is certainly not new.[144] The so-called 'capability-expectation gap' is a long running feature of CFSP/CSDP, since the Treaty of Maastricht.[145] And developments in PESCO, which have accelerated since Russia's invasion of Ukraine,[146] have not fundamentally changed this. Furthermore, until recently, efforts to develop EU military capabilities were primarily focused on creating 'expeditionary capabilities'[147]—ie military structures for low-intensity operations, to manage conflict, and project power outside the continent—rather than 'territorial capabilities'—ie resources towards defending territory, denying access to a foreign enemy, and projecting power within Europe.[148] In 2018, Simon Duke accurately

---

[141] See Federica Fazio, 'Collective defence in NATO: A legal and strategic analysis of Article 5 in light of the war in Ukraine' Dublin European Law Institute working paper 2/2024.

[142] See Camille Grand, 'Defending Europe with Less America', European Council on Foreign Relations Policy Brief, 3 July 2024; Maxime Lefebvre, 'L'Union européenne face à la guerre en Ukraine', Fondation Robert Schuman Policy Paper no 651, 9 January 2023. See also James Angelos, 'The Eastern Front', *The New York Times Magazine* (29 January 2023) 41 (reporting efforts to revitalize the German armed forces).

[143] See European Defence Agency, Defence Data 2022: Key Findings and Analysis, 2023 (reporting limited but uneven increase in defence spending across EU Member States). See also House of Commons Defence Committee report 'Ready for War?', HC 26, 4 February 2024 (stating that the UK would currently be unable to sustain a prolonged fight with a peer power).

[144] See also Urfan Khaliq, 'The European Union's foreign policies: an external examination of the capabilities-expectations gap' in Steven Blockmans and Panos Koutrakos (eds), *Research Handbook on the EU's Common Foreign and Security Policy* (Edward Elgar Publishing 2018) 459.

[145] See Christopher Hill, 'The Capability-Expectations Gap, or Conceptualizing Europe's International Role' (1993) 31 Journal of Common Market Studies 305.

[146] See Stefania Rutigliano, 'Ukraine Conflict's Impact on European Defence and Permanent Structured Cooperation' (2023) 8 European Papers 765.

[147] See Kaja Schilde, 'European Military Capabilities: Enablers and Constraints on EU Power?' (2017) 55 Journal of Common Market Studies 37.

[148] See Luis Simon, 'The "Third" Offset Strategy and Europe's "Anti-Access" Challenge' (2016) 39 Journal of Strategic Studies 417.

stated that military capabilities 'have become a (or even *the*) critical issue, not just for Europe's security and defence, but for the future of the European project itself'.[149] Yet, even after Russia's large-scale invasion of Ukraine, the EU still lacks boots on the ground.

4.3 Industrial capacity

Moreover, the EU also still lacks a common defence industrial capacity, and the measures adopted since 2022—including the ASAP, EDIRPA, and the proposed EDIP—have only partially changed that. This has to do with a number of weaknesses in EU defence production law, identified by the EU Court of Auditors,[150] and visible in the case of the ASAP. To begin with, most obviously, the ASAP budget is negligible—only €500 million for two years, which amounts to 0.04% of the €1,074 billion MFF 2021–2027, or even less (0.02%) if one considers also the separate €750 billion of the NGEU, which is on top of the MFF. Even when also accounting for the €300 million EDIRPA, the €7.9 billion EDF, which, however, is focused only on R&D, and now the proposed EDIP, worth €1.5 billion, the total EU expenditure on defence production is very small. Admittedly, the EU has spent a larger amount of resources to support Ukraine, including the EPF, whose envelope now is over €17 billion, a €18 billion Macro-Financial Assistance+ Facility for Ukraine 2023, and a €50 billion Ukraine Facility for 2024–2027, which will be examined in detail in Chapter 3. However, these figures pale when compared not only to the defence spending of the main European security provider, the US,[151] but also to the defence spending of EU Member States, including France,[152] or Germany—which has set up a €100 billion special fund to invest in rearmament.[153]

Yet, beyond the matter of sheer size, the ASAP also suffers from another relevant shortcoming, which is apparent when the final regulation is compared with the original Commission proposal of May 2023. The latter included a proposed Article 14, named 'Priority Rated Orders', that would have allowed the Commission to compel a private company to produce military materials needed for European security. Specifically, according to the proposed Article 14(2) the

---

[149] Simon Duke, 'Capabilities and CSDP: resourcing political will or paper armies' in Steven Blockmans and Panos Koutrakos (eds), *Research Handbook on the EU's Common Foreign and Security Policy* (Edward Elgar Publishing 2018) 154, 181.
[150] See European Court of Auditors news, 'European Defence Industry Programme: Auditors call for a more robust design', 3 October 2024.
[151] See Catie Edmonson, 'Congress Passed an $858 Billion Military Bill. Here is what's in it', *The New York Times* (16 December 2022).
[152] Loi n° 2023-703 du 1er août 2023 relative à la programmation militaire pour les années 2024 à 2030 et portant diverses dispositions intéressant la défense, JORF n°0177 du 2 août 2023.
[153] Gesetz zur Finanzierung der Bundeswehr und zur Errichtung eines 'Sondervermögens Bundeswehr', vom 1. Juli 2022 (BGBl. I S 1030).

Commission could, 'after the consultation of the Member State of establishment of the concerned undertaking and with its agreement, notify the latter of its intent to impose a priority rated order'. Moreover, under the proposed Article 14(3), '[w]here the notified undertaking declines the request ... the Commission may, in agreement with the Member State of establishment of that undertaking ... adopt an Implementing Act obliging the concerned undertakings to accept or perform the priority rated order, at a fair and reasonable price'. The proposed Article 14(5) clarified that a priority rated order shall 'take precedence over any performance obligation under private or public law'. Furthermore, to increase the coerciveness of the orders, the proposed Article 15 introduced penalties, stating that '[w]here an undertaking, intentionally or through gross negligence, does not comply with an obligation to prioritise priority rated orders ..., the Commission may, by decision, where deemed necessary and proportionate, impose periodic penalty payments'.

Admittedly, the possibility for the Commission to compel a specific economic undertaking to produce on demand defence-related goods needed for national security, trumping any other pre-existing obligation of contract, constituted a severe interference with private property and the right to freedom of enterprise, not to mention the right to due process and defence. As such, consistently with the legal principles enshrined in the legally binding EU Charter of Fundamental Rights,[154] the Commission proposal introduced several guarantees. Ex ante, the proposed Article 14 set up an administrative procedure that entitled the undertaking to a due process, with the possibility of making its views heard, and to provide explanations to object to the Commission's request. Moreover, the proposed Article 16 enshrined a right to be heard for the imposition of fines and periodic penalty payments. At the same time, ex post, the Commission proposal introduced an unlimited right of judicial review. Specifically, the proposed Article 15(5) stated that the ECJ 'shall have unlimited jurisdiction to review decisions whereby the Commission has fixed a fine or a periodic penalty payment. It may cancel, reduce or increase the fine or periodic penalty payment imposed'. Finally, to assuage worries still further, the Commission proposal explicitly limited in Article 15(7) the above-mentioned powers to a period of three years only.

With the guarantees of judicial review, the Commission's proposal to introduce priority-rated orders would have rendered the ASAP much more impactful. From a comparative law perspective, the executive authority to compel production by private companies to ensure the supply of materials and services necessary for national defence constitutes the hallmark of the US DPA. Admittedly, such a comparison may seem far-fetched, given the nature of the US military industrial complex. Yet, the DPA is not only the gold standard in the field, but also a model

---

[154] See also Federico Fabbrini, *Fundamental Rights in Europe* (OUP 2014).

that arguably the Commission considered in proposing the ASAP. This statute, which the US Congress approved at the dawn of the Korean War, empowers the US President, inter alia, to prioritize contracts and orders which are necessary for the national defence, designate scarce materials whose hording is prohibited, and ration energy resources. In the landmark 1952 Steel Seizure Case, *Youngstown Sheet & Tube Co v Sawyer*,[155] the US Supreme Court developed a tripartite scheme to evaluate executive powers and held that '[w]hen the President acts pursuant to an express or implied authorization of Congress, his authority is at its maximum, for it includes all that he possesses in his own right plus all that Congress can delegate'.[156] As a result, the DPA has remained a powerful instrument in the US President's toolbox to deal with issues of industrial capacity, and has been used as recently as during the Covid-19 pandemic, and now the war in Ukraine.

As pointed out above, however, the final text of the ASAP regulation did not include any provision on 'priority rate orders'. The co-legislator, therefore, ditched this part of the Commission's original proposal—with opposition to this coercive feature unsurprisingly emerging in the intergovernmental Council.[157] Yet, the choice to deprive the Commission of any teeth in its power to steer the defence industry, and to rely exclusively on market operators' good will and cooperation, ultimately undermined the goals of the ASAP. In fact, the Council of the EU's ambition enshrined in the March 2023 three-step plan to deliver 1 million rounds of ammunition to Ukraine within a year ultimately fell well short. As the High Representative had to acknowledge in January 2024, the EU reached only 'one-third of the objective, mainly taken from our stockpiles'.[158] Hence, despite the best intentions, national jealousies and governance obstacles in the EU decision-making system removed an empowerment in favour of the Commission from the ASAP regulation, which would have been necessary effectively to prioritize defence production. The Commission has now re-proposed the possibility of placing priority rated orders as part of the EDIP,[159] but it remains to be seen if this proposal will ultimately meet the Member States' approval.

In sum, the EU response to the war in Ukraine in CFSP/CSDP confirms that the EU's ability to provide for the common defence remains a work-in-progress, and that serious structural challenges in the EU constitution stand in the way of developing a fully-fledged EU defence union.[160] Before the war, the European Parliament had more ambitiously called for the creation of a real EU Defence

---

[155] 343 US 579 (1952).
[156] Ibid at 635 (Jackson J concurring).
[157] See also Federico Petrangeli, 'Il riassetto dei poteri dell'Unione europea in tempo di guerra' [2004] Osservatorio Costituzionale 39.
[158] High Representative/Vice-President Josep Borrell press remarks, 31 January 2024.
[159] See European Commission proposal (n 91), art 50.
[160] See also Ramses Wessel, 'Common foreign, security and defence policy' in Ramses Wessel and Joris Larik (eds), *EU External Relations Law* (Hart Publishing 2020).

Union, underpinned by strong and modern military capabilities.[161] In fact, in the aftermath of the Russian invasion of Ukraine, the European Parliament has called for a reinforcement of the EU capacity to act in a more challenging geo-political context,[162] and underlined 'the urgent need to establish a truly European defence equipment market', with increased financial support from the EU budget.[163] To get there, however, further steps are needed, including a significant increase in funding for single EU defence industrial production and procurement, and ultimately the creation of a real EU military force—all of which require amendments to the current treaty framework. Yet, with the war in Ukraine showing no sign of abating and with future uncertainties about the US commitment to European security,[164] especially in view of the elections of 2024,[165] the EU should more confidently address the question of the defence of the European continent.

5 Conclusions

This chapter has examined the EU's response to the war in Ukraine in the field of CFSP and CSDP, assessing the EU constitution's ability to provide for the common defence in time of war. The chapter mapped the most significant strategic, military assistance, and defence production measures deployed by the EU since 2022. As such, the chapter shed light on the EU strategic compass, the deployment of a military assistance mission (EUMAM) in favour of the Ukrainian army, the award of EU security commitments towards Ukraine, and the adoption of several pieces of legislation, namely the ASAP and EDIRPA, to boost the production and procurement of munitions and missiles with the aim of supporting Ukraine in the war against Russia.

As the chapter has maintained, the EU's response to Russia's aggression against Ukraine has been wide-ranging, and the EU constitution enabled the adoption of groundbreaking measures. The EU clarified its strategic posture; it offered security guarantees to Ukraine, providing weapons and military assistance; and it strengthened its defence industrial base. In particular, the ASAP, and related to this EDIRPA and the EDIP, pushed the EU into new territory, that of industrial defence

---

[161] European Parliament Resolution of 22 November 2016 on the European Defence Union, P8_TA(2016) 0435.

[162] See European Parliament resolution of 19 May 2022 on the social and economic consequences for the EU of the Russian war in Ukraine—reinforcing the EU's capacity to act, P9_TA(2022) 0219.

[163] European Parliament resolution of 18 January 2023 on the implementation of the common security and defence policy—annual report 2022, P9_TA(2023) 0010, para 34.

[164] Kjell Engelbrekt, 'Beyond Burden-sharing and European Strategic Autonomy: Rebuilding Transatlantic Security after the Ukraine War' (2022) 27 European Foreign Affairs Review 383.

[165] See Republican Party Vice-Presidential candidate J D Vance, 'The Math on Ukraine Doesn't Add Up', Op-Ed, *The New York Times* (12 April 2024) (calling for funding for Ukraine to cease, and criticizing NATO).

policy. Through constructive use of supranational legal bases in the treaties, the ASAP has granted the authority to the Commission to use resources from the EU budget to fund the industrial production of munitions and missiles urgently needed by Ukraine, thus helping to boost the EU's role in developing common defence capabilities.

Yet, as the chapter has pointed out, the EU's ability to provide for the common defence in time of war has proved still to be a work-in-progress. While the EU's diplomatic and military response to Russia's aggression has been underwhelming, and overshadowed by NATO, the EU's involvement in the military industrial complex remains limited. Indeed, the ASAP suffers from a number of weaknesses, including a very tiny biannual budget. Moreover, contrary to the original Commission proposal, the final text of the ASAP regulation did not empower the Commission to issue priority rated orders, compelling defence industries to produce specific defence goods on demand. From this point of view, therefore, the ASAP cannot be regarded as the EU's equivalent of the US DPA, a landmark piece of legislation which gives wide authority to the US executive to command the production of materials needed for the national defence. This state of affairs is hardly surprising, considering the constraints on EU defence policy. Nevertheless, it challenges the declared EU aspirations to establish a form of European sovereignty, and may be insufficient in light of the ongoing war in Ukraine, the violence of Russia's aggression, and the uncertainties about future US military commitment to European security.

3
To 'promote the general welfare'
Developments in fiscal and economic policy

1 Introduction

Wars are expensive. The war in Ukraine turned into one of the highest intensity armed conflicts in decades, requiring skyrocketing defence expenditures. Moreover, the protracted military campaign and the relentless Russian bombing of cities resulted in devastating damage to Ukraine's civilian infrastructure, including its energy grid. At the same time, maritime warfare in the Black Sea suffocated Ukraine's main export route. All this had unprecedented consequences on Ukraine's economic growth, its fiscal stability, and its ability to fund ordinary government expenditure. In July 2022, the Government of Ukraine presented to the Conference of donors a national recovery and post-war reconstruction plan of the country, which was worth over US$750 billion.[1] In September 2022, the World Bank, jointly with the European Commission and the Government of Ukraine, carried out a first rapid damage and needs assessment, and calculated that the cost of rebuilding the country would be around US$349 billion.[2] Since then, however, the war has continued, and the costs have increased with the latest—the third—World Bank rapid damage and needs assessment in February 2024, pricing the bill of reconstruction at US$486 billion.[3] In this context, a pressing need for the European Union (EU) as well as for the United States (US) and other partners has been to mobilize financial resources with the aim of assisting Ukraine to purchase defence weapons, to fund operational government expenses, and to rebuild, to the extent possible, critical infrastructures.[4]

The purpose of this chapter is to examine from an EU law and policy perspective the key legal instruments that the EU deployed from 2022 to 2024 to support

---

[1] See Ukraine's National Recovery Plan, 5 July 2022, Lugano Conference.
[2] See World Bank press release, 'Ukraine Recovery and Reconstruction Needs Estimated $349 Billion', 9 September 2022, https://www.worldbank.org/en/news/press-release/2022/09/09/ukraine-recovery-and-reconstruction-needs-estimated-349-billion.
[3] See World Bank press release, 'Updated Ukraine Recovery and Reconstruction Needs Assessment Released', 15 February 2024, https://www.worldbank.org/en/news/press-release/2024/02/15/updated-ukraine-recovery-and-reconstruction-needs-assessment-released.
[4] See OECD Policy Responses: Ukraine, 'Shaping the Path to Economic Recovery', 1 July 2022. See also Kiel Institute for the World Economy, 'Ukraine Support Tracker', https://www.ifw-kiel.de/topics/war-against-ukraine/ukraine-support-tracker/; and Ronja Ganster et al, 'Designing Ukraine's Recovery in the Spirit of the Marshall Plan', German Marshall Fund, September 2022.

The EU Constitution in Time of War. Federico Fabbrini, Oxford University Press. © Federico Fabbrini 2025.
DOI: 10.1093/oso/9780198963486.003.0003

Ukraine financially. This chapter, instead, does not consider other financial measures that the EU rolled out to mitigate the damage to the EU domestic economy resulting from Russia's illegal aggression, as this is dealt with in Chapter 5. In particular, the chapter examines the European Peace Facility (EPF),[5] the Macro-Financial Assistance Instrument for Ukraine (MFA+),[6] and the Ukraine Facility (UF),[7] and reflects on their significance for the consolidation of a fiscal capacity in the EU. As the chapter explains, at the beginning of the war in Ukraine, the EU resorted to the EPF, a novel funding instrument dedicated to foreign policy objectives, initially worth €5.6 billion and later increased to €17 billion, which is fully funded by Member States' transfers and subjected to their unanimous intergovernmental decision-making in the Council. Subsequently, however, as the war in Ukraine continued, the EU crafted the MFA+, a larger €18 billion financing tool approved jointly by the European Parliament and the Council, which enables the Commission to issue common debt, and to transfer these own resources to Ukraine as loans. Finally, building on the MFA+, in 2023 the Commission proposed to establish an even larger UF, which was ultimately approved by the European Council in early 2024. This UF, which is funded by issuing common EU debt, is worth €50 billion and will allow the EU to support Ukraine financially in the longer term, from 2024 until 2027, with both loans and grants, ie non-repayable support.

As the chapter argues, the EU constitution enabled the EU 'to promote the general welfare'[8] through the adoption of consequential legal measures in the field of fiscal and economic policy, which supported Ukraine in facing the budgetary costs of the war. In fact, Russia's large-scale invasion of Ukraine—which commenced in February 2022, exactly two years after the explosion of the Covid-19 pandemic in February 2020—quickly prompted the EU to replicate some of the novelties it used to respond to the pandemic. As is well known, to address the devastating socio-economic consequences of Covid-19, in 2020 the EU agreed to establish groundbreaking instruments, such a €100 billion unemployment reinsurance system called SURE,[9] and a €750 billion Recovery Fund, known as the Next Generation EU (NGEU).[10] As I have claimed elsewhere, the latter, in particular, endowed the

---

[5] Council Decision (CFSP) 2021/509 of 22 March 2021 establishing a European Peace Facility and repealing Decision (CFSP) 2015/528 [2021] OJ L102/14.

[6] Regulation (EU) 2022/2463 of the European Parliament and the Council of 14 December 2022 establishing an instrument for providing support to Ukraine for 2023 (macro-financial assistance +) [2022] OJ L322/1.

[7] Regulation (EU) 2024/792 of the European Parliament and the Council of 29 February 2024 establishing the Ukraine Facility [2024] OJ L1.

[8] US Const, preamble.

[9] Council Regulation (EU) 2020/672 of 19 May 2020 on the establishment of a European instrument for temporary support to mitigate unemployment risks in an emergency (SURE) following the Covid-19 outbreak [2020] OJ L159/1.

[10] Council Regulation (EU) 2020/2094 of 14 December 2020 establishing a European Union Recovery Instrument to support the recovery in the aftermath of the COVID-19 crisis [2020] OJ L433I/23; and Regulation (EU) 2021/241 of the European Parliament and of the Council of 12 February 2021 establishing the Recovery and Resilience Facility [2021] OJ L57/17.

EU with a fiscal capacity by empowering the Commission to raise funds by issuing common debt on the financial markets, to transfer these amounts to the Member States as grants and loans, and to levy new taxes to repay capital and interests on the debt in the longer term.[11] Formally speaking, the financial tools rolled out to address Covid-19 were designed to be temporary. Yet, NGEU and SURE provided a legal technique and a policy template that the EU promptly reused when facing the war in Ukraine. In particular, the MFA+ and the UF entail once again common borrowing and spending, which highlights the legacy of the NGEU model and suggests a trend towards consolidating a centralized fiscal capacity at the EU level of government.

Nevertheless, as this chapter maintains, structural weaknesses in the EU constitution's budgetary provisions hampered the consolidation of a fiscal capacity in the EU, and its ability to provide steady fiscal and economic support to Ukraine during the war. In particular, as the chapter highlights, the possibility for the Commission to issue common debt on behalf of the EU depends on an increase of the EU spending ceiling set in the EU budget—the Multi-Annual Financial Framework (MFF)[12]—which must be agreed unanimously by all Member States. This gives each Member State a veto that can be used, or, indeed, abused to obtain concessions on other, unrelated matters. Hence, the approval of the MFA+ was delayed in 2022 for many months by Hungary, which tactically opposed the measure to obtain the payment of funding that had been suspended due to rule of law backsliding. Similarly, the approval of the UF was again held to ransom by Hungary in late 2023, forcing the European Council to hold a special summit in early 2024 to greenlight an amendment to the MFF, including funding for Ukraine. These difficulties confirm that several substantive and governance shortcomings in the EU's constitutional set-up still limit the EU's ability to mobilize resources and leverage power on the international stage—a challenge worsened by the deterioration of the rule of law crisis.

As such, this chapter is structured as follows. Section 2 analyses the core measures adopted by the EU in the field of fiscal and economic policy in response to the war in Ukraine. It examines respectively the EPF, the MFA+, and the UF, discusses their main legal features, legal bases, funding mechanisms, and governance arrangements—thus highlighting their intergovernmental versus supranational features. Section 3 evaluates the EPF, the MFA+, and the UF in light of the legal and institutional innovations created by the EU and its Member States to respond to Covid-19; it points out that the war in Ukraine increased the need for the EU to reproduce funding mechanisms based on common debt akin to those rolled out

---

[11] See Federico Fabbrini, *EU Fiscal Capacity: Legal Integration after Covid-19 and the War in Ukraine* (OUP 2022).

[12] Council Regulation (EU, Euratom) 2020/2093 of 17 December 2020 laying down the multiannual financial framework for the years 2021 to 2027 [2020] OJ L433I/11.

during the pandemic; and it reflects on how the war in Ukraine contributed to the slow consolidation of a fiscal capacity in the EU. Section 4, however, underlines how this trend is slowed down by institutional shortcomings and constitutional constraints, which make it difficult for the EU to take decisions, and to upscale its financial firepower and influence in foreign affairs. Finally, section 5 concludes.

2 The core measures

2.1 The European Peace Facility

The EPF is a novel funding mechanism that the EU created in 2021 as part of the financial package for the period from 2021 to 2027, which is centred on the MFF and also includes (in response to Covid-19) the NGEU Recovery Fund. Notwithstanding its name, the EPF was specifically established as a special fund to finance the common costs of military operations by EU Member States under the EU Common Security and Defence Policy (CSDP), as well as actions to improve the military and defence capabilities of third states and partner international organizations. The EPF—which is adopted in the form of a Council decision— is based on Articles 28(1), 41(2), 42(4), and 30(1) TEU, which respectively allow the EU to act when the international situation so requires, to pool resources to this end, and to adopt initiatives unanimously in the Council, also at the request of the EU High Representative for Foreign Affairs and Security Policy.[13] The EPF is built as an off-budget fund, outside the MFF, because, as also pointed out in Chapter 2, Article 41(2) TEU explicitly prohibits charging to the EU budget 'expenditure arising from operations having military or defence implications'.

The EPF, as a tool of EU Common Foreign and Security Policy (CFSP) and CSDP, is exhibit A of intergovernmentalism in the EU. The Council Decision establishing the EPF is extremely long—76 articles and 5 annexes—and overcomplicated. The EPF, as clarified in Article 9, should be used to achieve 'the strategic priorities set by the European Council and the Council', and must be consistent with the CFSP goals of the EU.[14] Importantly, according to Article 36, 'assistance measures can be implemented through grants'. Yet, from a governance viewpoint the EPF is managed by a Facility Committee, composed by representatives from all 27 Member States, which must take decisions unanimously.[15] A large administrative bureaucracy operates under the direction of the Facility Committee.[16] Moreover, as a further guarantee to Member States, the Decision

---

[13] See Joris Larik, *Foreign Policy Objectives in EU Constitutional Law* (OUP 2016).
[14] Council Decision (CFSP) 2021/509 (n 5) art 8.
[15] Ibid art 11(14).
[16] Ibid arts 12, 13, and 15.

establishes a direct link between participation in decisions on, and contribution to the financing of, operation and assistance measures: in particular, pursuant to Article 5, 'a Member State which has abstained in a vote on a Council Decision ... is not obliged to contribute to the funding of that operation'.

From a financing viewpoint, the EPF is entirely resourced through Member States' transfers. According to Article 18(7)(a) of the Council Decision, the EPF revenues consist primarily of 'contributions payable by the contributing Member States'. As clarified in Article 26, Member States' contributions are determined on the basis of the Gross National Income (GNI), and are requisitioned by the Facility Committee annually.[17] Nevertheless, as a further guarantee to Member States' discretion—and yet another confirmation of the intergovernmental nature of the EPF—Article 27 states that '[a] Member State which has indicated its intention to abstain from the adoption of an assistance measure ... may identify other assistance measures to which it will make an additional contribution'. This means that, while the EPF is a common financial pot, each Member State still maintains full control on which measures its share of the funding is directed to. Furthermore, numerous reporting and accounting obligations are connected to the EPF, including a duty by EPF administrators to report to the Facility Committee on expenditure every three months,[18] and a right for the Council to review the Decision whenever a Member State so requires, and in any event at least every three years.[19]

At the explosion of the war in Ukraine, the EU quickly decided to mobilize the EPF, which had an initial budget of €5.6 billion, to provide financial support to the Ukrainian military. As explained in Chapter 2, the EPF was also utilized to fund the purchase of lethal weapons—an historic step, not least given that some EU Member States still abide by a policy of military neutrality.[20] In particular, in February 2022, the Council quickly approved a decision on an assistance measure for the supply of military equipment to the Ukrainian armed forces.[21] The decision empowered the High Representative to implement the measure,[22] making arrangements with the beneficiary, including ensuring compliance with international human rights law and humanitarian law,[23] and foresaw an initial disbursement of €450 million.[24] This amount was subsequently doubled in March 2022,[25] and tripled in April 2022

---

[17] Ibid art 29.
[18] Ibid art 38.
[19] Ibid art 75.
[20] TEU, art 42(2).
[21] See Council Decision (CFSP) 2022/338 of 28 February 2022 on an assistance measure under the European Peace Facility for the supply to the Ukrainian Armed Forces of military equipment and platforms designed to deliver lethal force [2022] OJ L60/1.
[22] Ibid art 4.
[23] Ibid art 3.
[24] Ibid art 2.
[25] See Council Decision (CFSP) 2022/471 of 23 March 2022 amending Decision (CFSP) 2022/338 on an assistance measure under the European Peace Facility for the supply to the Ukrainian Armed Forces of military equipment and platforms designed to deliver lethal force [2022] OJ L96/43.

to a total of €1.5 billion.[26] Subsequently, EPF funding to support the Ukrainian military was further increased in May 2022,[27] and in July 2022,[28] bringing the total size of support to €3.1 billion. This, combined with other EPF expenditure towards other third countries carried out in 2022, largely depleted in a single year a budget that had been designed for a seven-year timeframe. As a result, the Council decided in December 2022 for a €2 billion increase in the EPF for 2023,[29] and in June 2023, it agreed to a further €3.5 billion top-up of the EPF, bringing its size to €12 billion.[30]

Yet, the continuation of the war and the need to fund the Ukrainian army in its defence against the Russian aggression forced a further reorganization of the EPF. Following a request by the European Council in December 2023,[31] the Council agreed in March 2024 to increase the envelope of the EPF by a further €5 billion, ringfencing this new amount for Ukraine only, via a so-called Ukraine Assistance Fund (UAF).[32] Moreover, the Council decided to improve the governance arrangements for the implementation of the UAF, tasking the Facility Committee with deciding on the disbursement of this amount within a month.[33] At the same time, the Council agreed to limit after a transition period the ability of Member States to obtain reimbursement from the EPF for the national deliveries of ammunition from stocks to Ukraine,[34] thus promoting joint procurement of new weapons. The latest increase of the EPF—which brings it to a total of over €17 billion, more than three times the original EPF funding of €5.6 billion—constitutes a significant increase. However, the Council acknowledged that 'further comparable annual increases could be envisaged until 2027, based on Ukrainian needs'.[35] Be that as it may, thus far—due to opposition by Hungary—the UAF has not yet been rendered operational, creating uncertainties on its deployment.[36]

---

[26] See Council Decision (CFSP) 2022/636 of 13 April 2022 amending Decision (CFSP) 2022/338 on an assistance measure under the European Peace Facility for the supply to the Ukrainian Armed Forces of military equipment, and platforms, designed to deliver lethal force [2022] OJ L117/34.
[27] See Council Decision (CFSP) 2022/809 of 23 May 2022 amending Decision (CFSP) 2022/338 on an assistance measure under the European Peace Facility for the supply to the Ukrainian Armed Forces of military equipment, and platforms, designed to deliver lethal force [2022] OJ L145/40.
[28] See Council Decision (CFSP) 2022/1285 of 21 July 2022 amending Decision (CFSP) 2022/338 on an assistance measure under the European Peace Facility for the supply to the Ukrainian Armed Forces of military equipment, and platforms, designed to deliver lethal force [2022] OJ L195/93.
[29] Council Decision (CFSP) 2023/577 of 13 March 2023 amending Decision (CFSP) 2021/509 establishing a European Peace Facility [2023] OJ L75/23.
[30] Council of the EU press release, 'European Peace Facility: Council agrees on second top-up of the overall financial ceiling by 3.5 billion', 26 June 2023.
[31] European Council conclusions, 14–15 December 2023, EUCO 20/23, para 3.
[32] Council of the EU press release, 'Ukraine Assistance Fund: Council allocates €5 billion under the European Peace Facility to support Ukraine militarily', 18 March 2024.
[33] Council Decision (CFSP) 2024/890 of 18 March 2024 amending Decision (CFSP) 2021/509 establishing a European Peace Facility [2024] OJ L1/4, art 1.
[34] Ibid recital 10.
[35] Ibid recital 15.
[36] European Parliament resolution of 19 September 2024 on continued financial and military support to Ukraine by EU Member States, P10-TA(2024) 0012, para N.

2.2 The macro-financial assistance instrument

Given the limited resources available under the EPF, and arguably given the complications of this tool, in Autumn 2022, as the war in Ukraine worsened, the European Commission proposed to establish the MFA+ in the form of a regulation of the European Parliament and of the Council.[37] Going beyond the piecemeal support that the EU had given to the Ukrainian government in the initial months of the war,[38] the MFA+, worth €18 billion, was designed to provide predictable, continuous, orderly, and timely financial relief to Ukraine in 2023, thus supporting its rehabilitation and reconstruction and prospectively its preparation for EU membership.[39] The Commission's proposal was endorsed by the European Parliament and the Member States in the Council. The legal basis for the MFA+, in fact, is Article 212 TFEU—the Treaty provision dealing with economic, financial, and technical cooperation with third countries—which foresees the use of the ordinary legislative procedure, with the Council deciding by qualified majority voting (QMV). Yet, the MFA+ was connected to an amendment of the MFF, which raised the EU spending ceiling, enabling the Commission to issue debt—and under Article 312 TFEU this requires unanimity by all Member States. Hungary vetoed the MFF revision for several months, as a bargaining chip to obtain concession from the Commission on an unrelated measure. To tackle the problem of rule of law backsliding at play in Hungary, in fact, the Commission had suspended the transfer of NGEU funds to Hungary,[40] which was thus eager to use every available card to overcome the application of the rule of law conditionality regulation,[41] and obtain much needed EU transfers.

In the end, in order to circumvent Hungary's veto, in December 2022 the Council decided to amend the Commission proposal slightly, and passed it with the approval of the European Parliament.[42] Specifically, the Council introduced a back-up option to the original funding scheme proposed by the Commission, which envisaged guaranteeing the issuance of €18 billion of common debt exclusively

---

[37] See European Commission proposal for a Regulation of the European Parliament and the Council establishing an Instrument for providing support to Ukraine for 2023 (macro-financial assistance+), 9 November 2022, COM(2022) 597 final.
[38] See eg Decision (EU) 2022/1201 of the European Parliament and of the Council of 12 July 2022 providing exceptional macro-financial assistance to Ukraine [2022] OJ L186/1 (providing €1 billion in emergency funds).
[39] European Council conclusions, 23–24 June 2022, EUCO 24/22, para 11 (granting candidate status to Ukraine).
[40] European Commission press release, 'EU budget: Commission proposes measures to the Council under the conditionality regulation', 18 September 2022, IP/22/5623.
[41] Regulation (EU, Euratom) 2020/2092 of the European Parliament and of the Council of 16 December 2020 on a general regime of conditionality for the protection of the Union budget [2020] OJ LI433/1.
[42] European Parliament legislative resolution of 14 December 2022 on the Council position at first reading with a view to the adoption of a regulation of the European Parliament and of the Council establishing an instrument for providing support to Ukraine for 2023, P9_TA(2022) 0439.

through an increase in the spending ceiling of the MFF. Since that required an amendment to the MFF—a change on which Hungary had a right to veto—the Council foresaw the possibility of backing up the €18 billion of new common debt of the MFA+ through national guarantees, provided by 26 Member States pro quota.[43] In what was certainly not a coincidence, however, two days beforehand, the Council also approved the Hungarian National Recovery and Resilience Plan (NRRP),[44] thus ensuring that Hungary could access NGEU money in the future if the Commission were to unblock them pursuant to the rule of law conditionality regulation. Arguably thanks to this concession, Hungary ultimately agreed to an amendment of the MFF, which was approved by the Council in December 2022.[45] This increased the EU's spending ceiling, enabling the Commission to issue common debt to fund the MFA+, therefore ultimately ensuring that there was no need to resort to Member States' bilateral guarantees.

The MFA+ presents more supranational features than the EPF. The European Parliament and Council regulation establishing the MFA+ is only 21 articles long, and fairly linear. As clarified in Article 2, the objective of the instrument is to provide 'short-term financial relief to Ukraine ... and initial support towards post-war reconstruction', and the MFA+' areas of support include financing of Ukraine's funding need, restoring critical infrastructure, as well as alignment with the EU regulatory framework.[46] Based on Article 4 of its regulation, the MFA+ provides support in the form of loans, but the regulation mentions that Member States can provide additional amounts as bilateral grants. From a governance viewpoint, the MFA+ regulation vests the key decision-making power in the European Commission. Pursuant to Article 11, 'the support under the Instrument shall be made available by the Commission in installments'. The regulation, however, introduces a number of preconditions for the support under the MFA+, including 'that Ukraine continue[s] to uphold and respect effective democratic mechanisms ... and the rule of law'.[47] The Commission signs the memorandum of understanding (MoU) with Ukraine setting out priority actions;[48] reviews compliance with the ex ante conditionality;[49] and can reduce, suspend, or cancel support under the MFA+.[50]

---

[43] European Parliament press release, 'Parliament agrees to adapted €18 billion loan to Ukraine', 14 December 2022.
[44] Council of the EU press release, 'NextGenerationEU: Member States Approve National Plan of Hungary', 12 December 2022.
[45] Council Regulation (EU, Euratom) 2022/2496 of 15 December 2022 amending Regulation (EU, Euratom) 2020/2093 laying down the multiannual financial framework for the years 2021 to 2027 [2022] OJ L325/11.
[46] Regulation (EU) 2022/2463 (n 6) art 3.
[47] Ibid art 8.
[48] Ibid art 9.
[49] Ibid art 12.
[50] Ibid art 13.

From a financing viewpoint, the MFA+ instrument is based on the issuance of common EU debt, rather than Member States' transfers as in the EPF. Specifically, Article 16 of the MFA+ regulation states that 'in order to finance the support under the Instrument in the form of loans, the Commission shall be empowered, on behalf of the Union, to borrow the necessary funds on the capital markets or from financial institutions'. Loans to Ukraine, which are on very favourable terms, 'shall have a maximum duration of 35 years'[51] and the EU can offer an interest rate subsidy to Ukraine.[52] In case an amendment of the MFF were not to happen, Article 5(2) of the MFA+ regulation states that Member States contribute to guarantee the debt 'in the form of irrevocable, unconditional and on-demand guarantees through a guarantee agreement to be concluded with the Commission'. Such national guarantees are determined pro quota on the basis of each Member State's GNI,[53] but 'shall cease to be callable as of the date of application of an amendment to [the MFF Regulation]',[54] which—as mentioned above—is what happened in December 2022. The usual annual reporting obligation is imposed by the regulation on the Commission,[55] which must also constantly keep the European Parliament and the Council informed on disbursement operations.[56]

2.3 The Ukraine Facility

The MFA+ proved to be a successful instrument to support Ukraine, and the Commission disbursed all the €18 billion provided by the regulation, but its duration was limited to 2023 only. As the war continued, therefore, the EU institutions put forward a new financing tool, modelled on the MFA+, but designed for a longer period: the UF. Specifically, on 20 June 2023 the Commission proposed, as part of the mid-term revision of the MFF,[57] to establish a new UF, worth €50 billion for the period from 2024 to 2027, to secure long-term financial support to the Ukrainian government in its war efforts beyond the MFA+ instrument.[58] The UF would provide both grants and loans to Ukraine—along the model of the Recovery and Resilience Facility (RRF), the main programme funded under the NGEU Recovery Fund—and be funded both by empowering the Commission to issue additional common EU debt, guaranteed by the EU budget headroom, and

---

[51] Ibid art 16(2).
[52] Ibid art 17.
[53] Ibid art 5(3).
[54] Ibid art 6(f).
[55] Ibid art 20.
[56] Ibid art 15.
[57] European Commission Communication, Mid-term revision of the Multiannual Financial Framework 2021–2027, 20 June 2023, COM(2023) 336 final.
[58] European Commission Proposal for a Regulation of the European Parliament and of the Council on establishing the Ukraine Facility, 20 June 2023, COM(2023) 338 final.

by an increase in the EU budget itself. The Commission also proposed to amend the Own Resource Decision (ORD) with an adjusted packages of EU own resources,[59] and identified additional sources of EU revenues, including profits from the sales of the new Carbon Border Adjustment Mechanism (CBAM) certificates, and a novel statistical based own resources on company profits.[60]

The Commission's MFF reform package—which was worth over €75 billion and also included extra resources in the field of migration and technological development, as will be pointed out in Chapter 5—was subjected to extensive negotiations among the EU Member States. In a European Council meeting in December 2023, 26 EU Member States expressed their support for a MFF revision and the establishment of a UF.[61] However, in the same summit which blessed the opening of EU accession negotiations with Ukraine,[62] which will be discussed in Chapter 6, Hungary used its veto to block the approval of the UF.[63] As had been the case in December 2022, at the time of the approval of the MFA+ 2023, the Hungarian opposition was largely unrelated to the matter at hand. Rather, Hungary leveraged its veto power on the MFF to obtain the disbursement of EU funding which had been suspended by the Commission in light of rule of law backsliding at play in that Member State. In fact, the day before the European Council meeting, on 13 December 2023, the European Commission eventually took the much criticized decision to approve the payment of €10.2 billion of EU cohesion funding to Hungary.[64] This ultimately prompted Hungary to waive its veto on the opening of accession negotiations with Ukraine. Instead, however, Hungary blocked the approval of the UF and revision of the MFF, effectively blackmailing the EU in order to get an additional €21 billion of still suspended RRF funding for its NRRP.[65]

As a result, a special European Council summit was convened on 1 February 2024. Under pressure from the other Member States, Hungary eventually yielded and the European Council ultimately approved a revision of the MFF, worth €64.6 billion, of which €50 billion was set aside for the establishment of the UF.[66] Yet, at Hungary's insistence, the European Council agreed that '[o]n the basis of the Commission annual report on the implementation of the Ukraine Facility, the

---

[59] European Commission Communication, An adjusted package for the next generation of own resources, 20 June 2023, COM(2023) 330 final.
[60] European Commission Amended proposal for a Council Decision amending Decision (EU, Euratom) 2020/2053 on the system of own resources of the European Union, 20 June 2023, COM(2023) 331 final.
[61] See European Council meeting—Multiannual Financial Framework 2021-2027 Negotiating Box, 15 December 2023, EUCO 23/23.
[62] European Council conclusions, 15 December 2023, EUCO 20/23, para 15.
[63] Ibid para 24.
[64] See European Commission press release 'Commission considers that Hungary's judicial reform addressed deficiencies in judicial independence but maintains measures on budget conditionality', 13 December 2023, IP/23/6465.
[65] Ibid.
[66] European Council conclusions, 1 February 2024, EUCO 2/24, para 2.

European Council will hold a debate each year on the implementation of the Facility with a view to providing guidance'.[67] On substance, the European Council confirmed that the UF would consist of €33 billion of loans, and €17 billion of grants, which will be provided to Ukraine on the condition that the country 'continues to uphold and respect effective democratic mechanisms ... and the rule of law, and to guarantee respect for human rights'.[68] The European Council also 'stressed the need to foster Ukraine's ownership of its recovery and reconstruction efforts by means of a Plan to be prepared by the Ukrainian Government',[69] and clarified that '[t]he Council will play a key role in the governance of the [UF]. In this sense, a Council Implementing Decision shall be adopted by qualified majority for the adoption and amendments of the Ukraine Plan'.[70]

Following the European Council's blessing, on 29 February 2024 the Council and the European Parliament quickly approved the UF regulation, and the Council also simultaneously approved the related amendment to the MFF.[71] The UF regulation—which has as its legal bases Article 212 TFEU, on technical cooperation with third countries, and Article 322 TFEU, on common financial provisions—is longer than the MFA+ regulation, but follows its outlook. According to Article 3, the UF regulation's objective is to '(a) address the social, economic and environmental consequences of Russia's war of aggression, thereby contributing to the peaceful recovery, reconstruction, restoration and modernization of [Ukraine]; (b) foster ... [its] progressive integration into the Union'. Article 5 outlines preconditions for EU support under the UF, including Ukraine's continuing commitment to respect effective democratic mechanisms, the rule of law, and human rights.

From a funding perspective, Article 6 of the regulation lays out the EU financial commitments of the UF, which amount to €33 billion of loans and €17 billion of grants. As explicitly stated in Article 22 of the UF regulation, '[i]n order to finance support under the Facility in the form of loans, the Commission shall be empowered, on behalf of the Union, to borrow the necessary funds on the capital markets or from financial institutions'. Funding for the UF grants, instead, originates from the amendment of the MFF, which creates a corresponding Ukraine reserve worth €17 billion in the EU budget.[72] Spending under the UF is then divided into three pillars: first, a Ukraine Plan;[73] secondly, a Ukraine investment framework, based on EU guarantees worth €7.8 billion, to facilitate private investment;[74] and, thirdly, a pre-accession tool, with technical assistance to help Ukraine prepare for

---

[67] Ibid para 7.
[68] Ibid para 5.
[69] Ibid para 4.
[70] Ibid para 6.
[71] Council Regulation (EU, Euratom) 2024/765 of 29 February 2024 amending Regulation (EU, Euratom) 2020/2093 laying down the multiannual financial framework for the years 2021 to 2027 [2024] OJ L1.
[72] Ibid art 10b.
[73] Regulation (EU) 2024/792 (n 7) ch III.
[74] Ibid ch IV.

EU membership and incorporate the EU's *acquis*.[75] However, the Ukraine plan—modelled on the NRRP of the RRF—constitutes the core pillar of the UF regulation.

From a governance perspective, in fact, Article 16 of the UF regulation requires Ukraine to design a multi-annual plan, known as the Ukraine plan, which must set out the 'reform and investment agenda'.[76] The plan shall detail a 'timetable, and the envisaged qualitative and quantitative steps',[77] as well as 'an explanation of how the Plan corresponds to the recovery restoration, reconstruction and modernization needs stemming from the war'.[78] Ukraine must present its plan to the European Commission, which must assess its 'relevance, comprehensiveness and appropriateness'.[79] In case of a positive assessment of the Ukraine plan by the Commission, 'the Council shall … approve [it] by means of an implementing decision'.[80] On this basis, the Commission can conclude with Ukraine both a framework agreement[81] and a financing agreement.[82] While considering that Ukraine is at war the regulation introduces in Article 13 a provision for 'exceptional financing', in principle Ukraine will receive funding under the Facility only by complying with the plan, which the Commission monitors. In fact, according to Article 26(2), '[e]very quarter Ukraine shall submit a duly justified request for payment', which the Commission shall assess on the basis of compliance with the qualitative and quantitative steps of the plan. Moreover, contrary to what occurred under the MFA+, according to Article 26 of the UF regulation, the decision on the disbursement of EU funding is taken by the Council, rather than by the Commission. If the targets are not met, the EU can reduce or withhold payments. Finally, Ukraine and the Commission must take all appropriate measures to protect the financial interests of the EU,[83] and the usual auditing,[84] monitoring and reporting,[85] evaluation,[86] and information[87] provisions apply.

On 20 March 2024, the Commission awarded to Ukraine €4.5 billion of bridge financing, to provide the necessary liquidity and help finance the functioning of the state,[88] and in April 2024 it transferred to Ukraine another €1.5 billion.[89] On 20 March 2024, Ukraine also submitted its national plan to the Commission, which

---

[75] Ibid ch V.
[76] Ibid art 16.
[77] Ibid art 17(1)(c).
[78] Ibid art 17(1)(f).
[79] Ibid art 18.
[80] Ibid art 19.
[81] Ibid art 9.
[82] Ibid art 10.
[83] Ibid art 35.
[84] Ibid art 36.
[85] Ibid art 39.
[86] Ibid art 40.
[87] Ibid art 43.
[88] European Commission press release, 'Commission disburses first €4.5 billion of bridge financing to Ukraine under the Ukraine Facility', 20 March 2024.
[89] European Commission press release, 'Commission disburses addition €1.5 billion of bridge financing Ukraine', 24 April 2024.

positively assessed it on 15 April 2024.[90] The Council of the EU approved the Ukraine plan by qualified majority on 14 May 2024,[91] thus opening the door to another payment by the Commission of €1.9 billion of pre-financing.[92] Furthermore, following a positive assessment by the Council, on a proposal of the Commission of the achievement by Ukraine of the first quarterly milestones and targets set out in its national plan,[93] in July 2024 the Commission released €4.2 billion of regular payments to Ukraine, bringing the total support to approximately €12 billion in the six months since the approval of the UF.[94]

Yet, it is clear that also the funding from the UF will not suffice given the ever growing costs of the war in Ukraine. This is why on 20 September 2024 the European Commission proposed to create another instrument to support Ukraine financially through a new regulation to be jointly approved by the European Parliament and the Council on the basis of Article 212 TFEU.[95] Specifically, the Commission proposed to establish a new Macro-Financial Assistance Tool,[96] on the basis of which the EU would raise up to €35 billion on the financial markets,[97] and transfer these as a loan to Ukraine. At the same time—in line with a political agreement reached in June 2024 within the G7 (the Group of the seven most industrialized Western countries: the US, Germany, France, the United Kingdom, Italy, Japan, and Canada, to which the EU is associated as a member)—the Commission proposed to establish a Ukraine Loan Cooperation Mechanism (ULCM):[98] this would subsidize Ukraine's repayment of the loan's principal and interest by using the extraordinary revenues stemming from Russian Central Bank (RCB) assets immobilized in the EU due to sanctions[99]—an issue whose legality will be extensively discussed in Chapter 4. The Commission's plan seeks to provide up-front funding to Ukraine of up to an additional €35 billion, while using the windfall profits stemming from RCB assets as grants that Ukraine can use periodically to repay the loan. While the initiative is aimed at making Russia pay for the costs of

---

[90] European Commission proposal for a Council Implementing Decision on the approval of the assessment of the Ukraine Plan, 15 April 2024, COM(2024) 172 final.

[91] Council of the EU, press release, 'Ukraine Plan: Council greenlights regular payments under the Ukraine Facility', 14 May 2024, 399/24.

[92] European Commission news article, 'Commission disburses an additional €1.9 billion in pre-financing', 28 June 2024.

[93] See European Commission proposal for a Council implementing decision on establishing the satisfactory fulfilment of the conditions for the payment of the first instalment of the non-repayable financial support and of the loan support under the Ukraine Plan of the Ukraine Facility, 17 July 2024, COM(2024) 321 final.

[94] European Commission press release, 'Commission paves way for the release of close to €4.2 billion to Ukraine as first regular payment under the Ukraine Facility', 17 July 2024.

[95] European Commission proposal for a Regulation of the European Parliament and of the Council establishing a Ukraine Loan Cooperation Mechanism and providing exceptional macro-financial assistance to Ukraine, 20 September 2024, COM(2024) 426 final.

[96] Ibid art 9.

[97] Ibid art 14.

[98] Ibid art 3.

[99] Ibid art 2.

the war, it also highlights the urgency for the EU to come up with legally audacious ways to keep funding Ukraine.

3 The consequences

The EU's legal response to the war in Ukraine in the field of economic and financial affairs reveals a trend towards the consolidation of a fiscal capacity in the EU, confirming that wars are the most powerful engine of fiscal integration in federal unions of states.[100] The unprecedented geopolitical threat posed by the Russian military aggression at Europe's Eastern borders forced the EU institutions and Member States to resort to funding mechanisms analogous to those rolled out in response to the Covid-19 pandemic. At the start of Russia's large-scale aggression against Ukraine, the EU Member States deployed for the first time the EPF—a new tool designed to back up the EU voice in foreign affairs. Nevertheless, the limited size of the EPF, and arguably its complicated governance arrangements, quickly led the European Commission to propose an alternative funding instrument in the form of the MFA+. Grounded on a different treaty legal basis—and justified also in light of the EU grant of candidate status to Ukraine—the MFA+ enabled the Commission to raise €18 billion on the financial markets on behalf of the EU, and to transfer these to Ukraine in 2023 as concessionary loans subject to standard conditionality. The MFA+, in turn, served as the model for the UF, which had a longer duration and a larger size—with an envelope of €50 billion for the period from 2024 to 2027, to be partially disbursed also as grants.

While the EPF presents features which resemble the traditional EU budget, the MFA+ and the UF rather track the solution that the EU adopted to tackle the Covid-19 pandemic. As is well known, the second paragraph of Article 311 TFEU states that '[w]ithout prejudice to other revenue, the [EU] budget shall be finance wholly from own resources'. Yet, despite the letter and the spirit of the EU treaties, since the 1980s the MFF is mostly funded by Member States' transfers, based on GNI;[101] and as pointed out above, the same is true for the EPF. On the contrary, in response to the Covid-19 pandemic the EU experimented with novel financial instruments, legally engineering a constitutional transformation in the EU architecture of economic governance.[102] To address the devastating socio-economic damage caused by the pandemic, in particular, the EU set up the SURE mechanism, worth €100

---

[100] Tomasz Woźniakowski, *Fiscal Unions: Economic Integration in Europe and the United States* (OUP 2022); and Charles Tilly (ed), *The Formation of National States in Western Europe* (Princeton University Press 1975) (famously arguing that 'war make states and states make war').

[101] Ubaldo Villani-Lubelli and L Zamparini (eds), *Features and Challenges of the EU Budget* (Edward Elgar Publishing 2019).

[102] Bruno de Witte, 'The European Union's Covid-19 Recovery Plan: The Legal Engineering of an Economic Policy Shift' (2021) 58 Common Market Law Review 635.

billion, and subsequently the NGEU Recovery Fund, worth €750 billion.[103] Under SURE, adopted on the basis of Article 122 TFEU, the European Commission was empowered to raise €100 billion on the financial markets by issuing common debt on behalf of the EU, subject to €25 billion of Member States' guarantees.[104] In the case of the NGEU, instead, a complex legal arrangement centred on a EU Recovery Instrument (EURI),[105] also based on Article 122 TFEU, empowered the Commission to raise €750 billion by issuing common debt on behalf of the EU, with the general EU budget serving as a guarantee, and an increase in the headroom of the ORD.[106]

The MFA+ and the UF have different legal bases from SURE and NGEU, as they rely on Article 212 TFEU, on economic, financial, and technical cooperation with third countries, which is combined in the UF regulation with Article 322(1) TFEU, on common budgetary rules. Nevertheless, both the MFA+ and the UF largely follow in the footsteps of SURE and especially the NGEU as far as funding, governance, and values are concerned. From the point of view of funding, like SURE the MFA+ provides loans, rather than grants. Instead, like the NGEU, the UF entails both loans and grants. Moreover, both the MFA+ and the UF enable the Commission to issue debt on the financial markets through an increase of the EU spending ceiling, using the EU budget as a guarantee—exactly as in the NGEU. In fact, the Commission has now set up a unified funding strategy, whereby EU bonds to fund the NGEU and the various Ukraine-related programmes are now part of a bundled issuance, thus creating the bulk of a new EU treasury function in Brussels.[107]

At the same time, also from the point of view of governance, both the MFA+ and the UF draw from the example of the NGEU—and specifically the RRF. As I have argued elsewhere, the RRF established a new legal technology of European governance.[108] This can be conceptualized in five steps, each involving different institutions and the Member States. First, the EU identifies a number of objectives which must be achieved through this programme—with the Commission, European Parliament and the Council all being involved in this initial step of priority setting. Secondly, the Member States are asked to design multi-annual national plans, identifying country-specific paths to achieve these objectives, through clear milestones and targets. Thirdly, the Commission assesses and the Council approves

---

[103] Fabbrini (n 11).
[104] Ian Cooper, 'Support to mitigate unemployment risk in an emergency (SURE)' in Federico Fabbrini and Christy Petit (eds), *Research Handbook on Post-Pandemic Economic Governance and NGEU Law* (Edward Elgar Publishing 2024) 80.
[105] Council Regulation (EU) 2020/2094 (n 10).
[106] Council Decision (EU, Euratom) 2020/2053, of 14 December 2020, on the system of own resources of the European Union and repealing Decision 2014/335/EU, Euratom [2020] OJ L424/1, art 5(1).
[107] I am grateful to Emanuele Rebasti for making this point clear to me.
[108] See Federico Fabbrini, 'The Recovery and Resilience Facility as a New Legal Technology of European Governance' (2024) 46 Journal of European Integration 1.

the national plans, or if these fail to meet the EU priorities, calls for Member States to revise them. Fourthly, Member States implement their national plans, acting to achieve the milestones and targets indicated therein. Finally, the Commission recurrently monitors Member States' implementation of their national plans and the achievement of the milestones and targets indicated therein—thus deciding on the continuing disbursement of financial aid based on their performance. The RRF model has been replicated among others in the RePowerEU regulation,[109] which will be examined in Chapter 5, in the Social Climate Fund,[110] and even the new Stability and Growth Pact preventive arm.[111]

Similarly, the RRF model of 'spending conditionality'[112] based on compliance with milestones and targets was used also for funding Ukraine. As mentioned above, the MFA+ foresees that Ukraine and the Commission will enter into a MoU outlining the specific objectives to be achieved with EU funding over one year, and empowers the Commission to evaluate compliance as a condition for the payment of instalments. Similarly, the UF primarily requires Ukraine to develop a multi-annual Ukraine plan, with detailed reforms and investments. The Ukraine plan is assessed by the Commission and approved by the Council, and the Commission regularly monitors its implementation with the Council deciding on the periodic disbursement of funds based on Ukraine's reaching the previously agreed qualitative and quantitative goals set out in the plan.

Finally, also from the point of view of values, the instruments used to support Ukraine draw from the example of the NGEU. As is well known, a core piece of the puzzle establishing the NGEU—besides the EURI, the ORD, the RRF, and inter-institutional agreement between the Council, the Commission, and the European Parliament on budgetary discipline, on cooperation in budgetary matters, and on sound financial management, as well as on new own resources, including a roadmap towards the introduction of new own resources[113]—is the rule of law conditionality regulation.[114] This conditions the disbursement of EU funding to

---

[109] Regulation (EU) 2023/435 of the European Parliament and of the Council of 27 February 2023 amending Regulation (EU) 2021/241 as regards REPowerEU chapters in recovery and resilience plans and amending Regulations (EU) No 1303/2013, (EU) 2021/1060 and (EU) 2021/1755, and Directive 2003/87/EC, [2023] OJ L63/1.

[110] Regulation (EU) 2023/955 of the European Parliament and of the Council of 10 May 2023 establishing a Social Climate Fund and amending Regulation (EU) 2021/1060 [2023] OJ L130/1.

[111] See Regulation (EU) 2024/1263 of the European Parliament and of the Council of 29 April 2024 on the effective coordination of economic policies and on multilateral budgetary surveillance and repealing Council Regulation (EC) No 1466/97 [2024] OJ L/1.

[112] Niall Moran, 'Milestones and targets" in Federico Fabbrini and Christy Ann Petit (eds), *Research Handbook on Post-Pandemic Economic Governance and NGEU Law* (Edward Elgar Publishing 2024) 179.

[113] Interinstitutional Agreement between the European Parliament, the Council of the European Union and the European Commission on budgetary discipline, on cooperation in budgetary matters and on sound financial management, as well as on new own resources, including a roadmap towards the introduction of new own resources [2020] OJ L433I/28.

[114] Regulation (EU, Euratom) 2020/2092 (n 41).

the respect by EU Member States of the basic rule of law principle enshrined in Article 2 TEU, which again the Commission is empowered to evaluate.[115] Along the same lines, while the EPF conditions funding to continuing respect of international human rights law and humanitarian law, the MFA+ and the UF require Ukraine to abide by democratic and rule of law principles to receive continuing financial support from the EU. Albeit arguably these criteria are phrased in the MFA+ and the UF in a lighter form to account for the fact that Ukraine is a country at war, they replicate at least in spirit the EU rule of law conditionality rules.

The adoption of the MFA+ and the UF, therefore, reveals the importance of path dependency in the functioning of the EU. As political science literature on historical institutionalism[116] and legal scholarship research on emergency legislation[117] have both pointed out, once norms are adopted in time of emergency and become entrenched, they set a precedent for future action. Interestingly, all measures enacted by the EU to address the Covid-19 pandemic only created a temporary fiscal capacity.[118] The SURE regulation provided that its funding would 'end on 31 December 2022'.[119] Similarly, the NGEU Recovery Fund was designed to be a one-off, exceptional tool: as stated by the European Council 'the powers granted to the Commission to borrow are clearly limited in size, duration and scope'[120] with the RRF designed to run 'until 31 August 2026'.[121] Yet, SURE and NGEU offered the policy template and legal technique which the EU could resort to in order to address a new crisis arising even before the Covid-19 pandemic dissipated. And the MFA+ and the UF confirm a trend towards the consolidation of a centralized fiscal capacity in the EU.

4 The challenges

4.1 Funding

Nevertheless, the road towards the consolidation of a fiscal capacity in the EU remains fraught with difficulties and uncertainties.[122] As the difficult approval

---

[115] See further Niels Kirst, 'Rule of law conditionality' in Federico Fabbrini and Christy Ann Petit (eds), *Research Handbook on Post-Pandemic Economic Governance and NGEU Law* (Edward Elgar Publishing 2024) 195.
[116] See Kurt Dopfer, 'Toward a Theory of Economic Institutions: Synergies and Path Dependency' (1991) 25 Journal of Economic Issues 535.
[117] See Oren Gross and Fionnuala Ní Aoláin, *Law in Times of Crises: Emergency Powers in Theory and Practice* (CUP 2006).
[118] See Alicia Hinarejos, 'Legacy and Limits of NGEU' (2024) 118 American Journal of International Law 157
[119] Council Regulation (EU) 2020/672 (n 9) art 12(3).
[120] European Council conclusions, 17–21 July 2020, EUCO 10/20, para A4.
[121] Regulation (EU) 2021/241 (n 10) art 18(4)(f).
[122] See also Franz Mayer, 'NextGenerationEU and the Future of European Integration: Foreseeing the Unforeseeable' (2024) 118 American Journal of International Law 172.

of both the MFA+ and the UF highlight, the EU is hampered by constitutional constraints and institutional shortcomings which severely undermine its ability to raise a fiscal capacity and rise to the geopolitical challenges it is facing. At the time of the approval of the NGEU, a debate occurred on whether EU efforts to establish a fiscal capacity were limited by national or EU constitutional rules.[123] In the end, legal concerns were largely overcome—including in the Member State most reluctant to accept fiscal integration: Germany. In particular, in an important ruling delivered in December 2022, the Bundesverfassungsgericht (BVerfG) rejected the legal challenges that had been raised against the NGEU and the ORD.[124] As the BVerfG clarified in a 7:1 judgment, the establishment of the NGEU and the empowerment of the European Commission to issue €750 billion of common debt violated neither the EU treaties nor the German Basic Law. According to the BVerfG, the Recovery Fund was compatible with Articles 122, 125, and 311 TFEU, and did not constitute an ultra vires action by the EU, thus complying with the integration agenda foreseen in the Basic Law, particularly as the size of the NGEU funded by raising common debt was inferior to the size of the MFF, resourced via Member States' transfers. The BVerfG ruling marked a departure from its precedents and, albeit with caveats that may come to haunt it later, endorsed a path towards EU common debt.[125]

However, other EU constitutional rules weaken the EU's ability to mobilize financial resources as needed. On the one hand, as previously mentioned, Article 41(2) TEU explicitly prohibits charging to the EU budget 'expenditure arising from operations having military or defence implications'. This means that, despite recent efforts to use the MFF for defence production, discussed in Chapter 2, CSDP expenses have to be covered by separate funds, like the EPF, set up outside the EU budget.[126] On the other hand, Title II of Part VI of the TFEU, which sets the 'Financial Provisions' of the EU, lays out daunting rules.[127] In particular, according to Article 310(1) TFEU, the revenues and expenditures of the EU budget 'shall be in balance', which means the EU cannot fund itself at deficit. Moreover, Article 312 TFEU states that the MFF must set 'the amounts of the annual ceilings on commitments appropriations by category of expenditures and of the annual ceilings on payment appropriations', which means that the budget allocation by policy area is fixed in advance. Finally, it should be mentioned that the EU has only limited

---

[123] Brady Gordon, *The Constitutional Boundaries of European Fiscal Federalism* (CUP 2022).
[124] BVerfG, 2 BvR 547/21, 2 BvR 798/21, Final Judgment of 6 December 2022.
[125] See Elena Kempf and Katerina Linos, 'Shaming the Court: The German Constitutional Court's NGEU Reversal' (2024) (on file with author) (explaining the BVerfG reversal through public and political pressure against the previous Eurosceptic case law of the Court).
[126] See Stéphane Rodrigues, 'Financing European Defence: The End of Budgetary Taboos' (2023) 8 European Papers 1155, 1157.
[127] See also Ana Belen Macho Perez, 'The Own Resource Decision (ORD) and EU public finances' in Federico Fabbrini and Christy Ann Petit (eds), *Research Handbook on Post-Pandemic Economic Governance and NGEU Law* (Edward Elgar Publishing 2024) 255.

taxing powers: under Article 113 TFEU—which is located in Chapter 2 of Title VII TFEU on 'Tax Provisions'—the EU is only empowered to harmonize indirect taxes when this is necessary to ensure the establishment and functioning of the internal market and to avoid distortion of competition. This means, however, that the EU cannot introduce direct taxes.

4.2 Decision-making

The substantive constraints on the consolidation of an EU fiscal capacity, at the same time, interplay with governance shortcomings, which also stem directly from the EU treaties. In Chapter 2, it was pointed out how intergovernmentalism and the unanimity rule profoundly influence decision-making in CFSP/CSDP, by subjecting decisions to Member States' bargaining and unilateral vetoes. The institutional features of the EPF, detailed above, reflect this state of affairs. The EPF has a highly cumbersome governance structure, with a 27-member Facility Committee at the helm, and Member States still have multiple prerogatives, including the right to opt out of funding operations they dislike. While in the end—also thanks to the constructive abstention foreseen by the second paragraph of Article 31(1) TEU[128] Member States in Council collectively agreed to deploy the EPF to support Ukraine and to increase its size over time—it is clear that this is not congenial to fast and vigorous decision-making. In fact, as mentioned above, for idiosyncratic reasons in October 2024 Hungary was still blocking the operationalization of the UAF, approved by the Council in March 2024, severely limiting the effectiveness of the latest EPF budgetary increase.

Furthermore, intergovernmental governance also afflicts decision-making procedures about EU public finances[129]—another area close to 'core state powers'.[130] Pursuant to Article 312 TFEU, the Council must approve the MFF, or amendments thereof, unanimously, after obtaining the consent of the European Parliament. In fact, even if the European Council formally has no role under Article 312 TFEU by praxis it also has to approve unanimously the outlines of the MFF, and relatedly decisions to raise its spending ceiling and enable the issuance of EU common debt. Furthermore, under Article 311 TFEU the Council must also unanimously approve the ORD, or amendments thereof, and this decision must also be ratified by each Member State in accordance with its constitutional requirements

---

[128] Ramses Wessel and Viktor Szép, 'The implementation of Article 31 of the Treaty on European Union and the use of Qualified Majority Voting', study commission by the European Parliament Constitutional Affairs Committee, November 2022, 60–63.

[129] See also Federico Fabbrini, *Economic Governance in Europe: Comparative Paradoxes and Constitutional Challenges* (OUP 2016).

[130] See Philipp Genschel and Markus Jachtenfuchs (eds), *Beyond the Regulatory Polity? The European Integration of Core State Powers* (OUP 2014).

(usually parliamentary procedure). The dominant role of the European Council and the Council in budgetary affairs contrasts instead with the marginal role of the European Parliament.[131] While the European Parliament must approve the MFF, and often votes on the legislation governing how to spend EU funds—such as the RRF,[132] or indeed the MFA+ and the UF—it is excluded from voting on the ORD, and consequently has less influence in the EU budgetary decision-making process.

The procedural requirement to obtain unanimous agreement by the 27 Member States every time the EU wants to increase spending, and borrow money, explains why both the approval of the MFA+ and of the UF—which technically required only QMV in the Council—was effectively long delayed by Hungary, which had a veto to any amendment of the MFF needed to raise the EU spending ceiling and enable the Commission to issue common debt. However, the unanimity requirement means that a single Member State can veto efforts by the others to enable further EU borrowing and spending—even for unrelated reasons. This is exactly what happened in the case of both the MFA+ and the UF. In December 2022, Hungary vetoed an amendment to the MFF, which was needed to raise the EU budget ceiling to issue €18 billion of new common debt for the MFA+; and, in December 2023, Hungary vetoed a broader revision of the MFF, thus preventing the approval of the UF. In both circumstances, the Hungarian veto was unrelated to the matter at stake: rather, Hungary leveraged its necessary vote in order to obtain the disbursement of NGEU funding which had been frozen due to the rule of law backsliding problem. Yet, the shrewd blackmail by the Hungarian government had consequences on the EU's ability to assist war-torn Ukraine financially.

Needless to say, the EU is not alone in facing challenges in mobilizing financial resources. To some extent, this is a structural problem of federal unions of states.[133] The US, for example, does not have a balance budget obligation, but legislation dating to the First World War set a debt ceiling, which requires the federal government to obtain congressional authorization for issuing debt over a threshold fixed in advance, and this has in recent times regularly caused political stand-offs.[134] In fact, in the context of the war in Ukraine, even the US has had difficulties in providing continuing financial support to Ukraine. Specifically, the US was able to

---

[131] See Alastair McIver, 'Accountability: European Parliament' in Federico Fabbrini and Christy Ann Petit (eds), *Research Handbook on Post-Pandemic Economic Governance and NGEU Law* (Edward Elgar Publishing 2024) 225; and Menelaos Markakis, *Accountability in Economic and Monetary Union* (OUP 2020).

[132] Stefania Baroncelli, 'The recovery and resilience facility' in Federico Fabbrini and Christy Ann Petit (eds), *Research Handbook on Post-Pandemic Economic Governance and NGEU Law* (Edward Elgar Publishing 2024) 110.

[133] See also Shawn Donnelli, 'Clocks, Caps, Compartments and Carve-Outs: Creating Federal Fiscal Capacity Despite Strong Veto Powers' (2023) 11 Politics & Governance 92.

[134] See Jacob Charles, 'The Debt Limit and the Constitution: How the Fourteenth Amendment Forbids Fiscal Obstructionism' (2013) 62 Duke Law Review 1227: and Neil H Buchanan and Michael C Dorf, 'How to Choose the Least Unconstitutional Option: Lessons for the President (and Others) from the Debt Ceiling Standoff' (2012) 112 Columbia Law Review 1175.

provide extensive military and financial aid to Ukraine in 2022 and 2023[135]—with the US Government Accountability Office (GAO) estimating over US$113 billion of federal funding provided for US agencies as of 31 December 2023 to provide arms to Ukraine, aid civilians, impose sanctions, and more.[136] However, in 2023 the Republican Party took control of the US House of Representatives, and the faction dominated by supporters of former President Donal Trump, who opposed further aid to Ukraine, blocked for months the request advanced by President Biden, a Democrat, to refinance Ukraine in 2024.[137] Eventually, however, in April 2024 the US Congress—with a majority of Democrats joining a minority of Republicans in the House—managed to pass bipartisan legislation authorizing financial appropriations to fund Ukraine (as well as Israel and Taiwan).[138] The bill authorized the US federal government to give an additional US$50 billion in security assistance for Ukraine, almost matching the €50 billion of the EU's UF.

With that said, however, the decision-making difficulties faced by the US in mobilizing resources are of a different order of magnitude than those faced by the EU. To begin with, in the US decisions on revenues and expenditures are constitutionally taken exclusively by the federal government, without involvement of the 50 states.[139] Secondly, votes on taxing and spending bills are made by the two Houses of Congress—the House of Representatives and the Senate—by simple majority. In fact, since 1974, the filibustering rule, which normally requires a 60-vote majority in the 100-member Senate to advance legislation,[140] has been discontinued for budgetary laws approved through a fast-track process known as 'reconciliation', that can be used once a year for spending appropriations.[141] Finally, the US political dispute over funding for Ukraine appears to be different from the one affecting the EU. Certainly, the level of polarization of the US political parties is an undeniable fact,[142] and the radicalization of the Republican Party on matters of foreign affairs and the rule of law is a growing concern.[143]

---

[135] See also US Secretary of the Treasury Janet Yellen, 'American Economic Aid to Ukraine Is Vital', Op-Ed, *The New York Times* (28 February 2023).

[136] US Government Accountability Office, 'Ukraine: Status and Use of Supplemental US Funding, as of First Quarter, Fiscal Year 2024', 30 May 2024, https://www.gao.gov/products/gao-24-107232.

[137] See Siobhan Hughes, 'Republicans Block Ukraine Aid Bill, Putting New Pressure on Border Talks', *The Wall Street Journal* (6 December 2023).

[138] See Act making emergency supplemental appropriations for the fiscal year ending September 30, 2024, and for other purposes, Pub L No 118–50.

[139] See Allen Schick, *The Federal Budget: Politics, Policy, Process* (Brookings Institution Press 2007); and Max Edling, *A Revolution in Favor of Government: Origins of the U.S. Constitution and the Making of the American State* (OUP 2003) 163.

[140] See Catherine Fisk and Erwin Chemerinsky, 'The Filibuster' (1997) 49 Stanford Law Review 181.

[141] Congressional Budget Act of 1974, Pub L No 93–344.

[142] See also Lawrence Rosenthal, *Empire of Resentment* (New Press 2020); and Steven Levitsky and Daniel Ziblatt, *Tyranny of the Minority* (Crown Publishing 2023).

[143] See also Pew Research Centre, 'Growing Partisan Divisions over NATO and Ukraine', May 2024 (reporting no national consensus in the US on whether supporting Ukraine is in the US national interest, and highlighting that only a 51% majority of survey respondents identifying as Republican believe the US benefits from NATO).

Yet—if taken at face value—opposition by pro-Trump Republicans towards funding Ukraine was based on substantive policy reasons: as claimed by J D Vance funding for Ukraine appeared a distraction from the core US foreign policy threat, namely China.[144] This appears different from what has happened in the EU, where Hungary's opposition towards approving the MFA+ and the UF (or, indeed, the operationalization of the UAF) had effectively nothing to do with the substance of the decision at stake. Rather, approval of Ukraine funding served as a useful leverage for Hungary to obtain concessions on other matters—all related to its ongoing rule of law crisis.

4.3 Rule of law

As is well known, since the early 2010s a number of EU Member States have experienced legal and political developments that have openly challenged basic constitutional principles such as the independence of the judiciary, the separation of powers, and the fairness of the electoral process.[145] This backsliding is particularly acute among those Member States who joined the EU in the 2004–2007 enlargement, and is part of a broader right-wing, populist political trend at play in former Communist countries[146]—including also in Eastern Germany. In particular, Hungary under the leadership of Prime Minister Viktor Orban, and Poland during the rule of the PiS party, have become the paradigmatic cases of the rule of law backsliding.[147] The rule of law crisis constitutes a major danger for the EU, not only because it threatens the mutual trust which is indispensable for the functioning of the EU's internal market, and Area of Freedom, Security and Justice—but also because it undermines the very identity of the EU.[148] In fact, in recent years the European Court of Justice (ECJ) has taken important steps to uphold the rule of law[149]—in cases that were brought before it. In infringement cases started by the Commission, the ECJ ruled incompatible with EU law national laws that imposed the early retirement of judges, or the subjection of their renewal to the decision of

---

[144] Republican Party Vice-Presidential candidate J D Vance, 'The Math on Ukraine Doesn't Add Up', Op-Ed, *The New York Times* (12 April 2024).

[145] See Laurent Pech and Kim Lane Scheppele, 'Illiberalism Within: Rule of Law Backsliding in the EU' (2017) 19 Cambridge Yearbook of European Legal Studies 3.

[146] See also Beatrice Monciunskaite, 'To Live and to Learn: The EU Commission's Failure to Recognise Rule of Law Deficiencies in Lithuania' (2022) 14 Hague Journal of the Rule of Law 49.

[147] See Wojciech Sadurski, *Poland's Constitutional Breakdown* (OUP 2019); and Andras Sajo, *Ruling by Cheating: Governance in Illiberal Democracy* (CUP 2021).

[148] Koen Lenaerts and José Gutiérrez-Fons, 'Epilogue. High Hopes: Autonomy and the Identity of the EU' (2023) 8 European Papers 1495.

[149] See Case C-64/16 *Associação Sindical dos Juízes Portugueses* ECLI:EU:C:2018:117 (affirming the principle of judicial independence as a core feature of the rule of law) and Case C-896/19 *Repubblika v Il-Prim Ministru* ECLI:EU:C:2021:311 (affirming the principle that Member States must refrain from adopting rules which would undermine the independence of the judiciary).

a political authority;[150] in preliminary reference proceedings, the ECJ held that national judges executing an EU arrest warrant must consider the rule of law situation in the requesting Member State, while abiding by the principle of mutual trust;[151] and in the action for annulment brought by Hungary and Poland against the rule of law conditionality regulation, the ECJ forcefully defended the legality of that tool.[152]

However, despite the role of the ECJ, the primary task to police rule of law backsliding falls on the EU political branches of government—and the steps they have taken have been largely unsatisfactory.[153] The Commission and the Council established an annual rule of law dialogue, designed to nudge Member States to abandon illiberal practices.[154] However, as this process proved to be toothless,[155] in December 2017 the Commission activated the Article 7 TEU procedure against Poland,[156] and in September 2018 the European Parliament approved a resolution to initiate the same process against Hungary.[157] The Article 7 TEU procedure would allow for the suspension of voting rights of a Member State found to have committed a serious and persistent breach of the values enshrined in Article 2 TEU. Yet, the procedure proved to be a paper tiger, as no meaningful progress was made on the matter by the Council for several years.[158] It is also for this reason that—in preparation for the new MFF—the Commission proposed to introduce a mechanism to freeze funds for EU Member States who fail to respect the rule of

---

[150] See eg Case C-791/19 *Commission v Poland* ECLI:EU:C:2021:596 (declaring incompatible with EU law Polish legislation setting up a Disciplinary Chamber concerning judges); Case C-204/21 *Commission v Poland* ECLI:EU:C:2023:442 (declaring illegal a consequence of the Disciplinary Chamber system).

[151] See Case C-216/18 PPU *LM* ECLI:EU:C:2018:586 (holding that the execution of an arrest warrant from Ireland to Poland can be suspended only if in the particular circumstances of the case there is a risk of breach of the fundamental rights of the person concerned to a fair trial); Case C-563/21 PPU *Openbaar Ministerie* ECLI:EU:C:2022:100 (reaching the same holding in the execution of an arrest warrant from the Netherlands to Poland).

[152] Case C-156/21 *Hungary v Parliament and Council* ECLI:EU:C:2022:97; and Case C-157/21 *Poland v Parliament and Council* ECLI:EU:C:2022:98.

[153] See Kim Lane Scheppele, 'The Treaties Without a Guardian: The European Commission and the Rule of Law' (2023) 29 Columbia Journal of European Law 93; Daniel Kelemen, 'The European Union's Failure to Address the Autocracy Crisis: MacGyver, Rube Goldberg and Europe's Unused Tools' (2023) 45 Journal of European Integration 223.

[154] See European Commission Communication 'A New EU Framework to Strengthen the Rule of Law', 11 March 2014, COM(2014) 158 final.

[155] Renata Uitz, 'The Perils of Defending Rule of Law through Dialogue' (2019) 15 European Constitutional Law Review 1.

[156] European Commission reasoned proposal in accordance with Article 7(1) Treaty on European Union for a Council Decision on the determination of a clear risk of a serious breach by the Republic of Poland of the rule of law, 20 December 2017, COM(2017) 835 final.

[157] European Parliament resolution of 12 September 2018 on a proposal calling on the Council to determine, pursuant to Article 7(1) of the Treaty on European Union, the existence of a clear risk of a serious breach by Hungary of the values on which the Union is founded, P8_TA(2018) 0340.

[158] See also European Parliament resolution of 16 January 2020 on ongoing hearings under Article 7(1) TEU regarding Poland and Hungary, P9_TA(2020) 0014.

law[159]—a plan which would ultimately come to light with the rule of law conditionality regulation in the framework of the NGEU Recovery Fund.

Yet, the success of this instrument still remains a matter of debate.[160] Because in the EU intergovernmental system of governance rule-of-law backsliding Member States have multiple opportunities to blackmail the EU, they were able to gain concessions on the enforcement of the rule of law conditionality regulation as a price to greenlight key decisions. The EU approval of funding for Ukraine proves the point: before the approval of the MFA+ in December 2022 the Council gave its conditional green light to the Hungarian NRRP, and in December 2023 the Commission also authorized the disbursement of some EU funding to Hungary. In other words, Hungary's ransom paid off. This state of affairs makes a mockery of respect for the rule of law in the EU, and raises the question of whether the use of the veto can be in breach of the EU principle of sincere cooperation enshrined in Article 4(3) TEU. In fact, the European Parliament has openly stated as much:[161] in a January 2024 resolution on the situation in Hungary and frozen EU funds, the European Parliament stated that the 'actions of the Prime Minister of Hungary, who decided to block the decision on the essential MFF revision, including the Ukraine aid package … are in violation of the principle of sincere cooperation, as enshrined in the Treaties',[162] and clarified that 'in no way can the EU give in to blackmail and trade the strategic interests of the EU and its allies by renouncing its values',[163] thus condemning the decision of the Commission to disburse some EU funding to Hungary.[164]

Be that as it may, the dependence on the consent of 27 Member States for any EU financial operation is bound to continue to create challenges for the EU in the long term, fundamentally weakening its ability to respond to unforeseen economic challenges and to consolidate a fiscal capacity.[165] If one adds to this that the European Parliament finds itself largely in an inferior position to the Council and the European Council in deciding fiscal issues, it appears that the governance infrastructure for decision-making on funding is democratically inadequate for the consolidation of a permanent fiscal capacity. In this context, therefore, a number

---

[159] European Commission proposal for a regulation of the European Parliament and the Council on the protection of the Union's budget in case of generalised deficiencies as regards the rule of law in the Member States, 2 May 2018, COM(2018) 324 final.

[160] See also Daniel Kelemen and Tommaso Pavone, 'Where Have the Guardians Gone? Law Enforcement and the Politics of Supranational Forbearance in the European Union' (2023) 75 World Politics 779.

[161] See European Parliament resolution of 18 January 2024 on the situation in Hungary and frozen EU funds, P9_TA(2024) 0053.

[162] Ibid para 3.

[163] Ibid.

[164] Ibid para 5.

[165] See also Paul Dermine, *The New Economic Governance of the Eurozone: A Rule of Law Analysis* (CUP 2022).

of constitutional reforms are clearly needed to consolidate an EU fiscal capacity. In particular, the EU should overcome unanimity requirements on decisions about borrowing and spending, and make sure that the European Parliament—the sole EU institution directly elected by European citizens—gains a voice equal to that of the Council in the fiscal domain.

5 Conclusion

This chapter has examined the EU's legal response to the war in Ukraine in the field of fiscal and economic policy, assessing the EU constitution's ability to promote the general welfare in time of war. As the EU was re-emerging from the Covid-19 pandemic, it faced another unprecedented economic challenge due to the war in Ukraine. In response to the illegal Russian invasion, the EU mobilized financial resources to support Ukraine. In particular, the EU deployed the EPF for the first time. It then established the MFA+ 2023, and it eventually set up the UF, providing even longer and greater funding to help Ukraine from 2024 until 2027.

As this chapter has claimed, the EU constitution enabled the EU to 'promote the general welfare' and roll out important fiscal measures. The EU's efforts to support Ukraine increased over time through the use of funding mechanisms which tracked the model employed to address the Covid-19 pandemic. In particular, while the EPF is a new mechanism of EU spending in CFSP, the MFA+ and the UF also rely on the issuance of common EU debt, and are based on a governance framework that largely reproduces the successful experiment of the NGEU. As such, the war in Ukraine reveals a trend towards the consolidation of a fiscal capacity in the EU.

Nevertheless, as the chapter has explained, the process of fiscal integration in the EU remains very much in the making. Indeed, constitutional constraints and governance problems hamper the ability of the EU to raise resources and rise to the geopolitical challenges it faces. While the EPF is a purely intergovernmental arrangement, Hungary's idiosyncratic veto delayed the approval of the MFA+ and the UF. Otherwise, the EU treaties currently prevent the use of EU resources for CSDP purposes, and severely constrain the ability of the EU to borrow money and spend. In this context, the EU is likely to struggle in its efforts to support a neighbour—and now candidate Member State—like Ukraine financially. Despite the progress made towards the consolidation of an EU fiscal capacity, a number of reforms to the EU fiscal constitution appear inevitable, therefore, if the EU wants to endow itself with the long-term means to act autonomously on the international stage.

4
To 'establish justice'
Developments in justice and home affairs

1 Introduction

Wars are devastating. The Russian illegal aggression against Ukraine, with its relentless bombing of civilian infrastructures, including hospitals and schools, caused a dramatic death toll, a catastrophic displacement of refugees, and probable cases of war crimes. According to the United Nations (UN) High Commissioner for the Refugees (UNHCR), the Russian indiscriminate shelling of cities and the military occupation of almost one-fifth of the country's territory forced 3.7 million people to seek internal displacement, and over 6.4 million people to find refuge in neighbouring countries.[1] The UN Office of the High Commissioner for Human Rights reported credible allegations of war crimes and crimes against humanity in the context of Russia's armed attack against Ukraine.[2] Non-governmental human rights organizations have documented summary executions and other killings of civilians, conflict-related sexual violence, enforced disappearances, and torture—all war crimes—by Russian armed forces in occupied areas of Ukraine, notably in the city of Bucha;[3] and proven reports of forced relocation of children from Ukraine to Russia have led the International Criminal Court (ICC) to issue arrest warrants against Russian President Vladimir Putin and the head of the Russian Commission for Children Rights.[4] Furthermore, the Grand Chamber of the European Court of Human Rights (ECtHR) ruled unequivocally in June 2024 that Russia's occupation of Crimea in 2014—the prelude to the 2022 large-scale invasion—caused systemic human rights abuses, including torture, inhumane and degrading treatments, enforced disappearances, unlawful detentions,

---

[1] See UNHCR, 'Ukraine Situation: Flash Update #63', 5 February 2024, file:///C:/Users/feder/Downloads/UKRAINE%20SITUATION%20FLASH%20UPDATE%20%2363.pdf.

[2] See Office of the UN High Commissioner for Human Rights press release, 'UN Commission concludes that war crimes have been committed in Ukraine, express concerns for the suffering of civilians', 23 September 2022, https://www.ohchr.org/en/press-releases/2022/10/un-commission-concludes-war-crimes-have-been-committed-ukraine-expresses.

[3] See Human Rights Watch, 'Delivering Justice for Human Rights in Ukraine', 23 May 2023, https://www.hrw.org/news/2023/05/23/delivering-justice-war-crimes-ukraine.

[4] See ICC press release, 'Situation in Ukraine: ICC judges issue arrest warrants against Vladimir Vladimirovich Putin and Maria Alekseyevna Lvova-Belova', 17 March 2023, https://www.icc-cpi.int/news/situation-ukraine-icc-judges-issue-arrest-warrants-against-vladimir-vladimirovich-putin-and

and deprivation of property, resulting in countless violations of the European Convention on Human Rights.[5]

The purpose of this chapter is to analyse from an European Union (EU) law and policy perspective the core measures adopted by the EU in the fields of justice and home affairs to react to these horrific facts and such blatant breaches of international law by Russia. This includes both policies falling within the Area of Freedom, Security and Justice (AFSJ)—immigration and criminal justice cooperation[6]—as well as sanctions and other solidarity measures—which in the EU treaty are technically outside the AFSJ, but were closely connected to it in the war context. By and large, in fact, the EU's response to the war has been inspired by the desire to remedy the injustice Ukraine has faced from Russia. Needless to say, there is a long-standing and very rich debate in political theory and moral philosophy on what constitutes a just or an unjust war[7]—and this chapter has no pretension to contribute to it. But from a legal and policy perspective, the EU's response to Russia's illegal aggression against Ukraine has largely been driven by the awareness that the war in Ukraine was unjust. Russia's aggression certainly constituted an illegal breach of international law. Consequently, the EU deployed forceful countermeasures to inflict a cost on Russia, secure accountability, and restore a modicum of justice for Ukraine, including in the forms of compensation or reparations.[8]

As the chapter argues, the EU constitution enabled the EU to take consequential measures 'to establish justice'[9] in favour of Ukraine, and in response to Russia's aggression the EU enacted unprecedented legal acts in the field of justice and home affairs to express solidarity with Ukraine, to sanction Russia, and to prepare the terrain for compensating the damage caused by the war. The EU welcomed Ukrainian refugees and set up solidarity mechanisms to facilitate the export of Ukrainian goods. Moreover, between February 2022 and June 2024, the EU approved 14 packages of wide-ranging sanctions designed to target Russian President Vladimir Putin and his inner circle of oligarchs financially, to repel Russia politically, and to weaken its ability economically to continue the illegal war of aggression. Furthermore, the EU also developed, in partnership with other international organizations, new mechanisms to investigate cases of war crimes committed by the Russian military in Ukraine, and to quantify the damages caused by this aggression. Finally, the EU also took the unprecedented step of targeting the extraordinary profits stemming from the sovereign assets of the Russian Central Bank

---

[5] ECtHR, *Ukraine v Russia (re Crimea)*, Applications nos 20958/14 and 38334/18, Judgment of 25 June 2024 (GC).

[6] See Jörg Monar, 'Justice and home affairs' in Erik Jones, Anand Menon, and Stephen Weatherill (eds), *The Oxford Handbook of the European Union* (OUP 2012) 613.

[7] See notably Michael Walzer, *Just and Unjust Wars: A Moral Argument with Historical Illustrations* (Basic Books 1997).

[8] See also Restoring Justice for Ukraine, Political Declaration, The Hague, 2 April 2024, para 22.

[9] US Const, preamble.

(RCB), immobilized as a result of the sanctions, and seizing them to support financially Ukraine's military resistance and its economic recovery and reconstruction.

Nevertheless, as this chapter maintains, the EU's response to the war in Ukraine in the field of justice and home affairs exposed a number of challenges, revealing shortcomings in the EU constitution's resilience during wartime. On the one hand, EU action faced issues of effectiveness—largely a consequence of the rule of law backsliding at play within the EU. In fact, Hungary—a Member State which is increasingly at odds with EU principles of democracy and the rule of law—repeatedly delayed the approval of sanctions against Russia; and Poland and other Eastern European Member States unilaterally suspended the EU solidarity lanes, citing concerns that Ukrainian imports would damage their domestic markets. On the other hand, EU action in the field of justice and home affairs raised issues of legality—both in terms of the respect for EU fundamental rights and the rule of law, and compliance with international obligations. EU restrictive measures—including a sweeping ban on Russian media—were subjected to deferential review by the EU judicature, especially in the first years of the war. Moreover, several other EU initiatives designed to inflict a cost on Russia for its illegal war have escaped judicial review *tout court*. In particular, the decision to seize the extraordinary revenues held by private entities stemming from the immobilized assets of the RCB was shrouded in secrecy—with draft legislative texts never published—and poses significant international law challenges, including compliance with rules on foreign sovereign immunity, which are designed to protect sovereign assets reciprocally.

There is an extensive comparative literature that highlights how constitutions in democratic systems are put under stress in wartime.[10] Empirical experience reveals that in times of conflict or emergency governments increasingly act in secrecy,[11] restricting fundamental rights, and conveniently side-stepping international obligations in the name of national security.[12] Indeed, the objective to preserve the *salus rei publicae* regularly trumps other constitutional values during emergencies, and an often heard refrain is that in times of war the laws are silent.[13] From this point of view, the war in Ukraine exposed analogous challenges in the EU constitution in wartime. The EU political branches of government adopted groundbreaking measures to respond to Russia's aggression, motivated by a desire to support Ukraine and remedy the injustice it had suffered. Yet, some of these

---

[10] This literature is particularly extensive in the United States, following 9/11. See eg David Cole and James Dempsey, *Terrorism and the Constitution* (The New Press 2002); Bruce Ackerman, *Before the Next Attack: Preserving Civil Liberties in an Age of Terrorism* (Yale University Press 2006); Scott Matheson, *Presidential Constitutionalism in Perilous Times* (Harvard University Press 2009).

[11] See David Cole, Federico Fabbrini, and Arianna Vedaschi (eds), *Secrecy, National Security and the Vindication of Constitutional Law* (Edward Elgar Publishing 2013).

[12] See Federico Fabbrini and Vicki Jackson (eds), *Constitutionalism Across Borders in the Struggle Against Terrorism* (Edward Elgar Publishing 2016).

[13] The statement is originally by Cicero, Pro Milone, 11 ('*silent enim leges inter arma*'). For a more recent reappraisal see William Renquist, *All the Laws but One: Civil Liberties in Wartime* (Random House 1998).

measures raised difficult legal issues in terms of respect for human rights and the rule of law, including the need for transparency—and were initially subjected to deferential scrutiny by the judiciary, or fell *tout court* outside judicial review. However, the EU constitution enshrines principles, including respect for fundamental rights and international law, which ought to apply beyond peacetime. This chapter, therefore, provides cautionary tales on the ability of the EU's constitution to constrain action by the political branches, and guidelines on how to strengthen checks and balances and the rule of law in the EU constitution during wartime— mainly through an expansion of the European Court of Justice (ECJ) jurisdiction.

As such, the chapter is structured as follows. Section 2 examines the core solidarity, sanctions, and investigation and compensation measures adopted by the EU in response to the war in Ukraine. Section 3 discusses the consequences of war-related developments in justice and home affairs, emphasizing also the novel use of treaty legal bases to adopt secondary sanctions, expand the list of EU crimes, and utilize the extraordinary revenues resulting from immobilized RCB assets. Section 4, however, critically considers some of the EU measures adopted in the field of justice and home affairs during the war in Ukraine, particularly from the perspective of the protection of human rights and respect for the rule of law and international obligations. Section 5, finally, concludes.

2 The core measures

2.1 Solidarity

The EU responded in solidarity to the devastations of the war in Ukraine. In the fields of asylum and migration, in particular, the EU addressed the massive exodus of Ukrainian refugees fleeing their war-torn homeland with a groundbreaking open-door policy, which diametrically contrasted with the approach used to address the migration crisis in 2015 and 2016.[14] In March 2022, the Council of the EU decided to resort to a 2001 Directive for the common EU management of a sudden influx of refugees,[15] and to grant temporary protections to Ukrainiancitizens and third-country nationals benefiting from international protection in Ukraine, who resided in Ukraine before the outbreak of war on 24 February 2022.[16] The

---

[14] See Janine Silga, 'Differentiation in the EU Migration Policy: The "Fractured Values" of the EU' (2022) 7 European Papers 909.

[15] Council Directive 2001/55/EC of 20 July 2001 on minimum standards for giving temporary protection in the event of a mass influx of displaced persons and on measures promoting a balance of efforts between Member States in receiving such persons and bearing the consequences thereof [2001] OJ L212/12.

[16] Council Implementing Decision (EU) 2022/382 of 4 March 2022 establishing the existence of a mass influx of displaced persons from Ukraine within the meaning of Article 5 of Directive 2001/55/EC, and having the effect of introducing temporary protection [2022] OJ L71/1.

so-called temporary protection directive (TPD) had been adopted as part of the 1999 Tampere agenda to build a genuine AFSJ, but had never been used before. On the basis of this Council decision, individuals fleeing Ukraine were granted temporary protection status, with the right to circulate freely across the EU, and access work and social benefits, hence facilitating better burden sharing between Member States. The decision attributed temporary protection for an initial period of one year, but with automatic six months extensions for a maximum of another year—hence until March 2024.[17] However, in September 2023 the European Commission proposed to prolong the measure until March 2025,[18] and the Council agreed to this the following month.[19] Moreover, in June 2024, the Council further extended the temporary protection mechanism until March 2026.[20]

At the same time—although this is technically a trade measure, rather than an AFSJ one—the EU also facilitated the export of Ukrainian produce, an initiative which it labelled 'Solidarity Lanes'. As a vast agricultural country, Ukraine was one of the leading global exporters of wheat, maize, and sunflower products. The Russian military invasion of Ukraine and the naval blockade of the Black Sea (which was only partially forestalled between July 2022 and July 2023 by the Black Sea Grain Initiative, brokered by the UN and Turkey), disrupted Ukrainian exports— also causing global food shortages in several developing countries. To mitigate that, in May 2022 the European Parliament and the Council approved legislation which—in the framework of the Association Agreement with Ukraine—waived customs duties and suspended tariff rate quotas on Ukrainian imports in the EU internal market.[21] Moreover, the EU concluded a road transport agreement with Ukraine, allowing Ukrainian haulers to transit through and operate in the EU, without the need for permits, and recognizing Ukrainian driving licences.[22] The trade facilitation measure applied for a year, but was renewed for a second one.[23] In January 2024, the Commission proposed to extend it until June

---

[17] Ibid recital 21.
[18] European Commission Proposal for a Council Implementing Decision extending temporary protection as introduced by Implementing Decision (EU) 2022/382, 19 September 2023, COM(2023) 546 final.
[19] Council Implementing Decision (EU) 2023/2409 of 19 October 2023 extending temporary protection as introduced by Implementing Decision (EU) 2022/382 [2023] OJ L/1.
[20] Council of the EU press release, 'Ukraine refugees: Council extends temporary protection until March 2026', 25 June 2024, 575/24.
[21] See Regulation (EU) 2022/870 of the European Parliament and of the Council of 30 May 2022 on temporary trade-liberalisation measures supplementing trade concessions applicable to Ukrainian products under the Association Agreement between the European Union and the European Atomic Energy Community and their Member States, of the one part, and Ukraine, of the other part [2022] OJ L152/103.
[22] See European Commission news article, 'Supporting Ukraine exports and improving connections to the EU: EU strengthens cooperation with Ukraine and Moldova', 29 June 2022.
[23] See Regulation (EU) 2023/1077 of the European Parliament and of the Council of 31 May 2023 on temporary trade-liberalisation measures supplementing trade concessions applicable to Ukrainian products under the Association Agreement between the European Union and the European Atomic Energy Community and their Member States, of the one part, and Ukraine, of the other part [2023] OJ L144/1.

2025,[24] albeit with additional safeguards designed to avoid the possibility that Ukrainian imports 'adversely affect the Union market or the market of one or several member states'[25]—a measure which was approved in May 2024.[26] Similarly, in March 2024 the Commission proposed to renew the road transport agreement, although with safeguard measures in case of negative impact on regional markets,[27] and in June 2024 the EU and Ukraine extended the agreement until June 2025, with a tacit renewal for another six months.[28]

2.2 Sanctions

The EU also responded to Russia's illegal aggression against Ukraine by adopting, between February 2022 and June 2024, 14 rounds of far-reaching sanctions, and other measures designed to inflict a cost on Russia—including the suspension of the EU-Russia visa facilitation agreement.[29] While the EU had already adopted restrictive measures against Russia in the aftermath of the invasion of Crimea,[30] since February 2022 it immediately strengthened them, and expanded them in the subsequent two years. As Christine Abely has pointed out, the EU sanctions were comprehensive and coordinated with other nations, especially the United States (US) and the other allies.[31] Indeed, the G7 (the Group of the seven most industrialized Western countries: the US, Germany, France, the United Kingdom, Italy, Japan,

---

[24] See European Commission proposal for a Regulation of the European Parliament and the Council on temporary trade-liberalisation measures supplementing trade concessions applicable to Ukrainian products under the Association Agreement between the European Union and the European Atomic Energy Community and their Member States, of the one part, and Ukraine, of the other part, 31 January 2024, COM(2024) 50 final.

[25] Ibid art 4.

[26] See Regulation (EU) 2024/1392 of the European Parliament and of the Council of 14 May 2024 on temporary trade-liberalisation measures supplementing trade concessions applicable to Ukrainian products under the Association Agreement between the European Union and the European Atomic Energy Community and their Member States, of the one part, and Ukraine, of the other part [2024] OJ L.

[27] See European Commission press release 'Commission proposes to prolong road transport agreement with Ukraine and Moldova and introduces updates to the agreement with Ukraine', 5 March 2024, IP/24/1305.

[28] See European Commission press release 'EU and Ukraine update and extend Road Transport Agreement', 20 June 2024, IP/24/3382.

[29] See Council Decision (EU) 2022/333 of 25 February 2022 on the partial suspension of the application of the Agreement between the European Community and the Russian Federation on the facilitation of the issuance of visas to the citizens of the European Union and the Russian Federation, [2022] OJ L54/1, repealed by Council Decision (EU) 2022/1500 of 9 September 2022 on the suspension in whole of the application of the Agreement between the European Community and the Russian Federation on the facilitation of the issuance of visas to the citizens of the European Union and the Russian Federation [2022] OJ L234I/1.

[30] See Council Decision 2014/145/CFSP of 17 March 2014 concerning restrictive measures in respect of actions undermining or threatening the territorial integrity, sovereignty and independence of Ukraine [2014] OJ L78/16.

[31] Christine Abely, *The Russia Sanctions: The Economic Response to Russia's Invasion of Ukraine* (CUP 2023) Appendix (reporting the list of jurisdictions joining in the sanctions against Russia).

and Canada, to which the EU is associated as a member) often served as the platform to agree on sanctions, which were then formally approved by each party in accordance with domestic legal systems. In the EU, this required a two-step process, with first a Council decision adopted in the field of Common Foreign and Security Policy (CFSP) on the basis of Article 29 TEU, and then a Council regulation on the basis of Article 215 TFEU, which provides the legal basis for the adoption of restrictive measures. Moreover, Article 75 TFEU—an AFSJ provision—allows the EU to adopt a framework for the freezing of funds and financial assets, which is one of the most widespread tools in this domain. The EU had used this process for several decades, notably in the framework of the post-9/11 so-called war on terrorism.[32]

The EU restrictive measures following Russia's invasion of Ukraine, however, were on a scale not seen before.[33] Specifically, the EU blacklisted approximately 2,000 individuals and entities, including Russian President Vladimir Putin and his government officials, all members of the Duma, and various oligarchs connected to the regime, subjecting them to travel bans and assets freezing;[34] it prohibited transactions related to the reserves and assets of the RCB held in Western banks;[35] and it removed several Russian commercial banks from the Belgian-based SWIFT (Society for Worldwide Interbank Financial Telecommunication) system, which secures inter-bank clearing, thus cutting them off from the international financial system.[36] Moreover, EU sanctions targeted the Russian disinformation and propaganda machine, by suspending the broadcasting licences of state-owned television channels such as *Russia Today* and *Sputnik*.[37] At the same time, EU sanctions also targeted the Russian economy, introducing export bans on dual use technology, and prohibiting EU investment into Russia.[38] Crucially, EU sanctions then step by step phased in a number of import bans on Russian fossil fuels—a choice that proved costly for the EU economy, as will be discussed in Chapter 5, but that was relevant to target Russia's main sources of revenue.

---

[32] See also Christina Eckes, *EU Counter-Terrorist Policies and Fundamental Rights: The Case of Individual Sanctions* (OUP 2009).

[33] Abely (n 31) 26.

[34] Council of the EU press release, 'Russia's military aggression against Ukraine: EU imposes sanctions against President Putin and Foreign Minister Lavrov and adopts wide ranging individual and economic sanctions', 25 February 2022.

[35] Council Decision (CFSP) 2022/335 of 28 February 2022 amending Decision 2014/512/CFSP concerning restrictive measures in view of Russia's actions destabilising the situation in Ukraine [2022] OJ L57/4, art 1(1).

[36] Council Decision (CFSP) 2022/346 of 1 March 2022 amending Decision 2014/512/CFSP concerning restrictive measures in view of Russia's actions destabilising the situation in Ukraine [2022] OJ L63/5, art 1(1).

[37] Council Decision (CFSP) 2022/351 of 1 March 2022 amending Decision 2014/512/CFSP concerning restrictive measures in view of Russia's actions destabilising the situation in Ukraine [2022] OJ L65/5, art 1(1) and Annex.

[38] See eg Council Decision (CFSP) 2022/578 of 8 April 2022 amending Decision 2014/512/CFSP concerning restrictive measures in view of Russia's actions destabilising the situation in Ukraine [2022] OJ L111/70.

Furthermore, the EU sanctions against Russia were characterized by two unprecedented legal features. On the one hand, for the first time the EU also introduced secondary sanctions, targeting natural or legal persons who facilitated the circumvention of already-imposed sanctions.[39] On the other hand, the EU added the violation of restrictive measures to the list of 'EU crimes' included in Article 83(1) TFEU. Pursuant to this provision, the EU has competence to 'establish minimum rules concerning the definition of criminal offences and sanctions in the areas of particularly serious crime with a cross-border dimension'. Article 83(1) TFEU lists a number of such 'areas of crime [including …] terrorism, trafficking [… and] organized crime' but empowers the Council to identify 'other areas of crime that meet the criteria specified in this paragraph'. Consequently, in October 2022 the Council, with the consent of the European Parliament, unanimously decided to identify the violation of EU restrictive measures as a crime falling under Article 83(1) TFEU,[40] and shortly afterwards the Commission proposed a directive on the definition of criminal offences and penalties for the violation of EU restrictive measures.[41] This directive was approved by the co-legislators, and entered into force in April 2024, with a one-year transposition time for the Member States to implement it into their national legal systems.[42]

2.3 Criminal investigations and compensation

Besides targeting Russia with sanctions to deter its military aggression against Ukraine, however, the EU also took steps to re-establish justice, both by setting up new mechanisms to investigate war crimes and paving the way towards compensation for war damage. With regard to investigations, in March 2022 all EU Member States decided collectively to refer the situation in Ukraine to the ICC, which, as mentioned above, eventually issued arrest warrants for Russian President Putin, and subsequently also for some of his top generals.[43] Moreover, as foreseen by EU legislation in the area of the AFSJ,[44] a number of EU Member States established a

---

[39] See Council Decision (CFSP) 2022/1907 of 6 October 2022 amending Decision 2014/145/CFSP concerning restrictive measures in respect of actions undermining or threatening the territorial integrity, sovereignty and independence of Ukraine [2022] OJ L259I/98, art 1(1).
[40] Council Decision (EU) 2022/2332 of 28 November 2022 on identifying the violation of Union restrictive measures as an area of crime that meets the criteria specified in Article 83(1) of the Treaty on the Functioning of the European Union [2022] OJ L308/18.
[41] Commission Proposal for a Directive of the European Parliament and of the Council on the definition of criminal offences and penalties for the violation of Union restrictive measures, 2 December 2022, COM(2022) 684 final.
[42] Directive (EU) 2024/1226 of the European Parliament and of the Council of 24 April 2024 on the definition of criminal offences and penalties for the violation of Union restrictive measures and amending Directive (EU) 2018/1673 [2024] OJ L/1.
[43] See ICC press release, 'Situation in Ukraine: ICC judges issue arrest warrants against Sergei Kuzhugetovich Shoigu and Valery Vasilyevich Gerasimov', 25 June 2024, https://www.icc-cpi.int/news/situation-ukraine-icc-judges-issue-arrest-warrants-against-sergei-kuzhugetovich-shoigu-and.
[44] Council Framework Decision of 13 June 2002 on joint investigation teams [2002] OJ L162/1.

joint investigation team (JIT) with Ukraine and the ICC Office of the Prosecutor, tasked to investigate war crimes with a view to a future international criminal prosecution.[45] Furthermore, in May 2022 the European Parliament and the Council amended the regulation establishing Eurojust—the EU agency for criminal justice cooperation—giving it the authority to preserve, analyse, and store evidence relating to core international crimes, including war crimes, crimes against humanity, and genocide.[46] And, following an announcement of the European Commission,[47] a Centre for the Prosecution of the Crime of Aggression Against Ukraine (ICPA) started operations in July 2023 within Eurojust.[48]

Yet, the EU also explored avenues to compensate Ukraine for the war damage it suffered, closely coordinating with the Council of Europe (CoE) and the G7 on ways to use Russian sovereign assets immobilized in Western banks as a result of sanctions, which according to estimates were worth almost US$300 billion.[49] In May 2023, the CoE Committee of Ministers established, with the representatives of the EU, the US, Canada, and Japan, the Enlarged Partial Agreement on the Register of the Damage Caused by the Aggression of the Russian Federation against Ukraine.[50] In October 2023, the CoE Parliamentary Assembly called for the creation of a comprehensive compensation mechanism to ensure a just peace in Ukraine.[51] And in April 2024, the CoE Parliamentary Assembly approved a resolution drafted in January 2024 by the Committee on Political Affairs and Democracy[52] calling for the confiscation of Russian assets immobilized in Western financial institutions as a countermeasure for Russia's violation of international law, and a way to support the reconstruction of Ukraine, redressing the damage caused by the war.[53] Moreover, in December 2023, the G7 committed to 'direct extraordinary revenues held by private entities stemming directly from Russia's

---

[45] See Suhong Yang and Yudan Tan, 'The Joint Investigation Team in Ukraine: Challenges and Opportunities for the International Criminal Court' (2023) 8 European Papers 1121.

[46] Regulation (EU) 2022/838 of the European Parliament and of the Council of 30 May 2022 amending Regulation (EU) 2018/1727 as regards the preservation, analysis and storage at Eurojust of evidence relating to genocide, crimes against humanity, war crimes and related criminal offences [2022] OJ L148/1.

[47] European Commission President Ursula von der Leyen, Statement, 2 February 2023.

[48] See Eurojust press release, 'History in the Making: The International Centre for the Prosecution of the Crime of Aggression against Ukraine starts operations at Eurojust', 3 July 2023, https://www.eurojust.europa.eu/news/history-making-international-centre-prosecution-crime-aggression-against-ukraine-starts-operations-at-eurojust.

[49] See Elena Fabrichnaya and Guy Faulconbridge, 'What and where are Russia's $300 billion in reserves frozen in the West', *Reuters* (28 December 2023).

[50] See CoE Committee of Ministers Resolution establishing the Enlarged Partial Agreement on the Register of the Damage Caused by the Aggression of the Russian Federation against Ukraine, CM/Res (2023) 3, 12 May 2023.

[51] See CoE Parliamentary Assembly Resolution Ensuring a just peace in Ukraine and lasting security in Europe, 2516(2023), 12 October 2023.

[52] See CoE Parliamentary Assembly Committee in Political Affairs, Report, 'Support for the Reconstruction of Ukraine', 25 January 2024.

[53] CoE Parliamentary Assembly Resolution Support for the Reconstruction of Ukraine, 2539(2024), 16 April 2024.

immobilized sovereign assets to support Ukraine, consistent with applicable contractual obligations and in accordance with applicable laws'.[54]

In line with this, the European Council in both October and December 2023 adopted identically worded conclusions calling 'for decisive progress, in coordination with partners, on how extraordinary revenues held by private entities stemming directly from Russia's immobilised assets could be directed to support Ukraine and its recovery and reconstruction, consistent with applicable contractual obligations, and in accordance with EU and international law'.[55] It had indeed emerged that, given favourable interest rates, the main EU-based Central Securities Depositories (CSDs) had reported record profits from RCB immobilized assets in the fiscal year 2023.[56] On this basis, the EU High Representative for Foreign and Security Policy and the Commission put forward legal texts to seize these extraordinary revenues—which, however, were never published. In February 2024, the European Council 'welcome[d] the agreement reached on the Council Decision and Council Regulation concerning extraordinary revenues held by private entities stemming directly from Russia's immobilised assets to support Ukraine'.[57] And a few days afterwards, the Council of the EU announced in a press release that it had adopted a decision and a regulation clarifying the obligations of EU-based CSDs holding assets and reserves of the [RCB] that are immobilized as consequence of EU's restrictive measures.[58]

When the Council decision[59] and regulation[60] were eventually published in the EU *Official Journal* on 14 February 2024, it appeared that the EU embraced a narrower approach to the use of frozen RCB sovereign assets, avoiding a full seizure, and rather confiscating only the extraordinary revenues that they generated. With its decision and regulation, which were identical content-wise, the Council required CSDs to account the extraordinary cash balances accumulating due to EU restrictive measures separately and prohibited them from disposing of the ensuing net profits. The regulation also empowered the Commission to impose reporting requirements on CSDs. Significantly, however, both acts stated that 'unexpected and extraordinary revenues [from RCB frozen assets ...] do not constitute

---

[54] G7 Leaders' Statement, 6 December 2023, 3.

[55] European Council conclusions, 27–28 October 2023, EUCO 14/23, para 6; and European Council conclusions, 14–15 December 2023, EUCO 20/23, para 6.

[56] See Laura Dubois, 'Frozen Russian assets yielded €4.4bn in 2023, says Euroclear', *The Financial Times* (1 February 2024).

[57] European Council conclusions, 1 February 2023, EUCO 2/24, para 37.

[58] See Council of the EU press release, 'Immobilized Russian assets: Council decides to set aside extraordinary revenues', 12 February 2024, 114/24.

[59] See Council Decision (CFSP) 2024/577 of 12 February 2024 amending Decision 2014/512/CFSP concerning restrictive measures in view of Russia's actions destabilising the situation in Ukraine [2024] OJ L.

[60] See Council Regulation (EU) 2024/576 of 12 February 2024 amending Regulation (EU) No 833/2014 concerning restrictive measures in view of Russia's actions destabilising the situation in Ukraine [2024] OJ L.

sovereign assets. Therefore the rules protecting sovereign assets are not applicable to these revenues'.[61] Moreover, they mentioned that the Council would decide 'on a possible establishment of a financial contribution to the Union budget that shall be raised on those net profits to support Ukraine and its recovery and reconstruction, as well as detailed arrangements therefor, consistent with applicable contractual obligations, and in accordance with Union and international law'.[62]

In March 2024, the European Council 'reviewed progress on the next concrete steps towards directing extraordinary revenues stemming from Russia's immobilized assets for the benefit of Ukraine',[63] and referred to a proposal by the High Representative and the Commission—which, once again, was not published. In April 2024, the European Council 'welcome[d] the progress on the proposals to direct extraordinary revenues stemming from Russia's immobilizes assets for the benefit of Ukraine and call[ed] for their swift adoption'.[64] On 7 May 2024, the Committee of Permanent Representative validated a presidency compromise proposal on legal texts concerning the extraordinary revenues stemming from immobilized Russian assets to support Ukraine,[65] which the Council formally approved on 21 May 2024.[66] Specifically, through two almost identically worded acts—a decision[67] and a regulation[68]—the Council required CSDs to pay windfall profits stemming from RCB immobilized assets as a 'financial contribution'[69] to the EU, and decided that 90% of this financial contribution would be transferred to the European Peace Facility (EPF), while 10% would finance the Ukraine Facility (UF)[70]—two fiscal tools to support Ukraine which were examined in depth in Chapter 3.

Moreover—on the basis of a political agreement reached by the G7 meeting held in June 2024 to secure an extraordinary revenue acceleration (ERA) loan of US$50 billion to Ukraine, 'to be serviced and repaid by future flows of extraordinary revenues stemming from the immobilization of Russian sovereign assets

---

[61] See Council Decision (CFSP) 2024/577 (n 59) recital 18; Council Regulation (EU) 2024/576 (n 60) recital 20.
[62] See Council Decision (CFSP) 2024/577 (n 59) art 1; Council Regulation (EU) 2024/576 (n 60) art 20.
[63] European Council conclusions, 21–22 March 2024, EUCO 7/24, para 4.
[64] European Council conclusions, 17–18 April 2024, EUCO 12/24, para 3.
[65] Council of the EU, General Secretariat of the Council, Council Decision and Regulation concerning the extraordinary revenues stemming from immobilized Russian assets to support Ukraine: Preparation for adoption, 7 May 2024, Doc 9555/24.
[66] Council of the EU press release, 'Extraordinary revenues generated by immobilized Russian assets: Council greenlights the use of net windfall profits to support Ukraine's self-defence and reconstruction', 21 May 2024.
[67] Council Decision (CFSP) 2024/1470 of 21 May 2024 amending Decision 2014/512/CFSP concerning restrictive measures in view of Russia's actions destabilising the situation in Ukraine [2024] OJ L.
[68] Council Regulation (EU) 2024/1469 of 21 May 2024 amending Regulation (EU) No 833/2014 concerning restrictive measures in view of Russia's actions destabilising the situation in Ukraine [2024] OJ L.
[69] Council Decision (CFSP) 2024/1470 (n 67) art 1(2).
[70] Council Regulation (EU) 2024/1469 (n 68) Annex.

held in the [EU] and other relevant jurisdictions'[71]—the European Commission in September 2024 also put forward a proposal for a regulation of the European Parliament and the Council establishing a Ukraine Loan Cooperation Mechanism (ULCM).[72] As explained in Chapter 3, the Commission proposed to establish a new macro-financial assistance tool,[73] on the basis of which the EU would raise up to €35 billion on the financial markets,[74] and transfer these as an up-front loan to Ukraine. At the same time, the Commission proposed to subsidize Ukraine's repayment of the loan's principal and interest[75] by using the extraordinary revenues stemming from RCB immobilized assets.[76] In the Commission's plan the ULCM would have a budget of €45 billion, with contributions coming also from other nations subjecting RCB assets to sanctions freeze, notably the US, which, however, has struggled to honour its pledge given outstanding legal questions.[77] The Commission decision to move forward with the ULCM legislation regardless, therefore, puts the EU at the forefront of the international effort to seize RCB assets in response to the war in Ukraine.[78]

3 The consequences

The EU action in the fields of justice and home affairs since the outbreak of the war in Ukraine has been wide ranging. Several of the EU initiatives in this field were adopted on the basis of existing EU legislation. Most obviously, the TPD had been on the books since 2001, but never used: the war in Ukraine, however, provided the catalyst to overcome political opposition in the Council, which eventually triggered it to handle an unprecedented flux of almost six million refugees in the EU.[79] However, other EU initiatives were facilitated by the EU constitution, as newly applied by the EU institutions in a time of war. In particular, legislation was approved by the Council and the European Parliament under Article 85 TFEU to expand the tasks of Eurojust and empower it to investigate war crimes.[80] Moreover, the

---

[71] See G7 Leaders' Communiqué, 13–15 June 2024, 3.

[72] European Commission proposal for a Regulation of the European Parliament and of the Council establishing a Ukraine Loan Cooperation Mechanism and providing exceptional macro-financial assistance to Ukraine, 20 September 2024, COM(2024) 426 final.

[73] Ibid art 9.

[74] Ibid art 14.

[75] Ibid art 3.

[76] Ibid art 2.

[77] See Alan Rappeport, '$50 Billion in Aid to Ukraine Stalls over Legal Questions', *The New York Times* (17 September 2020).

[78] See European Commission press release, 'Commission proposes up to €35 billion MFA loan for Ukraine at the EU's contribution to the EU-G7 support of up to €45 billion', 20 September 2024.

[79] See Sylvain Thiéry, 'La protection temporaire de l'Union européenne en faveur des ressortissants ukrainiens: Perspectives d'avenir après un an d'application' (2023) 8 European Papers 779.

[80] On the use of JIT see Cornelia Riehle, '20 Years of Joint Investigation Teams in the EU' (2023) 24 ERA Forum 163.

treaty legal bases on sanctions—Article 29 TEU and Article 215 TFEU—were used flexibly by the Council first to introduce secondary sanctions, and subsequently to pave the way for the use of the extraordinary revenues generated by immobilized RCB assets—a form of seizure light.

The question of secondary sanctions had long troubled the EU institutions, especially vis-à-vis the US which regularly applied them as an ordinary foreign and trade policy tool.[81] In fact, in 1996 the Council of the EU had adopted legislation— the so-called blocking statute—designed to nullify the extraterritorial effects of secondary sanctions imposed by third countries.[82] Moreover, following the US withdrawal from the 2015 Iran nuclear deal—the Joint Comprehensive Plan of Action[83]—and the reintroduction of US secondary sanctions on legal entities conducting business with Iran, the EU had promoted the establishment of the Instrument in Support of Trade Exchanges (INSTEX). INSTEX, formally set up as a private company governed by French law, operated as a payment clearing house, netting European payments against Iranian payments, avoiding financial transactions which, given the global dominance of the dollar, fall under the sword of Damocles of US sanctions. Nevertheless, INSTEX never successfully took off the ground, and was ultimately discontinued in 2023.

In response to the war in Ukraine, however, the EU itself now embraced the idea of secondary sanctions, aligning with the US in introducing new extraterritorial measures designed to avoid the circumvention of its targeted measures against Russia. Ironically, this happened shortly after the ECJ had offered the first interpretation of the blocking statute in 2021, in *Bank Melli Iran*,[84] holding that it prohibited persons from complying with secondary sanctions, 'even in the absence of an order directing compliance issued by the administrative or judicial authorities of the third countries which adopted those laws'.[85] Yet, as a growing body of scholarship has pointed out, the EU increasingly projects the effects of its law outside its borders: this is particularly evident in the field of data protection,[86] as well as in the areas of competition law[87] and environmental law—witness the adoption of the Carbon Border Adjustment Mechanism (CBAM) which introduces a customs duty on goods produced outside the EU in disregard of carbon

---

[81] See Henry Farrell and Abraham Newmann, *Underground Empire: How America Weaponized the World Economy* (Random House 2023).
[82] Council Regulation (EC) No 2271/96 of 22 November 1996 protecting against the effects of the extra-territorial application of legislation adopted by a third country, and actions based thereon or resulting therefrom [1996] OJ L309/1.
[83] Joint Comprehensive Plan of Action, Vienna, 14 July 2015.
[84] Case C-124/20 *Bank Melli Iran* ECLI:EU:C:2021:1035.
[85] Ibid para 51.
[86] See also Federico Fabbrini, Edoardo Celeste, and John Quinn (eds), *Data Protection beyond Borders: Transatlantic Perspective on Extraterritoriality and Sovereignty* (Hart Publishing 2021).
[87] See eg Bernadette Zelger, 'EU Competition Law and Extraterritorial Jurisdiction: A Critical Analysis of the ECJ's Judgment in Intel' (2020) 16 European Competition Journal 613.

emission rules.[88] So the introduction of secondary sanctions in relation to the war in Ukraine aligns with this extraterritorial trend.

Moreover, the Council of the EU also resorted to the legal bases on sanctions to bring about a significant justice measure, namely the forfeiture of the extraordinary revenues generated by the immobilized assets of the RCB. Through a unanimous decision, the Council directed CSDs to account as separate revenues the windfall profits arising from favourable interest rates, and subsequently it ordered CSDs to transfer these revenues to the EU as financial contributions for the EPF and the UF. This is a significant development, not only because for the first time the EU has taken steps towards the expropriation of foreign sovereign assets, but also because Article 345 TFEU states that 'the Treaties shall in no way prejudice the rules in Member States governing the system of property ownership'. In fact, the Council decision and regulation explicitly affirm that the profits from RCB immobilized assets do not constitute sovereign assets, and can therefore be forfeited.

Finally, the EU also used for the first time since the entry into force of the Lisbon Treaty another legal basis of EU primary law, namely Article 83 TFEU, by expanding the lists of EU crimes.[89] Specifically, in 2022 the Council, with the consent of the European Parliament, included a new EU crime—the violation of restrictive measures—in the legislative competence of the EU; and in 2024, the Council and the European Parliament jointly adopted a directive establishing minimum rules on the definition of criminal offences and criminal sanctions for individuals who are guilty of violating the restrictive measures adopted in response to the war in Ukraine.

4 The challenges

4.1 Decision-making

While the EU response to the war in Ukraine in the field of justice and home affairs has been unprecedented, it has not been flawless—both from an institutional and a legal perspective. In fact, the EU justice and home affairs constitution revealed shortcomings in time of war. To begin with, EU action faced a question of policy effectiveness, largely resulting from the institutional decision-making system that applies in the field. In particular, sanctions adopted by the Council of the EU ex Article 29 TEU have to be agreed unanimously—which is the standard decision-making rule in foreign affairs pursuant to Articles 24 and 31 TEU. Yet, the

---

[88] See Goran Dominion and Dan Esty, 'Designing Effective Border-Carbon Adjustment Mechanisms: Aligning the Global Trade and Climate Change Regimes' (2023) 65 Arizona Law Review 1.

[89] See Jacob Oberg, 'The Definition of Criminal Sanctions in the EU' (2013) 3 EU Criminal Law Review 273.

requirement to obtain unanimous agreement by the 27 Member States in Council repeatedly delayed EU measures designed to impose a cost on Russia, or weakened it via national exceptions. Hence, for example, the adoption of the sixth package of sanctions, banning the import into the EU of Russian crude oil and petroleum products, ended up covering only seaborn imports, exempting oil delivered by pipeline,[90] essentially to appease Hungary, which in fact renegotiated an oil supply deal with Russia in 2024.[91] Similarly, Greece, Cyprus, and Malta—three shipping nations—delayed the eighth package of sanctions against Russia, over opposition to the introduction of an oil price cap. And Hungary again kept hostage the approval of the 14th package of sanctions for weeks in 2024, until it obtained an exception allowing the development of a Russian-sponsored nuclear reactor.

Furthermore, structural weaknesses in the EU governance and enforcement system also undermined the capacity of the EU to provide solidarity with Ukraine in time of war. In particular, Poland, together with other bordering EU Member States (Hungary, Slovakia, and Romania), unilaterally disapplied the EU trade measures designed to facilitate Ukraine's export of agricultural products, and free movement of hauliers, as this caused the entrance into these Member States' markets of cheaper goods and labour, and consequently caused protests by farmers and truck drivers.[92] However, the unilateral action by these Member States breached EU law, since pursuant to Article 3 TFEU the 'common commercial policy' is an exclusive competence of the EU. Yet, in the absence of strong response by the EU institutions, Ukraine commenced dispute settlement proceedings before the World Trade Organization (WTO).[93] The matter, ultimately, was settled amicably,[94] without the need for WTO adjudication, and the latest EU trade facilitation measures introduced safeguards to avoid adverse effects on the EU market or the market of one or several EU Member States[95]—a measure designed to ensure domestic tranquillity, as will be discussed further in Chapter 5. However, the incident revealed gaps in the EU's stance towards Ukraine.

This outcome, however, is not accidental; rather, it is the result of the process of rule of law backsliding at play in the EU—a state of affairs that predates Russia's aggression against Ukraine but which has worsened ever since, as explored in Chapter 3. Indeed, several academics have pointed out that the war served as 'a

---

[90] See European Council conclusions, 30–31 May 2022, EUCO 21/22, para 5.
[91] See 'Hungary Welcomes Russia Crude Supply Deal after Ukraine Halts Lukoil Transit', *The Moscow Times* (10 September 2024).
[92] See Constant Meheut, 'Thousands Wait at Ukraine Border after Polish Truckers Blockade It', *The New York Times* (10 November 2023).
[93] See World Trade Organization, 'Ukraine initiates WTO dispute complaints against Hungary, Poland, and Slovak Republic', 21 September 2023, https://www.wto.org/english/news_e/news23_e/ds619_620_621rfc_21sep23_e.htm.
[94] See Ukraine Ministry for Communities, Territories and Infrastructure Development press release, 'Oleksandr Kubrakov met with Minister of Infrastructure of Poland Dariusz Klimczak to discuss unblocking the border', 16 January 2024.
[95] Regulation (EU) 2024/ 1392 (n 26) art 4.

pretext to wave the rule of law goodbye',[96] as the EU institutions charged to enforce rule of law compliance granted more leeway to backsliding Member States like Poland, which played a big role in supporting Ukraine, especially by hosting millions of refugees in accordance with the TPD. Yet the attitude by some EU Member States to disobey EU law at will, encouraged them to do so again in the context of the war in Ukraine, raising questions regarding the real degree of EU solidarity and resolve vis-à-vis Ukraine.[97] Moreover, the limited enforcement power of the EU institutions in policing compliance with the rule of law emboldened several Member States to paralyse decision-making repeatedly in the Council, weakening the speed and the coherence of the EU response to the war in Ukraine. In particular, Hungary has emerged during the war as the regular objector to the EU decision-making process, in the fields of justice and home affairs, as well as in other policy areas like CFSP and economic and fiscal policy.[98]

4.2 Domestic legality

From a legal perspective, furthermore, the EU adoption of sanctions and other measures in the field of justice and home affairs raises important questions of domestic legality—notably in terms of the protection of fundamental rights and respect for the rule of law. According to Article 2 TEU, the EU is founded on the values of democracy, the rule of law, and the protection of human rights, and, pursuant to Article 6 TEU, the EU protects and respects the rights, freedoms, and principles enshrined in the Charter of Fundamental Rights (CFR).[99] For this reason, the EU constitution foresees a complete system of judicial remedies. While according to Article 24 TEU the ECJ 'shall not have jurisdiction with respect to the ... provisions' of CFSP, an exception is made for judicial review of restrictive measures: as foreseen in Article 275 TFEU, the ECJ has jurisdiction to rule on action for direct annulment brought in accordance with Article 263 TFEU, 'reviewing the legality of decisions providing for restrictive measures against natural or legal persons adopted by the Council'. Furthermore, both Articles 75 and 215 TFEU identically provide that freezing of funds and restrictive measures 'shall include necessary provisions on legal safeguards'.

---

[96] Petra Bard and Dimitry Kochenov, 'War as a Pretext to Wave the Rule of Law Goodbye? The Case for an EU Constitutional Awakening' (2021) 27 European Law Journal 39.
[97] See Benedetta Lobina, 'Between a Rock and a Hard Place: The Impact of the Rule of Law Backsliding on the EU's Response to the Russo-Ukrainian War' (2023) 8 European Papers 1143.
[98] See also Andrew Higgins, 'How Hungary Undermined Europe's Bid to Aid Ukraine', *The New York Times* (17 December 2023).
[99] See Federico Fabbrini, *Fundamental Rights in Europe: Challenges and Transformations in Comparative Perspective* (OUP 2014).

In fact, in the past two decades, and notably in the context of the so-called war on terrorism, the ECJ built an extensive body of case law reviewing the legality of sanctions imposed on individuals and entities suspected of financing global terrorism.[100] In particular, in the *Kadi* saga[101] the ECJ affirmed that sanctions had to comply with the constitutional rights of suspected persons, including the right to due process, and that EU principles prevailed over the orders of the UN Security Council.[102] In its ruling, the ECJ overruled a prior decision by the then EU Court of First Instance,[103] and forcefully excluded the view that an EU act could 'escape all review by the [EU] judicature once it ha[d] been claimed that [it] ... concern[ed] national security and terrorism'.[104] In concrete terms, the ECJ held that the applicant, an individual blacklisted as a suspected terrorist financier, was entitled to due process, including receiving evidence to justify his blacklisting, and in a follow-up ruling the ECJ reaffirmed this view,[105] striking down a subsequent relisting decision by the Commission and the Council.[106]

Nevertheless, the case law of the ECJ on counter-terrorism sanctions also revealed that the EU Courts were remarkably deferential towards the EU political branches of government, particularly in the early years after 9/11.[107] After all, from a comparative perspective, this is a trend visible in the counter-terrorism case law of the US Supreme Court too: in particular, in the aftermath of 9/11, the US Supreme Court held in *Hamdi*[108] that the executive branch had a wide latitude in detaining a US citizen as an enemy combatant without the full application of constitutional due process rights; and only subsequently—through decisions like *Hamdan*[109] and *Boumediene*[110]—did it rule that the executive was bound to comply with the rule of law and that the Constitution prohibited the suspension of *habeas corpus* for detainees suspected of being involved in terrorist activities. As I have explained elsewhere, this reflects a conventional pattern in constitutional democracies in

---

[100] Ibid 79 ff.
[101] Joined Cases C-402/05 P and C-415/05 P *Yassin Abdullah Kadi and Al Barakaat International Foundation v Council of the EU and Commission* ECLI:EU:C:2008:461.
[102] Gavin Sullivan, *The Law of the List: UN Counterterrorism Sanctions and the Politics of Global Security Law* (CUP 2020).
[103] Case T-315/01 *Yassin Abdullah Kadi v Council of the EU and Commission* ECLI:EU:T:2005:332. See also Case T-306/01 *Ahmed Ali Yusuf and Al Barakaat International Foundation v Council of the EU and Commission* ECLI:EU:T:2005:331.
[104] *Kadi* (n 101) para 343.
[105] Case C-584/10 P *European Commission v Kadi (Kadi II)* ECLI:EU:C:2013:518.
[106] See Matej Avbelij, Filippo Fontanelli, and Giuseppe Martinico (eds), *Kadi on Trial: A Multifaceted Analysis of the Kadi Trail* (Routledge 2014).
[107] See also Case T-253/02 *Ayadi v Council of the EU* ECLI:EU:T:2006:200; and Case T-85/09 *Kadi v European Commission (Kadi II)* ECLI:EU:T:2010:418.
[108] *Yaser Hamdi v Donald Rumsfeld* 542 US 507 (2004).
[109] *Salim Hamdan v Donald Rumsfeld* 548 US 557 (2006).
[110] *Lakhdar Boumediene v George W Bush* 553 US 723 (2008).

times of emergencies—be they a terrorist attack[111] or a pandemic:[112] the judiciary tends to be extremely deferential to executives and legislatures in the aftermath of an emergency, tightening its scrutiny only as time goes by, and the memory of the threat recedes.

The approach of the EU judiciary during the war in Ukraine mirrors this pattern. While a number of actions for annulment challenging the EU sanctions against Russian individuals and entities were brought before the ECJ, the General Court—the lower EU Court, which has first-hand competence to adjudicate cases under Article 263 TFEU—initially rejected them on the merits. For example, in the *Abramovich* case,[113] the General Court upheld the sanctions imposed by the Council on a leading Russian oligarch, holding that 'with regard to developments in the situation in Ukraine, by also targeting businesspersons who are involved in activities in economic sectors providing a substantial source of revenue to the Russian Government, the Council could legitimately expect that such actions would cease or become too costly for those engaging therein, in order to promote an end to the blatant violation of the territorial integrity, sovereignty and independence of Ukraine'.[114]

Admittedly, as the war in Ukraine continued and time passed, the EU judicature has tightened its scrutiny of EU sanctions, requiring the EU political branches of government to provide more detailed reasons for the adoption of restrictive measures. In particular, in the *Mazepin* case,[115] delivered in March 2024—more than two years since the start of Russia's large-scale military act of aggression against Ukraine—the General Court annulled the sanctions imposed by the Council against the son of a Russian oligarch who was an F1 driver. The General Court held that EU courts 'must ensure the review, in principle, the full review, of the lawfulness of all Union acts',[116] and that the Council must base its decision on facts that are 'sufficiently specific, precise and consistent'.[117] In light of these legal principles, the General Court concluded that the Council had made an error of assessment and removed the applicant's name from the EU sanctions list—a decision it reached in at least one other case.[118]

Nevertheless, the General Court upheld other EU restrictive measures with broader implications for fundamental rights and democracy. In particular, in *RT*

---

[111] Federico Fabbrini, 'The Role of the Judiciary in Times of Emergency: Judicial Review of Counter-Terrorism Measures in the US Supreme Court and the European Court of Justice' (2010) 28 Oxford Yearbook of European Law 664.
[112] Federico Fabbrini, 'Covid-19, Human Rights and Judicial Review in Transatlantic Perspectives' (2025) 31 Columbia Journal of European Law.
[113] Case T-313/22 *Abramovich v Council of the EU* ECLI:EU:T:2023:830.
[114] Ibid para 142.
[115] Case T-743/22 *Mazepin v Council of the EU* ECLI:EU:T:2024:180.
[116] Ibid para 65.
[117] Ibid para 68.
[118] Case T-212/22 *Prigozhina v Council of the EU* ECLI:EU:T:2023:104.

France the General Court upheld a Council decision that—for the first time ever—temporarily suspended the broadcasting licence of *Russia Today*, a news channel controlled by the Kremlin.[119] Sitting as a grand chamber, the General Court rejected the challenge which was based on violation of the CFR-protected right of defence, the freedom of expression and information, freedom to conduct a business, and non-discrimination on the basis of nationality.[120] The General Court ruled that the measure adopted by the Council was proportionate as far as the restrictions of the right to freedom of information given the work of *Russia Today* as a propaganda machine, evident from the fact that 'during the period preceding the Russian Federation's military aggression against Ukraine and, above all, during the days following that aggression, the applicant engaged in a systematic action of broadcasting "selected" information, including manifestly false or misleading information, revealing a manifest imbalance in the presentation of the different opposing viewpoints, with the specific aim of justifying and supporting that aggression'.[121] The applicant lodged an appeal at the ECJ, but subsequently withdrew it,[122] so the General Court ruling has become final.

Moreover, in another recent ruling delivered in October 2024, the GC ruled that prohibition introduced by the Council in the eighth package of sanctions on providing legal advisory services to the Russian government and to entities established in Russia was valid.[123] The prohibition had been challenged by the Flemish bar association of Brussels, with the support of the federal bar association of Germany, and the Ordre des avocats de Genève. These associations claimed, inter alia, that the EU blanket prohibition to provide legal advisory services to any Russian entity was incompatible with the fundamental role of lawyers in a democratic society, that it breached the right to be advised by a lawyer enshrined in Article 47 CFR, and that it was disproportionate. Yet, in its ruling the GC rejected the challenge, holding that 'the fundamental right of access to a lawyer and to advice from him or her, enshrined in Article 47 of the Charter, must ... be recognised solely if there is a link to judicial proceedings'.[124] As a consequence, the GC found that legal advice 'in non-contentious matters'[125] fell outside the scope of protection, and that therefore the Council prohibition could 'be interpreted in a manner which upholds the right to be advised, defended and represented by a lawyer, guaranteed in Article 47 of the [CFR]'.[126]

---

[119] Case T-125/22 *RT France v Council of the EU* ECLI:EU:T:2022:483.
[120] See Viktor Szep and Ramses Wessel, 'Balancing Restrictive Measures and Media Freedom: *RT France v. Council*' (2023) 60 Common Market Law Review 1384.
[121] *RT France* (n 119) para 211.
[122] Case C-620/22 P *RT France v Council of the EU* ECLI:EU:C:2023:615.
[123] Case T-797/22 *Ordre néerlandais des avocats du barreau de Bruxelles v Council* ECLI:EU:T:2024:670.
[124] Ibid para 51.
[125] Ibid para 57.
[126] Ibid para 59.

In many ways the approach of the EU judicature in *RT France*, and now also in *Ordre néerlandais des avocats du barreau de Bruxelles*, seems to be in line with the idea of militant democracy—according to which democratic systems should legally authorize the exceptional restrictions of certain basic political rights to preemptively marginalize those purportedly undermining liberal democratic institutions.[127] In fact, the threat posed by foreign propaganda and disinformation cannot be underestimated,[128] and there are credible allegations of Russia's interreferences in European electoral processes, including for the European Parliament elections.[129] But it is undeniable that the *RT France* decision validated a severe restriction of free speech and freedom of the press. From a comparative perspective, the ruling thus evokes the jurisprudence followed by the US Supreme Court from the First World War to the early days of the Cold War—with cases such as *Schenck v United States*[130] and *Dennis v United States*[131] upholding restrictions of free speech on national security grounds. That jurisprudence, however, has since been overruled by the US Supreme Court. Modern US case law on the First Amendment to the US Constitution holds that government cannot punish or restrict speech unless that speech is 'directed to inciting or producing imminent lawless action and is likely to incite or produce such action'.[132] In fact, while in response to the war in Ukraine the US government has imposed sanctions on *Russia Today*, and accused it of acting as an arm of the country's intelligence agency, it has not outright banned its operation, as this would almost certainly amount to an unlawful restriction of constitutionally protected freedom of the press.[133]

4.3 International legality

Be that as it may, EU sanctions against Russian natural and legal persons under Article 275 TFEU have still been subjected to judicial review for compliance with EU fundamental rights principles and rule of law standards—thus enjoying a modicum of legality. Yet, there are other measures adopted by the EU to inflict costs on Russia and discourage it from continuing its war of aggression that have *tout court* escaped judicial review—despite raising several issues of compliance

---

[127] Jan-Werner Müller, 'Militant democracy' in Michel Rosenfeld and Andras Sajo (eds), *Oxford Handbook of Comparative Constitutional Law* (OUP 2012) 1253.

[128] See also Gergely Ferenc Lendvai, 'Media in War: An Overview of the European Restrictions on Russian Media' (2023) 8 European Papers 1235.

[129] See also European Parliament resolution of 25 April 2024 on new allegations of Russian interference in the European Parliament, in the upcoming EU elections and the impact on the European Union, P9_TA(2024) 0380.

[130] *Schenck v United States* 249 US 47 (1919).

[131] *Dennis v United States* 341 US 494 (1951).

[132] *Brandenburg v Ohio* 395 US 444 (1969).

[133] See Steven Lee Myers and Michael Crowley, 'U.S. Accuses Russian TV Network of Conducting Cover Intelligence Acts', *The New York Times* (13 September 2024).

with human rights and international law.[134] Pursuant to Article 3(5) TEU, the EU is bound to the 'strict observance' of international law, which is recalled also in Article 21 TEU, and EU Member States are subjected to the same obligation. In particular, some academics have criticized nationality-based bans from the Schengen zone against Russian citizens adopted by some EU Member States as a breach of EU law,[135] and one may wonder whether the suspension of the EU-Russia visa facilitation agreement, inflicting a cost on any Russian citizen seeking to obtain lawful entry into the EU, entails a form of collective punishment, which is prohibited by the Geneva Convention.[136] This treaty is formally binding on Member States only, as the EU is not a signatory, but its principles are regarded as part of customary international law, and so also apply to the EU.

Furthermore, the EU's decision to seize the extraordinary revenues stemming from RCB immobilized assets to support Ukraine has raised major legal issues too.[137] National criminal law legally permits the confiscation of property in execution of a criminal sentence. In fact, the EU directive defining criminal offences and penalties for the violation of EU restrictive measures foresees asset confiscation as a criminal penalty for the most severe violation of EU sanctions.[138] In addition, another EU directive recently adopted in response to the war in Ukraine has required Member States to 'take the necessary measures to enable the confiscation, either wholly or in part, of instrumentalities and proceeds stemming from a criminal offence subject to a final conviction'.[139] Moreover, the same directive also enables the 'non-conviction-based confiscation' in a 'limited' number of cases, including illness, death, or absconding of the suspected or accused person.[140] Nevertheless, as former ECJ judge Allan Rosas has pointed out, the outright seizure of assets without a prior criminal conviction—or similar—raises issues of both international and EU law.[141]

Since the beginning of the war in Ukraine, a number of academics, especially in the US, have proposed the seizure of the frozen assets of the RCB to compensate Ukraine.[142] Nevertheless, the matter has been heavily contested.[143] In fact, several

---

[134] See Veronika Bilkova, 'The Effects of the Conflict in Ukraine on the Human Rights Situation within the European Union' (2023) 8 European Papers 1037.

[135] See Sarah Ganty, Dimitry Kochenov, and Suryapratim Roy, 'Unlawful Nationality Based Bans from the Schengen Zone' (2023) 48 Yale Journal of International Law Online 1.

[136] Geneva Convention (IV) relative to the Protection of Civilian Persons in Time of War, art 33.

[137] See Illia Chernohorenko, 'Seizing Russian Assets to Compensate for Human Rights Violations in Ukraine: Navigating the Legal Labyrinth' (2023) 8 European Papers 1067.

[138] Directive (EU) 2024/1226 (n 42) art 10.

[139] Directive (EU) 2024/1260 of the European Parliament and of the Council of 24 April 2024 on asset recovery and confiscation [2024] OJ L/1, art 12.

[140] Ibid art 15.

[141] Allan Rosas, 'From Freezing to Confiscating Russian Assets?' (2023) 48 European Law Review 337.

[142] See Laurence H Tribe and Jeremy Lewin, '$100 Billion. Russia's Treasure in the U.S. Should be Turned Against Putin', Op-Ed, *The New York Times* (15 April 2022); and Philip Zelikow and Sumon Johnson, 'How Ukraine Can Build Back Better', *Foreign Affairs* (19 April 2022). See also Editorial, 'It's Time to Seize Russia's Reserves', *The Wall Street Journal* (21 February 2024).

[143] See Abely (n 31) 107. See also Editorial, 'The Pitfalls of Seizing Russian Assets to Fund Ukraine', *The Financial Times* (22 December 2023).

international law scholars have emphasized that the seizure of RCB immobilized assets would contravene the international law principles of state sovereign immunity.[144] While it seems unquestionable that *freezing* of RCB assets is compatible with state sovereign immunity,[145] since this is a temporary measure that can rightfully be regarded as a counter-measure,[146] there is little doubt that the *seizing* of assets does affect the sovereign rights of Russia as a state, since it results in the coercive transfer of property—a form of taking. For this reason, to date the US government has warned that it lacks legal authority to seize Russian assets,[147] although in April 2024 the US Congress passed legislation to authorize the President to do so,[148] as part of its latest appropriation bill to fund Ukraine (as well as Israel and Taiwan).[149]

From an international law perspective, the principle of foreign sovereign immunity is not codified in a binding international convention, but is generally regarded as a customary rule of international law. In a judgment concerning the immunity of Germany for the crimes committed by the Nazi Wehrmacht in occupied Italy during the Second World War, the International Court of Justice (ICJ) endorsed a particularly generous interpretation of foreign sovereign immunity from jurisdiction, ruling that the effort by Italian courts to adjudicate compensation claims against the Federal Republic of Germany was a breach of international law.[150] Moreover, in its recent 2023 ruling in a case between Iran and the US, the ICJ found that the US had breached international law by confiscating Iranian assets and using them to compensate victims of Iranian action.[151] While in that case the US and Iran had previously concluded a treaty of amity, economic relations, and consular rights which explicitly protected the property rights of natural and legal persons of either nation, one could extract from the opinion a general international law obligation to respect the separate legal personality of the state central bank.[152]

Given this international legal framework, an EU legal measure expropriating the underlying assets of the RCB frozen in European financial institutions would

---

[144] See Paul Stephen, 'Giving Russian Assets to Ukraine: Freezing Is not Seizing', *Lawfare* (26 April 2022); and Paul Stephen, 'Seizing Russian Assets' (2022) 17 Capital Markets Law Journal 13.
[145] But see Ron van der Horst, 'Illegal, Unless: Freezing the Assets of Russia's Central Bank' (2023) 34 European Journal of International Law 1021.
[146] See Anton Moiseinko, 'Legal: The Freezing of the Russian Central Bank's Assets' (2023) 34 European Journal of International Law 1007.
[147] See US Treasury Secretary Janet Yellen press statement, 18 May 2022.
[148] See Rebuilding Economic Prosperity and Opportunity (REPO) for Ukrainians Act 2024, s 102.
[149] See Act making emergency supplemental appropriations for the fiscal year ending September 30, 2024, and for other purposes, Pub L No 118–50.
[150] ICJ, *Jurisdictional Immunity of the State (Germany v Italy, Greece intervening)*, judgment of 3 February 2012.
[151] ICJ, *Certain Iranian Assets (Islamic Republic of Iran v United States of America)*, judgment of 30 March 2023.
[152] I am grateful to Paul Stephen for making this point clear to me.

clash with international law.[153] Admittedly, the EU has refrained from following this more radical position—still endorsed by the CoE Parliamentary Assembly which has called for the confiscation of 'all Russian Federation assets in [Member States'] custody ... for the recovery and reconstruction of Ukraine'.[154] Yet, with its recent legislation, the EU has now by law decided to forfeit the profits that CSDs have accumulated on immobilized RCB assets. Pursuant to the legislation approved by the Council of the EU in May 2022, CSDs must now transfer the windfall profits on RCB assets as 'a financial contribution' to the EU.[155] Currently, 90% of these extraordinary revenues are assigned to the EPF, and 10% to the UF. As mentioned above, however, the Commission has proposed to establish a longer-term ULCM which would periodically transfer profits to Ukraine as a subsidy to repay the principal and interest of an up-front EU loan worth €35 billion, and lasting for 35 years.

As a legal justification for the above-mentioned measures, the Council held that 'unexpected and extraordinary revenues [from frozen assets ...] do not constitute sovereign assets. Therefore the rules protecting sovereign assets are not applicable to these revenues'.[156] However, from a legal point of view this argument is questionable. Interest earned on capital still belongs to the owner, so by taking those profits the EU is still carrying out a forfeiture, ie a forced transfer of property. Moreover—from a strictly EU law perspective—'-finding a legal basis for confiscatory measures is not free from problems', as arguably Article 215 TFEU, the treaty provision regulating the adoption of restrictive measures, is not sufficient to this end.[157] This is all the more so considering that Article 345 TFEU—a provision of primary EU law since the inception of the integration process—explicitly states that: 'The treaties shall in no way prejudice the rules in Member States governing the system of property ownership.'

EU action therefore is likely to lead to litigation and, potentially, three levels of courts may have jurisdiction. First, at the international level, the EU cannot be sued before the ICJ, but Russia could possibly take the 27 EU Member States jointly to court. Secondly, Russia could start proceedings in front of national courts—in the case of the main EU CSD, Euroclear, basically before Belgian courts. In fact, the Council has empowered CSDs to set aside some of the extraordinary revenues to cover the costs of risks related to holding the assets[158]—including,

---

[153] See also 'Don't Seize: Capitalize', *The Economist* (2 March 2024) 10.
[154] Resolution 2539(2024) (n 53) para 12.3.
[155] Council Decision (CFSP) 2024/1470 (n 67) art 1(2); Council Regulation (EU) 2024/1469 (n 68) art 1(1).
[156] See Council Decision (CFSP) 2024/577 (n 59) recital 18; Council Regulation (EU) 2024/576 (n 60) recital 20; Council Decision (CFSP) 2024/1470 (n 67) recital 17; Council Regulation (EU) 2024/1469 (n 68) recital 18.
[157] Rosas (n 141) 345.
[158] See Council Decision (CFSP) 2024/577 (n 59) recital 24; Council Regulation (EU) 2024/576 (n 60) recital 26.

presumably, future litigation. Thirdly, Russia could arguably have *locus standi* to challenge the assets seizure directly before the ECJ under the action for direct annulment. However, the timeframe for bringing a case under Article 263 TFEU is very limited.

Be that as it may, beyond litigation it is plausible that EU efforts to seize the extraordinary revenues resulting from RCB immobilized assets would also lead to retaliation—the standard countermeasure in international law and foreign relations. In fact, there are early signs that this is what is happening, as evident from a recent decision made by Russian President Putin to put several European firms operating in Russia under controlled management, effectively suspending the property rights of foreign companies on a temporary basis and shifting their management to a Russian entity.[159] This has immediately led to calls to compensate the European businesses that were expropriated by Russia via a new EU fund,[160] which could potentially be financed with the revenues from Russia's frozen assets— hence effectively resulting in a zero sum financial game. In fact, the 14th package of sanctions approved by the Council of the EU in June 2024 has also introduced measures to protect EU operators allowing them to claim compensation before national courts for damages caused by sanctions implementation and Russian expropriations.[161]

Otherwise, it cannot go unnoticed that the reason behind seizing Russian assets, or the fruits thereof, is not only driven by a quest to establish justice. As analysed in detail in Chapter 3, given fiscal constraints and governmental shortcomings in the EU economic constitution, the EU has been struggling to find financial resources to fund Ukraine and support its war of resistance against Russia. From this point of view, therefore, revenues from RCB immobilized assets turned out to be a convenient alternative—and the European Council has acknowledged as much. In the February 2024 summit approving the establishment of the UF, the European Council explicitly stated that potential revenues to cover the costs of the grant component of the UF 'could be generated under the relevant Union legal acts, concerning the use of extraordinary revenues held by private entities stemming directly from the immobilizes [RCB] assets'.[162] In fact, as mentioned above, this is what the Commission proposed in September 2024 with the ULCM.[163] In conclusion, the EU's decision to seize the extraordinary profits resulting from RCB immobilized assets raises complicated transnational legal issues that 'do not lend

---

[159] See Antonella Scott, 'Caso Ariston, da Mosca un ricatto in vista del G7 sulle sanzioni', *Il Sole 24 Ore* (28 April 2024) (reporting the Russian effective seizure of the Italian firms Ariston and German firm BSH Hausgeräte ahead of the G7 summit scheduled to discuss expropriation of Russian assets).
[160] See Adriana Castagnoli, 'Creare un Fondo UE per risarcire le imprese', *Il Sole 24 Ore* (1 May 2024).
[161] See Council of the EU press release, 'Russia's War of Aggression against Ukraine: Comprehensive EU's 14th package of sanctions cracks down on circumvention and adopts energy measures', 24 June 2024, 558/24.
[162] European Council conclusions, 1 February 2024, EUCO 2/24, para 2(ii).
[163] European Commission proposal (n 72).

themselves to easy solutions.'[164] In this context, it would be important for the ECJ to have full jurisdiction, and provide legal certainty on the matter at stake. As the ECJ has ruled, the EU legal order is autonomous and must provide all legal remedies to deal with possible cases of illegality.[165] Yet, there are important measures that the EU adopts in the fields of foreign affairs and security which still escape judicial review, and this is an issue that has to be corrected *de jure condendo* to make sure that constitutional principles continue to apply also in wartime.

5 Conclusion

Russia's illegal and unjustified war of aggression against Ukraine has resulted in massive displacement of civilians, indiscriminate bombings of cities, including hospitals and schools, documented atrocities, and unspeakable human rights abuses—all amounting to war crimes. This chapter has examined how the EU has responded to Russia's brutal and devastating aggression and has endeavoured to restore a modicum of justice for Ukraine, focusing on core EU measures adopted in the field of justice and home affairs. As the chapter pointed out, since February 2022 the EU has taken groundbreaking initiatives to express solidarity with Ukraine, to sanction Russia, and to pave the way for investigations and compensation. This has resulted in remarkable developments in the AFSJ—including the application of the TPD, the enlargement of the Eurojust mandate, and the expansion of the list of EU crimes. Moreover, in connected areas, the EU has rolled out 14 rounds of restrictive measures, including secondary sanctions, and supported transnational efforts towards accountability and compensation. It is perhaps not an exaggeration to claim that Bucha, Irpin, and Adviivka—Ukrainian cities where some of the darkest moments of the war have occurred—have pushed forward EU action in justice and home affairs just as much as Maastricht, Amsterdam, and Lisbon—cities where important EU treaties were drafted.

Yet, as this chapter has pointed out, the EU's response to the war in Ukraine in the AFSJ has not been flawless. From an institutional perspective, several of the EU measures have been ineffective, or weakened by unilateral action of some Member States. From a legal perspective, moreover, some of the measures adopted by the EU have raised issues with regard to compliance with fundamental rights and the rule of law. While the EU judicature has exercised review on restrictive measures, increasing its scrutiny over time, it has often deferred to the political branches. Furthermore, other EU war-related measures have escaped judicial review *tout court*, despite raising questions of compatibility with international law and the rule of law. This is especially the case for the decision

---

[164] Rosas (n 141) 346.
[165] See Opinion 2/13 *Accession to the ECHR* ECLI:EU:C:2014:2454.

to forfeit the extraordinary profits resulting from the sovereign assets of the RCB frozen in European CSDs.

As this chapter has argued, in response to the war in Ukraine, the EU constitution enabled the EU institutions to take innovative policy measures in the field of the AFSJ and beyond, with the goal of restoring justice for Ukraine. Yet, as this chapter has also underlined, the EU constitution at times failed sufficiently to constrain EU action in times of war. In many ways, this is nothing new: as the experience of several democratic constitutional systems highlights, in times of war or emergency government action is often shrouded in secrecy, and results in limitations of human rights and the rule of law. Indeed, the refrain is that laws are silent in times of war—silent *enim leges inter arma*. Nevertheless, as the EU fights the injustice of an illegal Russian war of aggression in Ukraine, it is imperative that the fundamental principles of its legal order, including respect for human rights and the rule of law, continue to be upheld. From this point of view, therefore, strengthening the surveillance role of the ECJ—including by giving it full jurisdiction over any EU action, including in the field of foreign affairs—would be a necessary development in the EU constitution for the future.

5

To 'insure domestic tranquility'

Developments in energy and industrial policy

1 Introduction

Wars have unintended consequences. In particular, Russia's war against Ukraine, and the measures adopted by the European Union (EU) to sanction the aggressor, produced major turmoil on the energy markets. Many EU Member States had significant energy dependencies from Russia, with the EU as a whole importing 40% of its gas, 27% of its oil, and 46% of its coal from Russia in early 2022. Consequently, Russia could weaponize its resources leading to skyrocketing energy prices, a spike in inflation, and an economic slowdown. As reported by the EU Agency for the Cooperation of Energy Regulators (ACER), electricity prices sharply increased in 2022, from a prior average of €35/MWh, to over €300/MWh, with intra-day spikes of over €3,000/MWh.[1] Moreover, as highlighted by the EU statistical agency EUROSTAT, annual inflation more than tripled in the EU in 2022,[2] forcing the European Central Bank (ECB) to raise interest rates quickly in 2022/2023 by 450 basis point to an all-time high of 4%.[3] At the same time, as indicated by the Organisation for Economic Cooperation and Development (OECD), war-induced high inflation combined with post-pandemic bottlenecks to weaken economic growth.[4] All this threatened the competitiveness of the European economy, the welfare of households, and the liquidity of firms, and therefore could potentially break the EU's steadfast political and popular stance in support of Ukraine.

The purpose of this chapter is to examine from an EU law and policy perspective the key measures that the EU rolled out from 2022 to 2024 in the fields of energy and industry to respond domestically to Russia's aggression against Ukraine.

---

[1] ACER, 'Wholesale Electricity Market Monitoring 2022: Key Developments', 28 February 2023 https://acer.europa.eu/sites/default/files/documents/Publications/Electricity_MMR_2022-Key_Developments.pdf.

[2] EUROSTAT, 'Annual inflation more than tripled in the EU in 2022', 9 March 2023 https://ec.europa.eu/eurostat/web/products-eurostat-news/w/DDN-20230309-2.

[3] European Central Bank, 'Key ECB Interest Rates' https://www.ecb.europa.eu/stats/policy_and_exchange_rates/key_ecb_interest_rates/html/index.en.html.

[4] OECD press release, 'Russia's war of aggression against Ukraine continues to create serious headwinds for global economy, OECD says', 22 November 2022, https://www.oecd.org/newsroom/russia-s-war-of-aggression-against-ukraine-continues-to-create-serious-headwinds-for-global-economy.htm.

Many of these measures are of an economic nature, and as such are connected to the fiscal policies examined in Chapter 3, but they were deployed not to support Ukraine externally but rather to protect EU citizens and businesses internally from the war's side effects. Specifically, the chapter examines the emergency interventions in the energy markets that the EU adopted to tackle skyrocketing prices of gas and electricity. Moreover, it analyses the structural policies that the EU introduced to phase out Russian fossil fuels and accelerate the transition towards renewable energies, including through greater flexibility in the application of state aid rules and new EU funding to repower the green transition. Finally, the chapter also outlines the development of a brand new EU industrial policy for the net-zero age, mapping the legal measures that the EU adopted to promote a green deal industrial plan, to foster a regulatory environment for clean energies, and to strengthen trade defence instruments against unfair global competition.

As the chapter argues, the EU constitution enabled the EU 'to insure domestic tranquility',[5] mitigating the economic side effects of Russia's aggression against Ukraine and thus maintaining EU popular and political support in favour of Ukraine's defensive war. In particular, the EU institutions enacted ground-breaking measures to help European citizens and businesses weather the domestic consequences of the war and cushion the energy crisis resulting from Russia's aggression against Ukraine. Moreover, in line with the goal set by EU heads of state and government in the March 2022 Versailles Declaration to '(b) reducing our energy dependencies; and (c) building a more robust economic base'[6] the EU accelerated the phasing-out from Russian fossil fuels and launched a new industrial policy for the green transition. Among others, the EU introduced emergency measures to cap the price of oil and to correct the unjustified increases in the price of gas. It adjusted its state aid framework and approved new financing measures to support public investment in renewable energies. And it revised its industrial policy strategy to strengthen the competitiveness of its domestic clean industries, also by defending it against unfair global competition.

Nevertheless, as this chapter maintains, the EU's response to the energy crisis raised a number of challenges. On the one hand, emergency interventions in the energy markets posed issues of domestic legality, with especially the adoption by the Council of a solidarity contribution for energy producers who had made surplus profits being subjected to multiple legal challenges. On the other hand, EU measures adopted to facilitate the green transition and the decarbonization of industry—notably the relaxation of state aid rules—have threatened the level playing field at the heart of the EU internal market, given the differences in Member States' fiscal margins of intervention. Otherwise, the EU public investment in

---

[5] US Const, preamble.
[6] Informal meeting of the Heads of State or Government, Versailles Declaration, 10–11 March 2022, para 7.

strategic technologies and the green industrial deal has been negligible, due to constraints in the EU fiscal constitution. Yet, this state of affairs has significantly challenged the competitiveness of the EU industry especially in light of massive investments in clean energy made by other global players, such as the United States (US) through the 2022 Inflation Reduction Act (IRA).[7] This poses long-term challenges for the EU economy.

As such, this chapter is structured as follows. Section 2 examines the core measures adopted by the EU in the fields of energy and industry in response to the war in Ukraine, including interventions in the energy market, support for the green transition, and development of an industrial policy for the net-zero age, including the approval of a new regulatory framework, the promotion of supply chains resilience, and access to critical raw materials. Section 3 discusses the consequences of these war-related developments. Section 4, however, critically considers some of the challenges that EU action in energy and industry raised, including on the level playing field and funding. Section 5, finally, concludes.

2 The core measures

2.1 Interventions in the energy market

To deal with ever higher energy prices, the EU institutions adopted a barrage of legal measures. To begin with, in June 2022, the European Parliament and the Council adopted a regulation on the basis of Article 194(2) TFEU, on the EU's energy policy, laying out rules with regard to gas storage.[8] The regulation amended a prior piece of EU legislation on the security of gas supplies and set filling targets and filling trajectories for Member States with regard to the filling of underground gas storages facilities in their territories. Specifically, on the understanding that '[t]he escalation of the Russian military aggression against Ukraine since February 2022 has led to unprecedented price increases … which are likely to fundamentally change the incentives to fill underground gas storage facilities in the [EU]',[9] the regulation required Member States to fill 80% of their gas storages facility by 1 November 2022, and 90% by 1 November 2023, and subsequent years.[10] To this end, Article 6a(7) of the regulation required Member States to report progression

---

[7] Inflation Reduction Act of 2022, Pub L No 117–169.
[8] Regulation (EU) 2022/1032 of the European Parliament and of the Council of 29 June 2022 amending Regulations (EU) 2017/1938 and (EC) No 715/2009 with regard to gas storage [2022] OJ L173/17.
[9] Ibid recital 1.
[10] Ibid art 1(2) adding art 6a to Regulation (EU) 2017/1938 of the European Parliament and of the Council of 25 October 2017 concerning measures to safeguard the security of gas supply and repealing Regulation (EU) No 994/2010 [2017] OJ L280/1.

in their filling targets by 15 September and, in case of 'a substantial and sustained deviation'[11] from the target, empowered the Commission to 'take a decision as a measure of last resort to require the Member State concerned to take measures that effectively remedy the deviation'.[12] The regulation also introduced a reporting requirement for the Commission to the European Parliament and the Council by 28 February 2023, and annually thereafter, with an overview of the measures taken by Member States to fulfil the storage obligations.[13]

Furthermore, in August 2022, the Council of the EU adopted, on the basis of Article 122(1) TFEU, a regulation on coordinated demand-reduction measures for gas.[14] As stated in recital 5, 'the recent escalation of disruption of gas supply from Russia points to a significant risk that a complete halt of Russian gas supplies may materialise in the near future, in an abrupt and unilateral way'. As a result, the regulation introduced both a voluntary and a mandatory demand reduction mechanism for gas. Specifically, Article 3 required Member States to 'use their best efforts to reduce their gas consumption in the period from 1 August 2022 to 31 March 2023 at least by 15% compared to their average gas consumption in the period from 1 August to 31 March during the five' proceedings years. Furthermore, Article 4 established a mechanism to declare 'a Union alert', whereby the Council, on a proposal from the Commission, could take the 'political ... decision to trigger a mandatory Union-wide demand-reduction obligation'.[15] In this case, pursuant to Article 5, the regulation set a mandatory gas reduction of 15%. According to Article 6, Member States were 'free to choose the appropriate measures to reduce demand' provided these measures neither 'unduly distort competition or the proper functioning of the internal market in gas' nor 'endanger the security of gas supply of other Member States or of the [EU]'.[16] Article 8 of the regulation also granted the Commission monitoring powers. Yet, in case of 'risk that a Member State will not be able to fulfil the mandatory demand-reduction obligation', the Commission enforcement powers were limited to 'request the Member State to submit a plan setting out a strategy to effectively achieve the demand-reduction obligation'.[17]

Given its 'exceptional nature',[18] the regulation had an initial validity of one year.[19] However, in March 2023, the Council adopted an amending regulation, also based on Article 122(1) TFEU, which prolonged the demand-reduction

---

[11] Ibid art 6a(11).
[12] Ibid.
[13] Ibid art 1(5) adding art 17a to Regulation (EU) 2017/1938 (n 10).
[14] Council Regulation (EU) 2022/1369 of 5 August 2022 on coordinated demand-reduction measures for gas [2022] OJ L206/1.
[15] Ibid recital 11.
[16] Ibid art 6(1).
[17] Ibid art 8(2).
[18] Ibid recital 29.
[19] Ibid art 10.

period for demand-reduction measures until 31 March 2024.[20] As stated in recital 3, given that 'severe difficulties persist for the security of energy supply[, t]he global situation on the gas market has not improved since February 2022 and the [EU] continues to rely on certain volumes of Russian gas to meet its overall gas demand', the regulation extended the 2022 demand-reduction measures 'until the end of the winter of 2023-2024',[21] while also introducing additional reporting requirements for Member States.[22] However, the conditions to extend the regulation existing in March 2023 did not also recur the following year: therefore, in March 2024, the Council did not further renew the regulation but rather replaced it with a non-binding recommendation to continue a 15% voluntary demand reductions for gas.[23]

Furthermore, in October 2022 the Council of the EU adopted another regulation, also based on Article 122 TFEU, on emergency interventions to address high energy prices.[24] Recital 1 of regulation noted that the war in Ukraine 'resulted in substantial additional increases in, and volatility of, the price of electricity'—both in the wholesale and the retail market. At the same time, recital 5 pointed out that '[t]he stark increase of energy prices is substantially contributing to the general inflation in the euro area and slowing down economic growth in the [EU]'. Therefore, recital 8 stated that 'Russia's war of aggression against Ukraine, and the hybrid war which is thereby being carried out, have created a crisis situation which requires the adoption of a set of urgent, temporary and exceptional measures of an economic nature to address the unbearable effects on consumers and companies'. Content-wise, Article 1 of the regulation introduced three 'exceptional, targeted and time-limited measures' to mitigate the effects of high electric energy prices. First, it set targets to reduce electricity consumption; secondly, it introduced a cap on market revenues that producers receive from the generation of electricity; and, thirdly, it established a mandatory solidarity tax from EU companies with activities in the crude petroleum, natural gas, coal, and refinery sectors to contribute to the affordability of energy for households and companies.

More in detail, Article 3 of the regulation required Member States to 'endeavour to implement measures to reduce their total monthly gross electricity consumption by 10% compared to the average of gross electricity consumption in the corresponding months', while Article 4 required Member States to reduce consumption by at least 5% during peak hours. Moreover, Article 6 introduced a mandatory cap

---

[20] Council Regulation (EU) 2023/706 of 30 March 2023 amending Regulation (EU) 2022/1369 as regards prolonging the demand-reduction period for demand-reduction measures for gas and reinforcing the reporting and monitoring of their implementation [2023] OJ L93/1.
[21] Ibid recital 21.
[22] Ibid art 1(5) amending art 8 of Council Regulation (EU) 2022/1369 (n 14).
[23] Council of the EU press release, 'Security of gas supply: member states agree on recommendation to continue voluntary demand reduction measures', 4 March 2024.
[24] Council Regulation (EU) 2022/1854 of 6 October 2022 on an emergency intervention to address high energy prices [2022] OJ L261I/1.

on market revenues, specifying that producers of energy from the sources listed in Article 7—hence: wind energy, solar energy, geothermal energy, hydropower, biomass fuel, waste, nuclear energy, lignite, crude petroleum products, and peat— could receive 'a maximum of 180 EUR per MWh of electricity produced'.[25] On the basis of Article 10, then, 'Member States shall ensure that all surplus revenues resulting from the application of the cap on market revenues are used to finance measures in support of final electricity customers that mitigate the impact of high electricity prices on those customers, in a targeted manner'. To this end, the regulation left open to Member States the possibility, inter alia, to arrange 'direct transfers to final electricity customers',[26] clarifying also that: 'Where revenues obtained directly from the implementation of the cap on market revenues ... are insufficient to adequately support final electricity customers, Member States shall be allowed to use other appropriate means such as budgetary resources for the same purpose and under the same conditions'.[27]

Beside the cap on market revenues, Article 15 of the regulation also introduced a temporary solidarity contribution for companies in the crude petroleum, natural gas, coal, and refinery sectors for fiscal years 2022 and 2023. As the regulation made clear, this windfall tax 'should act as a redistributing measure to ensure that the companies concerned which have earned surplus profits as a result of the unexpected circumstances, contribute in proportion to the improvement of the energy crisis in the internal market'.[28] Specifically, Article 15 of the regulation identified the base for calculating the temporary solidarity contribution as 'the taxable profits, as determined under national tax rules, in the fiscal year 2022 and/or the fiscal year 2023 ... which are above a 20% increase of the average of the taxable profits ... in the four fiscal years starting on or after 1 January 2018', while Article 16 indicated that '[t]he rate applicable for calculating the temporary solidarity contribution shall be at least 33%' of the above-mentioned base. Pursuant to Article 17, Member States were free to use proceeds from the temporary solidarity contribution, inter alia, to provide 'financial support measures for final energy customers, and in particular vulnerable households'[29] and 'financial support measures to support companies in energy intensive industries provided that they are made conditional upon investments into renewable energies, energy efficiency or other decarbonisation technologies'.[30] The regulation, which had standard monitoring[31] requirements, 'shall apply until 31 December 2023'[32] but Article 20(2) tasked the

---

[25] Ibid art 6(1).
[26] Ibid art 10(4)(b).
[27] Ibid art 10(3).
[28] Ibid recital 51.
[29] Ibid art 17(1)(a).
[30] Ibid art 17(1)(c).
[31] Ibid art 19.
[32] Ibid art 22(2).

Commission to carry out a review of the windfall tax by 15 October 2024 'in view of the general situation of the fossil fuel sector and the surplus profits generated'.

As the energy crisis continued, however, pressure mounted to introduce a price cap on the costs of oil and gas. In October 2022,[33] the European Council flagged the possibility of 'a temporary dynamic price corridor on natural gas transactions'[34] or 'a temporary EU framework to cap the price of gas in electricity generation'[35], but due to German and Dutch reluctance progress on this matter was slow.[36] Eventually, however, in December 2022, the Council of the EU—in coordination with international partners, especially the US—introduced a price cap on Russian oil, at US$60 per barrel.[37] This measure was set up as part of an EU round of sanctions against Russia, examined in Chapter 4. Specifically, a Council decision enacted on the basis of Article 29 TEU,[38] and an identically worded Council regulation enacted on the basis of Article 215 TFEU,[39] followed by a Commission implementing regulation,[40] prohibited the maritime transport of crude oil and petroleum products, and relatedly the provision of technical assistance, brokering services, and financing or financial assistance, of petroleum which originates in Russia, except provided the price did not exceed the value of US$60 per barrel.[41] The price cap was operational as of 5 December 2022 for crude oil, and as of 5 February 2023 for petroleum products, with a commitment to review its operation every two months.

Furthermore, also in December 2022 the Council of the EU approved a package of three regulations—all based on Articles 122(1) TFEU—which sought to address 'skyrocketing energy prices in the [EU]'.[42] The package included a regulation on enhancing solidarity through better coordination of gas purchases, reliable price benchmarks, and exchange of gas across borders; a regulation laying down a framework to accelerate the deployment of renewable energy;[43] and, crucially,

---

[33] European Council conclusions, 20–21 October 2022, EUCO 31/22.
[34] Ibid para 18(c).
[35] Ibid para 18(d).
[36] Germany and the Netherlands, Joint non-paper on gas prices in the European Union, 11 October 2022.
[37] Council of the EU press release 'Russian oil: EU agrees on level of price cap', 3 December 2022.
[38] Council Decision (CFSP) 2022/2369 of 3 December 2022 amending Decision 2014/512/CFSP concerning restrictive measures in view of Russia's actions destabilizing the situation in Ukraine [2022] OJ L311 I/8.
[39] Council Regulation (EU) 2022/2367 of 3 December 2022 amending Regulation (EU) No 833/2014 concerning restrictive measures in view of Russia's actions destabilising the situation in Ukraine [2022] OJ L311 I/1.
[40] Commission Implementing Regulation (EU) 2022/2368 of 3 December 2022 amending Council Regulation (EU) No 833/2014 concerning restrictive measures in view of Russia's actions destabilising the situation in Ukraine [2022] OJ L311 I/5.
[41] Ibid Annex.
[42] Council Regulation (EU) 2022/2576 of 19 December 2022 enhancing solidarity through better coordination of gas purchases, reliable price benchmarks and exchanges of gas across borders [2022] OJ L335/1, recital 1.
[43] Council Regulation (EU) 2022/2577 of 22 December 2022 laying down a framework to accelerate the deployment of renewable energy [2022] OJ L335/36.

a regulation establishing a market correction mechanism (MCM) to protect EU citizens and the economy against excessively high prices.[44] The first regulation essentially promoted a mostly voluntary[45] mechanism to allow for 'demand aggregation and joint gas purchasing by undertakings established in the [EU]'.[46] To this end, Article 5 empowered the Commission to 'contract the necessary services of an entity established in the [EU] through a procurement procedure', tasking the gas purchasing consortium to seek offers from natural gas suppliers in third countries,[47] provided these were not subjected to EU restrictive measures, or directly or indirectly owned or controlled by Russia.[48] Moreover, the regulation also put in place measures to enhance the use of liquefied natural gas (LNG) facilities, gas storage facilities, and pipelines,[49] and to strengthen inter-state solidarity in case of a gas emergency.[50] Finally, to address the 'extremely high and volatile natural gas prices'[51] resulting from Russia's aggression against Ukraine, the regulation introduced special measures to prevent excessive gas prices and excessive intra-day volatility in energy derivatives markets. Specifically, Article 15 required trading venues to set up by 31 January 2023 'for each energy-related commodity derivative traded on it, an intra-day volatility management mechanism based on an upper and lower price boundary ("price boundaries") that defines the prices above and below which orders may not be executed ("intra-day volatility management mechanism")', while Article 16 gave to competent national authorities and to the European Securities and Market Authority (ESMA) a supervisory role.

While this intra-day volatility management mechanism was largely left to market forces to operationalize, the regulation establishing a MCM set up a publicly-enforced regime to handle exceptionally high energy prices—coming close to a form of price cap for gas. As the regulation pointed out, 'Russia's weaponisation of gas supply and market manipulation through intentional disruptions of gas flows have led to skyrocketing energy prices in the [EU]'[52] and '[f]ollowing the damage to the Nord Stream 1 pipeline which was likely caused by an act of sabotage in September 2022, there is no likelihood that gas supplies from Russia to the [EU] will resume at pre-war levels in the near future'.[53] As a result, the ordinary price-formation mechanisms for the EU gas market—which primarily relied on the standard pricing set at the Dutch Title Transfer Facility (TTF)—appeared no

---

[44] Council Regulation (EU) 2022/2578 of 22 December 2022 establishing a market correction mechanism to protect Union citizens and the economy against excessively high prices [2022] OJ L335/45.
[45] Council Regulation (EU) 2022/2576 (n 42) art 10(1).
[46] Ibid art 1(1)(a).
[47] Ibid art 7(1)(b).
[48] Ibid art 8.
[49] Ibid art 12.
[50] Ibid art 23.
[51] Ibid recital 41.
[52] Council Regulation (EU) 2022/2578 (n 44) recital 1.
[53] Ibid recital 3.

longer reliable.[54] To deal with this situation, therefore, the regulation introduced 'a temporary [MCM] for orders placed for trading TTF derivatives ... to limit episodes of excessively high gas prices in the [EU] which do not reflect world market prices'.[55] The regulation, however, pushed back the entry into force of the MCM to 1 February 2023,[56] and introduced two tight conditions for its activation: as clarified in Article 4, the price of gas shall 'exceed[] EUR 180/MWh for three working days', and this must be 'EUR 35 higher than the reference price' provided by the daily average price of the LNG, as calculated using several global benchmarks. If such conditions were met, the ACER would publish a notice,[57] requiring market operators not to trade commodities over the reference value, 'for a minimum of 20 working days'.[58] Yet, Article 5 introduced an automatic deactivation mechanism of the MCM 'if the reference price is below EUR 145/MWh for three consecutive working days', and—reflecting worries that the MCM may impair the functioning of financial markets[59]—Article 6 gave the Commission wide powers, also in consultation with ESMA, to 'suspend the MCM at any time by means of an implementing decision, where unintended market disturbances or manifest risks of such disturbances occur that negatively affect security of supply, intra-Union flows of gas or financial stability'.

Both the regulation on reliable price benchmarks and exchange of gas across borders, and the regulation establishing a MCM were initially valid for a period of one year.[60] However, both acts required the Commission to issue a report on the usefulness of these instruments,[61] and their review.[62] As a result, in December 2023 the Council extended until 31 December 2024 the validity of the price benchmark regulation,[63] and until 31 January 2025 the validity of the MCM regulation,[64] considering that 'severe difficulties persist for the Union's security of energy supply',[65] and that '[t]he level of gas prices could have a negative impact on the economic situation of the [EU], on its industrial competitiveness and on the purchasing power of its citizens'.[66]

---

[54] Ibid recital 5.
[55] Ibid art 1.
[56] Ibid art 12.
[57] Ibid art 4(3).
[58] Ibid art 4(7).
[59] See Ebbe Rogge, 'The European Energy Crisis, the Dutch TTF, and the Market Correction Mechanism: A Financial Markets Perspective' (2024) 17 Journal of World Energy Law and Business 184.
[60] Council Regulation (EU) 2022/2578 (n 44) art 12; Council Regulation (EU) 2022/2576 (n 42) art 31.
[61] Council Regulation (EU) 2022/2576 (n 42) art 30.
[62] Council Regulation (EU) 2022/2578 (n 44) art 10.
[63] Council Regulation (EU) 2023/2919 of 21 December 2023 amending Regulation (EU) 2022/2576 as regards the prolongation of its period of application [2023] OJ L.
[64] Council Regulation (EU) 2023/2920 of 21 December 2023 amending Regulation (EU) 2022/2578 as regards the prolongation of its period of application [2023] OJ L.
[65] Ibid recital 5.
[66] Ibid recital 9.

2.2 Promotion of the green transition

Besides the above-mentioned emergency measures, the EU responded to the energy crisis caused by Russia's aggression against Ukraine by accelerating the energy transition. In 2019, the EU had already set the goal to become the first carbon neutral continent,[67] and a core pillar of the post-pandemic EU economic recovery programme had centred on the green transition. The war in Ukraine, however, led to an acceleration of this path. In particular, in March 2022, the European Commission put forward a plan named RePowerEU, which outlined a roadmap for more affordable, secure, and sustainable energy.[68] The Commission plan rested essentially on a two-pronged strategy. On the one hand, the Commission envisioned broadening the flexibility of EU state aid laws, to enable Member States to support households and companies facing the energy crisis, while providing more incentives to improve energy efficiency and decarbonize. On the other hand, the Commission set the target to reduce faster the dependence on Russian fossil fuels through a series of measures speeding up the transition towards renewable energies.

On the state aid front, in March 2022 the European Commission approved a temporary crisis framework (TCF) for state aid measures to support the economy following the aggression against Ukraine by Russia,[69] which in view of the 'challenges resulting from the geopolitical situation ... set[ ] out the possibilities Member States have under EU State aid rules to ensure liquidity and access to finance for undertakings ... that face economic challenges under the current crisis'.[70] The TCF gave wide latitude to Member States to subsidize the cost of energy for households and companies, especially small and medium-sized enterprises (SMEs), until 31 December 2022. In July 2022, however, the Commission amended the TCF, further increasing the maximum amount of funding that Member States could provide to undertakings, while incentivizing investments in renewable energy.[71] And in October 2022 the Commission adopted a new TCF, which inter alia also coordinated the state aid framework with the recently adopted regulations on emergency interventions in the energy markets.[72] In connection with this, as mentioned

---

[67] European Commission Communication, 'The European Green Deal', 11 December 2019, COM(2019) 640 final.

[68] European Commission Communication, 'RePowerEU: Joint European Action for more affordable, secure and sustainable energy', 8 March 2022, COM(2022) 108 final.

[69] Communication from the Commission Temporary Crisis Framework for State Aid measures to support the economy following the aggression against Ukraine by Russia 2022/C 131 I/01, C/2022/1890 [2022] OJ C131/I1.

[70] Ibid para 21.

[71] Communication from the Commission Amendment to the Temporary Crisis Framework for State Aid measures to support the economy following the aggression against Ukraine by Russia 2022/C 280/01 [2022] OJ C280/1.

[72] Communication from the Commission Temporary Crisis Framework for State Aid measures to support the economy following the aggression against Ukraine by Russia 2022/C 426/01 [2022] OJ C426/1.

above, in December 2022 the Council of the EU also adopted a regulation laying down a framework to accelerate the deployment of renewable energy,[73] which set up for an initial period of 18 months special, simplified rules for the permit-granting process for the installation of inter alia solar energy equipment, heat pumps, and other renewal energy projects.

Subsequently, in March 2023 the European Commission amended the General Block Exemption Regulation (GBER),[74] and replaced the TCF with a new temporary crisis and transition framework (TCTF), with a stronger focus on facilitating the energy transition.[75] The TCTF enabled Member States to cushion the economic impact of Russia's aggression against Ukraine and, until 31 December 2023, to (i) grant limited amounts of aid to companies affected by the current crisis; (ii) ensure that sufficient liquidity remains available to businesses; (iii) compensate companies for the additional costs incurred due to exceptionally high gas and electricity prices; and (iv) incentivize additional reduction of electricity consumption. At the same time, the TCTF enabled Member States to provide state aid until 31 December 2025, to (i) accelerate the roll-out of renewable energy, storage, and renewable heat relevant for REPowerEU and (ii) decarbonize industrial production processes. In November 2023, however, the Commission prolonged the possibility of granting state aid until 30 June 2024,[76] and in May 2024—in response to farmers' protests—it further extended public support for firms in the agricultural and fisheries sectors.[77]

Yet, the European Commission's decision to give greater room for manoeuvre to Member States in subsidizing the energy transition caused concerns given differences in national budgetary capacity. As such, in May 2022 the European Commission further detailed the RePowerEU plan,[78] introducing steps to increase energy saving, diversify energy imports, ensure sufficient level of gas storage, enhance connectivity of the energy grids within the EU and between the EU and its neighbours, and financially support the clean energy transition. In its RePowerEU plan, in particular, the Commission proposed raising €20 billion additional resources from the auctioning of Emission Trading Scheme (ETS) rights and allocating these to the energy transition. Moreover, the Commission proposed to

---

[73] Council Regulation (EU) 2022/2577 (n 43).
[74] European Commission press release, 'State aid: Commission amends General Block Exemption rules to further facilitate and speed up green and digital transition', 9 March 2023.
[75] Communication from the Commission Temporary Crisis and Transition Framework for State Aid measures to support the economy following the aggression against Ukraine by Russia 2023/C 101/03 [2023] OJ C101/3.
[76] Communication from the Commission, Amendment to the Temporary Crisis and Transition Framework for State Aid measures to support the economy following the aggression against Ukraine by Russia C/2023/8045, [2023] OJ C.
[77] Communication from the Commission, Second amendment to the Temporary Crisis and Transition Framework for State Aid measures to support the economy following the aggression against Ukraine by Russia C/2024/3123, [2024] OJ C.
[78] See European Commission Communication, 'RePower EU Plan', 18 May 2022, COM(2022) 230 final.

redirect up to €225 billion from the post-pandemic Next Generation EU (NGEU) Recovery Fund—which the EU had funded through the issuance of common debt in the aftermath of the Covid-19 pandemic[79]—to finance energy transition measures in Member States affected by soaring energy costs as a result of Russia's weaponization of oil and gas.[80]

Eventually, in February 2023, the European Parliament and the Council approved the RePowerEU regulation,[81] which amended the 2021 regulation establishing the Recovery and Resilience Facility (RRF)[82] to further support the green transition financially. By recognizing the 'direct links between a sustainable recovery, building the [EU]'s resilience and energy security, reducing dependence on fossil fuels, in particular from Russia, and the [EU]'s role in a just and inclusive transition'[83] the RePowerEU regulation required Member States to amend their national recovery and resilience plans (NRRPs) by adding a new RePowerEU chapter, with reforms and investments designed to 'a) improving energy infrastructure ...; b) boosting energy efficiency ...; c) addressing energy poverty; d) incentivizing reduction of energy demands; e) addressing internal and cross-border energy transmission'.[84] To this end, the RePowerEU regulation made available to Member States an additional budget of €20 billion in grants,[85] and empowered them to request further loan assistance under the RRF,[86] tapping on the unused resources of the NGEU Recovery Fund. Moreover, the Regulation also enabled Member States to redirect up to 7.5% of cohesion spending,[87] as well as resources from the Brexit Adjustment Reserve,[88] towards RePowerEU targets.

2.3 Development of an industrial policy

If the war in Ukraine pushed the EU to reduce its energy dependence on Russia and accelerate the green transition, it also highlighted the need to increase the

---

[79] See Federico Fabbrini, *EU Fiscal Capacity: Legal Integration after Covid-19 and the War in Ukraine* (OUP 2022).
[80] See European Commission proposal for a regulation of the European Parliament and the Council amending Regulation (EU) 2021/241 as regards REPowerEU chapters in recovery and resilience plans and amending Regulation (EU) 2021/1060, Regulation (EU) 2021/2115, Directive 2003/87/EC and Decision (EU) 2015/1814, 18 May 2022, COM(2022) 231 final.
[81] Regulation (EU) 2023/435 of the European Parliament and of the Council of 27 February 2023 amending Regulation (EU) 2021/241 as regards REPowerEU chapters in recovery and resilience plans and amending Regulations (EU) No 1303/2013, (EU) 2021/1060 and (EU) 2021/1755, and Directive 2003/87/EC [2023] OJ L63/1.
[82] Regulation (EU) 2021/241 of the European Parliament and of the Council of 12 February 2021 establishing the Recovery and Resilience Facility [2021] OJ L57/17.
[83] Regulation (EU) 2023/435 (n 81) recital 2.
[84] Ibid art 1(8) adding a new art 21c(3) to Regulation (EU) 2021/241 (n 82).
[85] Ibid art 1(8) adding a new art 21a to Regulation (EU) 2021/241 (n 82).
[86] Ibid art 1(3) adding a new art 14(6) to Regulation (EU) 2021/241 (n 82).
[87] Ibid art 3.
[88] Ibid art 4.

resilience of the EU economic base, addressing strategic dependencies in multiple sectors, including the critical raw materials and semi-conductors needed to decarbonize industries.[89] In fact, the pressure to phase out fossil fuels and develop renewable energy technologies raised a novel awareness regarding the importance of an EU industrial policy designed to support the transition towards a green economy. The urgency of a dedicated green industrial policy, furthermore, was amplified by policy measures adopted in the aftermath of the pandemic by other developed economies, notably the US, which allocated major amounts of resources in the form of subsidies and tax credits to incentivize companies to invest in clean technologies. As a result, in late 2022 and early 2023 the largest EU Member States—Germany, France, and Italy—jointly and severally called for promoting an EU industrial policy fit for the 21st century, with measures to support the EU's competitiveness and facilitate the industrial adjustment to the net-zero age.[90]

Along these lines, in February 2023 the European Commission unveiled a 'Green Deal Industrial Plan for the Net-Zero Age'[91] which laid out detailed proposals to speed up net-zero industrial transformation in the EU. The Commission underlined how the war in Ukraine and the 'phase-out of Russian fossil fuels has accelerated a new industrial revolution',[92] and consequently put forward a strategy to lead the way on this path. To this end, the Commission proposed changing the EU regulatory environment, with a dedicated Net-Zero Industry Act (NZIA), defining simple and operational criteria for identifying net-zero supply chain projects of strategic interests. Moreover, the Commission unveiled opportunities for private investment in renewable energies, and proposed to set up a dedicated funding scheme, named Strategic Technologies for Europe Platform (STEP), designed to provide extra public funding to four EU programmes, namely InvestEU, Horizon, the Innovation Fund, and the European Defence Fund (EDF).[93] Finally, the Commission also identified a set of trade defence instruments to grow the EU internal market for green industrial technologies and protect it from unfair global competition.[94]

---

[89] Versailles Declaration (n 6) para 21.
[90] See Bunderministerium fur Wirschaft under Energie, Franco-German manifesto for a European industrial policy fit for the 21st century, 19 December 2022; Italian non-paper 'A European Resilience and Competitiveness Agenda: Reinforcing the EU Industrial Base, Relaunching Competitiveness', 2 February 2023; Ministero delle imprese e del made in Italy, Una visione condivisa per una strategia industriale dell'UE verso la transizione verde e digitale, 3 March 2023.
[91] European Commission Communication, 'A Green Deal Industrial Plan for the Net-Zero Age', 1 February 2023, COM(2023) 62 final.
[92] Ibid 1.
[93] See European Commission proposal for a Regulation of the European Parliament and of the Council establishing the Strategic Technologies for Europe Platform ('STEP') and amending Directive 2003/87/EC, Regulations (EU) 2021/1058, (EU) 2021/1056, (EU) 2021/1057, (EU) No 1303/2013, (EU) No 223/2014, (EU) 2021/1060, (EU) 2021/523, (EU) 2021/695, (EU) 2021/697 and (EU) 2021/241, 20 June 2023, COM(2023) 335 final.
[94] See also European Commission and High Representative Joint Communication, European economic security strategy, 20 June 2023, JOIN(2023) 20 final.

Based on the Commission's roadmap, between 2023 and 2024 the European Parliament and the Council adopted the Chips Act,[95] the Critical Raw Materials Act,[96] and the NZIA.[97] These regulations—all based on Article 114 TFEU, the EU's internal market clause, and, as far as the Chips Act is concerned, Article 173 TFEU, on industrial policy—enhanced the EU regulatory framework for innovative technologies for the green deal, and promoted the industrial transition. Furthermore—as part of a broader package of mid-term reforms of the EU budget, including the approval of the Ukraine Facility (UF) discussed in Chapter 3—in early 2024 the European Parliament and the Council approved the STEP regulation,[98] on the basis of TFEU Articles 164 (on the European social fund), 173 (on industry), 175, 177, and 178 (on cohesion policy), 182 (on technological development), and 192 (on environment). STEP set aside €1.5 billion 'from existing Union programmes'[99] to support 'the development or manufacturing of critical technologies throughout the [EU], or safeguarding and strengthening their respective value chains [... especially in] clean and resource efficient technologies, including net-zero technologies as defined in the [NZIA]'.[100] Finally, the European Parliament and the Council also upgraded the EU trade defence toolbox—which already included a regulation screening foreign direct investments,[101] and an international procurement instrument[102]—by enacting among others a regulation on foreign subsidies distorting the internal market[103] and the Anti-Coercion Instrument.[104]

---

[95] Regulation (EU) 2023/1781 of the European Parliament and of the Council of 13 September 2023 establishing a framework of measures for strengthening Europe's semiconductor ecosystem and amending Regulation (EU) 2021/694 (Chips Act) [2023] OJ L229/1.

[96] Regulation (EU) 2024/1252 of the European Parliament and of the Council of 11 April 2024 establishing a framework for ensuring a secure and sustainable supply of critical raw materials and amending Regulations (EU) No 168/2013, (EU) 2018/858, (EU) 2018/1724 and (EU) 2019/1020, [2024] OJ L.

[97] Regulation (EU) 2024/1735 of the European Parliament and of the Council of 13 June 2024 on establishing a framework of measures for strengthening Europe's net-zero technology manufacturing ecosystem and amending Regulation (EU) 2018/1724 [2024] OJ L.

[98] Regulation (EU) 2024/795 of the European Parliament and of the Council of 29 February 2024 establishing the Strategic Technologies for Europe Platform (STEP), and amending Directive 2003/87/EC and Regulations (EU) 2021/1058, (EU) 2021/1056, (EU) 2021/1057, (EU) No 1303/2013, (EU) No 223/2014, (EU) 2021/1060, (EU) 2021/523, (EU) 2021/695, (EU) 2021/697 and (EU) 2021/241 [2024] OJ L.

[99] Ibid art 3.

[100] Ibid art 2(1)(a).

[101] Regulation (EU) 2019/452 of the European Parliament and of the Council of 19 March 2019 establishing a framework for the screening of foreign direct investments into the Union [2019] OJ L79I/1.

[102] Regulation (EU) 2022/1031 of the European Parliament and of the Council of 23 June 2022 on the access of third-country economic operators, goods and services to the Union's public procurement and concession markets and procedures supporting negotiations on access of Union economic operators, goods and services to the public procurement and concession markets of third countries (International Procurement Instrument—IPI) [2022] OJ L173/1.

[103] Regulation (EU) 2022/2560 of the European Parliament and of the Council of 14 December 2022 on foreign subsidies distorting the internal market [2022] OJ L330/1.

[104] Regulation (EU) 2023/2675 of the European Parliament and of the Council of 22 November 2023 on the protection of the Union and its Member States from economic coercion by third countries [2023] OJ L.

With the war in Ukraine continuing and growing global economic competition, however, in April 2024 the European Council approved a 'new European competitiveness deal'.[105] The European Council conclusions—which built on a high-level report on the future of the EU internal market authored by former Italian Prime Minister Enrico Letta[106]—sketched an holistic approach to 'ensure [the EU] long-term competitiveness, prosperity and leadership on the global stage and to strengthen its strategic sovereignty',[107] with action in multiple policies including the single market, the capital markets union, industry, research and innovation, energy, and trade. The European Council roadmap was followed in May 2024 by the Council of the EU,[108] and in July 2024 European Commission President-elect Von der Leyen—in the political guidelines she presented for her re-election at the European Parliament—promised that she will present 'a new Clean Industrial Deal for competitive industries ... within the first 100 days of the mandate'.[109] In September 2024, finally, former ECB President Mario Draghi released a detailed and ambitious report on the future of EU economic competitiveness, which is likely to shape policy-making in the next EU institutional cycle.[110]

3 The consequences

EU action in the fields of energy and industry in response to the war in Ukraine has been highly consequential from both a formal and a substantive EU law perspective. From a formal point of view, the core measures adopted by the EU, especially interventions in the energy market, have revealed a growing confidence in utilizing Article 122(1) TFEU. This clause, which is located in Chapter 1 of Title VIII TFEU on 'Economic Policy', states that: 'Without prejudice to any other procedures provided for in the Treaties, the Council, on a proposal from the Commission, may decide, in a spirit of solidarity between Member States, upon the measures appropriate to the economic situation, in particular if severe difficulties arise in the supply of certain products, notably in the area of energy.' Article 122(2) TFEU, instead, affirms that: 'Where a Member State is in difficulties or is seriously threatened with severe difficulties caused by natural disasters or exceptional occurrences beyond its control, the Council, on a proposal from the Commission, may

---

[105] European Council conclusions, 17–18 April 2024, EUCO 12/24, section IV.
[106] See Enrico Letta, 'Much More than a Market: Speed, Security, Solidarity', 17 April 2024.
[107] European Council conclusions, 17-18 April 2024, EUCO 12/24, para 11.
[108] Council of the EU Conclusions, 'A competitive European industry driving our green digital and resilient future', 24 May 2024, Doc 9893/24.
[109] European Commission President-elect Ursula von der Leyen, 'Europe's Choice: Political Guidelines for the next European Commission 2024-2029', 18 July 2024, 8.
[110] See Mario Draghi, The Future of European Competitiveness. Part A. A Competitiveness Strategy for Europe, 9 September 2024.

grant, under certain conditions, Union financial assistance to the Member State concerned.'

Article 122 TFEU had been occasionally used by the EU before. Specifically, the predecessor of Article 122(1) TFEU, Article 103 of the Treaty establishing the European Economic Communities (TEEC), on conjunctural policy, had been utilized in the 1970s to deal with the oil crisis.[111] Moreover, more recently, Article 122 TFEU was used to address both the euro-crisis and the Covid-19 pandemic. In the first case, the Council had established the European Financial Stabilisation Mechanism (EFSM), providing loans to Greece, on the basis of Article 122(2) TFEU.[112] In the second case, Article 122(1) TFEU had been used to set up a framework for crisis-relevant medical counter-measures in the event of a health emergency.[113] Furthermore, as also pointed out in Chapter 3, the Council had adopted both SURE[114]—a temporary unemployment reinsurance system to mitigate lay-offs during the pandemic—and especially the EU Recovery Instrument (EURI)[115]—a key piece of legislation for the establishment of the NGEU Recovery Fund and the issuance of EU common debt—on the basis of Article 122 TFEU generally, without specifying which paragraph of this provision served as the legal basis.[116]

To tackle the energy crisis, however, the EU resorted to Article 122(1) TFEU five times in 2022, and three of the emergency acts adopted in the aftermath of Russia's aggression against Ukraine were subsequently renewed in 2023. As Merijn Chamon has argued, the increased reliance on Article 122 TFEU constitutes a 'paradigm-changing'[117] development, as it increases the ability of the EU to 'adopt far-reaching economic policy measures'.[118] In fact, Article 122(1) TFEU refers to the ability of the Council to intervene 'in particular if severe difficulties arise in the supply of certain products, notably in the area of energy'—which was the case at stake in the energy intervention acts enacted in response to Russia's aggression

---

[111] See eg Council Regulation (EEC) No 1893/79 of 28 August 1979 introducing registration for crude oil and/or petroleum product imports in the Community [1979] OJ L220/1.

[112] Council Regulation (EU) No 407/2010 of 11 May 2010 establishing a European financial stabilisation mechanism [2010] OJ L118/1.

[113] Council Regulation (EU) 2022/2372 of 24 October 2022 on a framework of measures for ensuring the supply of crisis-relevant medical countermeasures in the event of a public health emergency at Union level [2022] OJ L314/64.

[114] Council Regulation (EU) 2020/672 of 19 May 2020 on the establishment of a European instrument for temporary support to mitigate unemployment risks in an emergency (SURE) following the COVID-19 outbreak [2020] OJ L159/1.

[115] Council Regulation (EU) 2020/2094 of 14 December 2020 establishing a European Union Recovery Instrument to support the recovery in the aftermath of the COVID-19 crisis [2020] OJ L433I/23.

[116] See Bruno de Witte, 'The European Union's Covid-19 Recovery Plan: The Legal Engineering of an Economic Policy Shift' (2021) 58 Common Market Law Review 635, 654.

[117] Merijn Chamon, 'The Use of Article 122 TFEU: Institutional Implications and Impact on Democratic Accountability', report commissioned by the European Parliament Constitutional Affairs Committee, September 2023, 41.

[118] Ibid 21.

against Ukraine. Yet, this case is non-exhaustive and, as Article 122(1) TFEU states, more broadly the EU could intervene to adopt, in a spirit of solidarity, 'the measures appropriate to the economic situation'.

From a substantive point of view, furthermore, the action taken by the EU in the field of energy interventions contributes to strengthen solidarity as the core principle of EU energy law.[119] As has been argued in response to the war in Ukraine, 'in a very short period of time, the EU has adopted several legal instruments to address the energy crisis. All of these legal emergency instruments rely heavily on the idea of solidarity and highlight its role in the EU's crisis responses'.[120] This aligns with, and strengthens, the approach to solidarity embraced by EU courts just before the start of the war in Ukraine in the *OPAL* case: both the General Court[121] and the European Court of Justice (ECJ)[122] had ruled that the principle of energy solidarity enshrined in Article 194(1) TFEU constituted a legally binding principle of EU law. Consequently, the EU courts had struck down a decision by the Commission enabling the German energy market regulatory authority to exempt the Russian state-owned company Gazprom from having to comply with rules on third-party access and tariff regulation in the use of the OPAL pipeline (connecting the Nord Stream 1 pipeline to the power grid in Central and Western Europe).[123] The EU courts' decisions—which protected the energy interests of Poland and the Baltics states, which were worried that Gazprom's monopoly would increase dependence on Russian gas supplies and threaten energy security in Europe—affirmed the central value of solidarity in EU energy law. Emergency measures adopted since Russia's aggression against Ukraine have substantively confirmed this.

At the same time, from a substantive viewpoint, EU action to promote a new industrial policy for the net-zero era also constitutes a watershed.[124] For years, the idea that the EU could develop its own industrial policy was regarded as unorthodox, as the EU was primarily engaged in establishing an internal market and banning unfair competition between Member States. Yet, in response to the war in Ukraine the EU adopted the NZIA and the Critical Raw Materials Act, as well as a Chips Act and STEP. The first two are based on the standard Article 114 TFEU, the internal market legal basis. The Chips Act instead relies on both Article 114 and Article 173 TFEU, on industry—which are also the same legal bases of the Act in Support of Ammunition Production (ASAP), discussed in Chapter 2. STEP, finally, draws on multiple legal bases including industry, cohesion, and technological

---

[119] Kaisa Huhta and Leonie Reins, 'Solidarity in European Union Law and Its Application in the Energy Sector' (2022) 72 International & Comparative Law Quarterly 771.
[120] Ibid 733 (internal citation omitted).
[121] Case T-883/16 *Poland v Commission* ECLI:EU:T:2019:567.
[122] Case C-848/19 P *Germany v Poland* ECLI:EU:C:2021:958.
[123] Max Münchmeyer, 'The Principle of Energy Solidarity: *Germany v. Poland*' (2022) 59 Common Market Law Review 915.
[124] See Editorial Comments, 'Paying for the EU's Industry Policy' (2023) 60 Common Market Law Review 617.

development. In all these legal acts the use of the internal market, or industry, legal bases are pushed towards a new goal, namely positioning the EU to address in a supranational way a more threatening geo-strategic environment. In fact, all these measures have been designed to increase the resilience of EU supply chains, to reduce foreign dependences, and to adjust to the reality of the new, selective, globalization.[125]

As Armin Steinbach has argued, the new EU economic security strategy, and the measures adopted in response to the war in Ukraine, reveal a 'turn to strategic autonomy'.[126] Since at least the time of the Covid-19 pandemic, the EU had been debating at policy level how to strengthen its strategic autonomy[127]— admittedly a vague political, rather than legal, concept, which generally referred to the idea of increasing the EU's ability to make decisions independently, while taking into account its interests and values.[128] Yet, following Russia's aggression against Ukraine, the EU has now enacted legislative measures that consistently push in that direction. 'Driven by security-of-supply concern, the EU has rapidly become independent from Russian energy supplies and redirected efforts away from market-driven dependence to security-centred diversification. The goal of reducing dependence has driven the EU's more general push towards a EU-based production of key technologies, notably through the EU [NZIA].'[129] This has consequential implications for EU law and policy, especially as efforts to strengthen EU economic competitiveness continue in the new EU institutional cycle, in line with the Draghi report.[130]

4 The challenges

4.1 Domestic legality

The measures adopted by the EU to intervene in the energy markets have been subjected to a number of legal challenges before EU courts.[131] In particular, several

---

[125] See Harold James, 'The new globalization and the economic consequences of Brexit' in Federico Fabbrini (ed), *The Law & Politics of Brexit. Volume V. The Trade & Cooperation Agreement* (OUP 2024) 29.
[126] Armin Steinbach, 'The EU's Turn to "Strategic Autonomy": Leeway for Policy Action and Points of Conflict' (2023) 34 European Journal of International Law 973.
[127] See also Thomas Verellen and Alexandra Hofer, 'The Unilateral Turn in EU Trade and Investment Policy' (2023) 28 European Foreign Affairs Review 1.
[128] See Editorial Comments, 'Keeping Europeanism at Bay? Strategic Autonomy as a Constitutional Problem' (2022) 59 Common Market Law Review 313.
[129] Steinbach (n 126) 1005.
[130] See Editorial Comments, 'A European Industrial Policy and the EU's Turning Point' (2024) 49 European Law Review 317.
[131] See Leigh Hancher, 'EU Energy Market Regulation after the 2022 Energy Crisis: the reforms so far and the challenges ahead', SIEPS European Policy Analysis, January 2024.

major undertakings in the petroleum sector have brought action for annulment pursuant to Article 263 TFEU, challenging the legality of the windfall tax introduced by the Council regulation on emergency interventions to address high energy prices.[132] Similarly, energy companies in the renewable sector have challenged the legality of the cap on market revenues also set by the same Council regulation on emergency interventions in the electricity sector.[133] These private undertakings have equally complained, inter alia, that Article 122 TFEU provided an invalid legal basis for the Council to adopt such measures, that the interventions violated the principle of proportionality enshrined in Article 5(4) TEU, that they infringed the right to property as protected in Article 17 of the EU Charter of Fundamental Rights (CFR), and that—with regard to the solidarity contribution on surplus profits—Article 122 TFEU violated the general principle of legal certainty and the presumption against retroactivity.

Furthermore, a direct action for annulment before the ECJ has also been lodged by Poland against the Council, challenging the legality of the regulation on the coordinated demand reduction for gas.[134] In its plea, Poland also challenged the use of Article 122 TFEU as a valid legal basis, and claimed that the act should have been based on Article 194(2) TFEU, on energy, in conjunction with Article 192(2)(c) TFEU, on environmental policy. Poland's challenge essentially had to do with the voting procedure. Under Article 122 TFEU the Council decides by qualified majority voting (QMV). According to Article 194(2) TFEU, instead, EU measures in the field of energy 'shall not affect a Member State's right to determine the conditions for exploiting its energy resources, its choice between different energy sources and the general structure of its energy supply, without prejudice to Article 192(2)(c) [TFEU]', which introduces a special legislative procedure, under which the Council acts by unanimity. As such, Poland primarily claimed that the main objective of the gas demand reduction regulation is to have a significant effect on the conditions for exploiting energy resources, the choice between different energy sources and the general structure of a Member State's energy supply, while further alleging also a breach of the principle of energy solidarity.

At the time of writing, none of these cases has yet been adjudicated by either the General Court or the ECJ. In substantive terms, the introduction through legislation of either a revenue cap or a special levy on firms that have made extraordinary profits due to alteration of standard market conditions may not appear unreasonable. In fact, the legality of some windfall taxes introduced during the energy crisis has been upheld at national level. In Italy, for example, the Corte Costituzionale ruled in early June 2024 that the introduction by Italian legislation of a temporary

---

[132] See Case T-803/22 *Petrogas E&P Netherlands v Council*, pending; Case T-802/22 *ExxonMobil Producing Netherlands v Council*, pending.
[133] Case T-759/22 *Electrawinds Shabla South v Council*, pending.
[134] Case C-675/22 *Poland v Council*, pending.

tax on surplus profits for energy companies was neither arbitrary nor disproportionate.[135] In particular, the Corte Costituzionale ruled that, in the context of the energy crisis, it was not unreasonable for the Italian legislature 'to identify the enormous price increase of energy products in the exceptional situation at play and the specific market in which energy companies operate—when certain conditions occur—as a sign of wealth'.[136] The Corte Costituzionale therefore opened the door to a temporary solidarity contribution—providing a jurisprudential path that may also be followed by EU courts.

However, in procedural terms, the introduction of emergency measures in the energy market raises additional questions, which go beyond those adjudicated at national level. On the one hand, there is an important formal legal point raised by Poland in its challenge, on the choice of legal basis. Since Article 122(1) TFEU explicitly states that this legal basis must be used 'without prejudice to any other procedure provided for in the Treaties', the Council should 'attach special attention to the context in which the measure would be adopted, if that measure could also be adopted pursuant to a different legal basis'.[137] Admittedly, in a prior dispute the ECJ had rejected a challenge by Poland against the European Parliament and the Council, ruling that the use of Article 191 TFEU on environmental policy, which requires QMV in the Council, rather than Article 192(2)(c) TFEU, which requires unanimity, was legal because the effect of the contested act on Poland's energy mix was only indirect.[138] Yet, that case concerned the ETS, a clearly environmental measure, rather than gas reduction, which could more likely have been adopted as an energy measure—as in the case of the 2022 gas storage regulation. Furthermore neither of the two legal bases under dispute in the 2018 *Poland v Parliament and Council* case included a 'without prejudice' clause such as that in Article 122(1) TFEU.

On the other hand, the substantively more significant legal issue to be addressed is whether a Council regulation adopted on the basis of Article 122(1) TFEU can serve as a valid way to introduce a solidarity contribution, which is effectively a direct tax. As the use of Article 122 TFEU as a legal basis for EU action has significantly increased in recent years, a number of judgments have now been delivered by both national and EU courts on this provision. For example, in *Pringle* the ECJ ruled in the abstract that Article 122 TFEU could not be used to establish a permanent stability mechanism to finance euro-zone countries,[139] and in *Anagnostakis* it held that Article 122 TFEU 'cannot serve as a basis for adopting a

---

[135] Corte Costituzionale, sentenza 111/2024.
[136] Ibid para 7.1.3 (my translation. The original text is: 'non appare arbitrario che il fortissimo aumento dei prezzi dei prodotti energetici nell'eccezionale situazione congiunturale e lo specifico mercato in cui le imprese energetiche operano siano stati identificati dal legislatore – al verificarsi di una serie di condizioni – come un indice rivelatore di ricchezza').
[137] Chamon (n 117) 23.
[138] Case C-5/16 *Poland v Parliament and Council* ECLI:EU:C:2018:483.
[139] Case C-370/12 *Pringle* ECLI:EU:C:2012:756, para 116.

measure or a principle enabling, in essence, a Member State to decide unilaterally not to repay all or part of its debt'.[140] Furthermore, in December 2022 the German Bundesverfassungsgericht (BVerfG) ruled that Article 122 TFEU constituted a lawful legal basis for the adoption of the NGEU.[141] Nevertheless, none of these cases concerned the use of Article 122 TFEU for the introduction of tax measures imposing a burden on legal persons.

Yet, it is legally questionable whether this clause can be used to introduce a windfall tax on legal persons. From a strictly legal perspective, Chapter II of Title VII of the TFEU—laying out the EU primary law 'Tax provisions'—only empowers the Council acting unanimously to harmonize laws on indirect taxation. Furthermore, from a constitutional perspective, the fact that a direct tax can be imposed on legal persons by the Council, without any involvement of the European Parliament, raises significant democratic questions.[142] It is indeed a fundamental principle of constitutionalism since the American Revolution that there cannot be taxation without representation. However, because under Article 122 TFEU the European Parliament has no role, 'the democratic legitimacy of the decision-making procedure pursuant to that provision' is problematic.[143] Surely, the solidarity contribution was introduced in response to the war in Ukraine as a form of redistribution on a purely temporary and exceptional basis. However, it remains to be seen if this can suffice to uphold it.

4.2 Level playing field

The EU's responses to the energy crisis unleashed by Russia's aggression against Ukraine, furthermore, have also caused other domestic legal challenges. In particular, building on the state aid flexibility introduced during Covid-19, the EU effort to accelerate the phasing out of Russian fossil fuels and to support the green transition of firms and households has significantly affected the conventional EU competition law framework enshrined in Title VII, Chapter I, Section 2 of the TFEU. Since the inception of the EU integration project, the TEEC put in place rigid state aid rules limiting the amount of subsidies that Member States could provide to their national champions, so as to ensure a fair level playing field in the internal market.[144] Certainly, Article 107 TFEU—today's core treaty provision on

---

[140] C-589/15 P *Anagnostakis v Commission* ECLI:EU:C:2017:663, para 71.
[141] 2 BvR 547/21, 2BvR 798/21, Judgment of 6 December 2022.
[142] See Alastair McIver, 'Accountability: European Parliament' in Federico Fabbrini and Christy Ann Petit (eds), *Research Handbook on Post-Pandemic Economic Governance and NGEU Law* (Edward Elgar Publishing 2024) 225; and Menelaos Markakis, *Accountability in Economic and Monetary Union* (OUP 2020).
[143] Chamon (n 117) 34.
[144] See Andrea Biondi, 'The Rationale of State Aid Control: A Return to Orthodoxy' (2010) 12 Cambridge Yearbook of European Legal Studies 35; Frank Benyon, *Direct Investment, National Champions and EU Treaty Freedoms* (Hart Publishing 2010).

state aid—authorizes some specific forms of state subsidies. However, through the adoption of the TCF and then the TCTF and the reform of the GBER, the EU largely widened Member States' room for manoeuvre to grant aid to support businesses and households in weathering the high costs of energy, and to invest in renewables threatening the level playing field at the base of the EU internal market.[145]

Yet, as Juan Jorge Piernas Lopez has pointed out, 'the wide scope of this Temporary Framework raises doubts as to its complementarity with the existing State aid rules, apart from raising cohesion concerns linked to dissimilar financial capacity of Member States'.[146] In fact, the Commission's decision to empower Member States to subsidize their domestic firms and households has resulted in very different degrees of national intervention—which have largely depended on the budgetary resources, the so-called fiscal space, of each Member State. Admittedly, as a result of the war in Ukraine the Commission extended in 2022 and 2023 the suspension of the Stability and Growth Pact[147]—the centrepiece of EU fiscal rules, imposing spending constraints on Member States, which had been put on hold in 2020 following the outbreak of the Covid-19 pandemic. This empowered all Member States to run deficits to support their economies. However, as European Commissioners for the Economy and for the Internal Market Paolo Gentiloni and Thierry Breton jointly pointed out, because of the different fiscal headroom of each EU Member State, governments' interventions created disparities, threatening the level playing field of the EU internal market.[148]

In fact, as reported by the European Commission Vice-President in charge of Competition Policy Margrethe Vestager in January 2023, €672 billion in state aid was approved under the TCF in 2022 by the 27 EU Member States—but a total of €350 billion in subsidies was given by Germany alone, with France and Italy spending €150 billion and €50 billion each, hence a total of 82% was absorbed by the three largest Member States only.[149] In particular, German government subsidies to the domestic industry caused widespread concerns. Consequently, the Commission's crisis-related state aid policy has increasingly been subjected to criticism—especially by smaller, less protectionist Member States.[150] However,

---

[145] See also Juan Jorge Piernas Lopez, 'State aid' in Federico Fabbrini and Christy Ann Petit (eds), *Research Handbook on Post-Pandemic Economic Governance and NGEU Law* (Edward Elgar Publishing 2024) 93; and Irene Agnolucci, 'Will COVID-19 Make or Break EU State Aid Control?' (2022) 13 Journal of European Competition Law and Practice 3.

[146] Juan Jorge Piernas Lopez, 'The Transformation of EU State Aid Law ... and Its Discontents' (2023) 60 Common Market Law Review 1623, 1652.

[147] See European Commission press release, 'European Semester Spring Package', 23 May 2022, IP/22/3182.

[148] Paolo Gentiloni and Thierry Breton, 'I 200 miliardi della Germania sulle bollette: serve una risposta europea comune e solidale', Op-ed, *Il Corriere della Sera* (3 October 2022).

[149] European Commission Executive Vice-President Margrethe Vestager, Letter, 13 January [2023], Annex.

[150] See Commission's consultation on the Temporary Crisis and Transition Framework, Joint non-paper by Denmark, Finland, Ireland, the Netherlands, Poland and Sweden, 23 December 2023, joined also by the Czech Republic, Hungary, Latvia and Slovakia on 2 February 2023.

if through the application of state aid law the Commission has emerged 'as a "de facto crisis management authority"',[151] it has struggled to compensate this through appropriate supranational balancing measures—due to difficulties in raising EU funding.

4.3 Funding

The prevailing EU strategy to address the socio-economic damage caused by the war in Ukraine and its resulting energy crisis has been to empower Member States to spend more of their national resources. Instead, the EU has struggled to mobilise supranational resources to support the green transition and facilitate the development of a net-zero industry. As mentioned above, the RePowerEU regulation made available to Member States an additional €20 billion of grants, raised through the auction of further ETS quotas, assigned on the basis of a methodology reported in Annex I, which privileged Poland and Italy. Furthermore, the RePowerEU regulation also empowered Member States to request unused loans from NGEU.[152] As a result, by September 2023 four Member States—namely Greece, Poland, Portugal, and Slovenia—had requested additional loan support, while six countries—Belgium, the Czech Republic, Spain, Croatia, Lithuania, and Hungary—had requested loan support under the NGEU for the first time[153] (thus joining the seven who had requested loans from the start: namely, Greece, Italy, Cyprus, Poland, Portugal, Romania, and Slovenia).

Nevertheless, beyond these EU resources designed to finance new RePowerEU chapters in NRRPs, no other real sources of supranational funding for the energy transition have been made available. On the one hand, the NZIA, the Critical Raw Materials Act and the Chips Act have exclusively changed the regulatory framework, without providing any new source of public funding, on the expectation that private funding will mobilize by itself.[154] On the other hand, the STEP regulation has only redeployed existing resources. The 2023 European Commission work programme had mentioned a plan to create a new 'European Sovereignty Fund',[155]

---

[151] Piernas Lopez (n 146) 1624.
[152] Rosalba Famà, 'RePowerEU' in Federico Fabbrini and Christy Petit (eds), *Research Handbook on Post-Pandemic Economic Governance and NGEU Law* (Edward Elgar Publishing 2024) 128.
[153] See European Commission Recovery and Resilience Task Force, 'Final overview of Member States' loan requests under the RRF. Note to the Council and European Parliament', 1 September 2023 https://commission.europa.eu/system/files/2023-09/01092023-Final-overview-of-MS-loan-requests-under-the-RRF_en.pdf.
[154] But see Christy Ann Petit, 'Covid-19 and Financial Union' in Federico Fabbrini and Christy Petit (eds), *Research Handbook on Post-Pandemic Economic Governance and NGEU Law* (Edward Elgar Publishing 2024) 43 (discussing difficulties of advancing towards the completion of the Capital Markets Union).
[155] See Guillaume Ragonnaud and Marin Mileusnic, 'Strategic Technologies for Europe Platform', European Parliament Research Service, February 2024.

and President Ursula von der Leyen had previously endorsed this idea as a way to strengthen European sovereignty building on the experience of NGEU.[156] In fact, the June 2023 Commission proposal for a regulation establishing STEP had called for reinforcing the firepower of existing EU instruments with 'an additional total amount of EUR 10 billion'[157] as part of a mid-term revision of the Multi-annual Financial Framework (MFF), worth a total of €75 billion.[158] During the legislative process, the European Parliament even called for an increase of the STEP budget by an extra €3 billion.[159] However, due to opposition in the Council, the final version of the STEP regulation only set aside a budget of €1.5 billion of funding for the net-zero transition, drawing these resources 'from existing Union programmes'.[160]

As highlighted in Chapter 3, the EU constitutional architecture in the field of economic governance poses major constraints on the ability of the EU to raise financial resources. Substantively, Article 310 TFEU requires the EU to balance its budget, which is primarily financed by national transfers. Furthermore, institutionally, Article 312 TFEU requires the MFF to be approved by unanimity, while Article 311 TFEU imposes unanimous approval in the Council, and parliamentary ratification, for the adoption of the Own Resource Decision—the key EU revenues act. Given this cumbersome unanimity-based decision-making system and national control on the size of the EU budget, it is unsurprising that—even before Hungary vetoed in December 2023 the approval of the MFF revision, with the connected UF—the 27 heads of state and government of the European Council had already decided to cut back the size of STEP to just €1.5 billion,[161] as it would eventually remain.[162] Just as much as this constitutional framework slowed the EU's capacity to 'promote the general welfare' and mobilize resources to fund Ukraine externally, it also hampered its action to 'insure domestic tranquillity' and support internally the industrial transition and economic competitiveness in the face of an energy crisis and global supply chain bottlenecks.

Ironically, moreover, constitutional fiscal constraints are also re-emerging in the EU at the national level too.[163] In particular, in November 2023 the BVerfG declared unconstitutional and void Germany's second supplementary budget act of 2021, which provided for the transfer of an authorization to borrow €60 billion, granted in response to the Covid-19 pandemic and not needed in 2021, to

---

[156] European Commission President Ursula von der Leyen, speech, 4 December 2022.
[157] European Commission proposal (n 93) 7.
[158] European Commission Communication, Mid-term revision of the Multiannual Financial Framework 2021–2027, 20 June 2023, COM(2023) 336 final, 10.
[159] European Parliament press release, 'A STEP towards supporting EU competitiveness and resilience in strategic sectors', 17 October 2023.
[160] Regulation (EU) 2024/795 (n 98) art 3.
[161] See European Council meeting, Multiannual Financial Framework 2021–2027 Negotiating Box, 15 December 2023, EUCO 23/23, para 12.
[162] European Council conclusions, 1 February 2024, EUCO 2/24, para 13.
[163] Clara Bösche, 'La crise allemand du *Schuldenbremse*: un symptôme à prendre au sérieux en Europe', Fondation Robert Schuman Policy Paper no 734, 29 January 2024.

the Energy and Climate Fund, since renamed the Climate and Transformation Fund.[164] Because the German Basic Law enshrines a debt brake rule, an authorization to borrow can only be taken by the lower house of Parliament on the basis of an extraordinary emergency. On a legal challenge from the opposition, the BVerfG ruled that the government and the parliamentary majority had violated the constitutional debt brake by authorizing additional borrowing for Covid-19 related purposes, but shifting these resources to a different political objective, namely the promotion of climate protection and transformation. The BVerfG ruling, however, caused a €60 billion hole in the budget of the state, significantly restricting its ability to continue funding the green transition.

Yet, the structural weaknesses in the EU fiscal constitution—combined with the constraints stemming from national basic laws—are increasingly problematic, given steps by other international players to invest heavily and drive the green transition. This is most visible in the 2022 IRA, a piece of US legislation promoted by President Joe Biden which, despite its name, is primarily geared towards investing in domestic energy production, while promoting clean energy. Among others, the IRA authorizes US$783 billion in federal spending on energy and climate change, including tax credits to spur investment in clean energy and manufacturing. The IRA has proved to be extremely popular, lulling a number of EU-based firms to shift production in the US to seize the fiscal benefits resulting from this groundbreaking programme. And additional pieces of US legislation—including the 2022 CHIPS and Science Act[165]—have provided further financial incentives for firms to reshore in the US, authorizing roughly US$280 billion in new federal funding to boost domestic research and manufacturing of semiconductors, including US$39 billion of grants for chips manufacturing. In light of these global developments, the measures adopted by the EU in the field of energy and industry appear largely unsuitable to support the competitiveness of the EU economy, unless more funding is made available ahead.

5 Conclusions

This chapter has examined the EU's response to the war in Ukraine in the field of energy and industry, assessing the EU constitution's ability to insure domestic tranquillity. As Russia's weaponization of fossil fuels resulted in an energy crisis, which threatened domestic firms and households, and therefore potentially the EU's unwavering support for Ukraine, the EU adopted a number of emergency interventions to regulate the energy markets. The chapter analysed these measures, while also mapping the EU legal acts passed to support the green transition

---

[164] BVerfG, 2 BvF 1/22, Judgment of 15 November 2023.
[165] CHIPS and Science Act of 2022, Pub L No 117–167.

and the decarbonization of industry, and overviewing the novel tools put in place to develop an industrial policy for the net-zero age.

As the chapter has maintained, the EU's response to Russia's aggression against Ukraine has been wide-ranging, and the EU's constitution has empowered the EU to take highly consequential measures. In particular, the EU repeatedly used emergency powers under the treaties to cap excessive energy prices and revenues; it strengthened transnational solidarity in the energy sector; and leveraged internal market competences to push for a green industrial deal.

Nevertheless, the EU's effort to ensure domestic tranquillity in time of war has been hampered by several challenges. Some of the EU's energy emergency measures, including a windfall tax on surplus profits, have been challenged in court as an illegal exercise of direct tax power. The EU's decision to relax state aid law and allow Member States to subsidize domestic firms and households heavily have threatened the level playing field at the heart of the EU internal market. And the EU has provided only limited supranational funding to drive the green transition and finance strategic developments. Compared to the US IRA, therefore, the EU's action has appeared weaker, confirming that structural constraints in the EU's fiscal constitution pose a long-term challenge for the EU's economic competitiveness.

6
To 'secure the blessings of liberty'
Developments in enlargement and reforms

1 Introduction

Wars have transformative consequences. On 28 February 2022, four days after Russia's invasion of Ukraine, the Ukrainian President, Prime Minister, and Chairman of Parliament jointly submitted to the European Union (EU) institutions their country's application for EU membership.[1] In fact, opinion polls in Ukraine have consistently revealed a very strong popular support in favour of joining the EU, with over 90% of respondents confirming that the latter is seen by a country at war as a shield against the imperialist threats of Russia.[2] Ukraine's EU membership application was quickly followed by that of Moldova, which in late October 2024 will also hold a constitutional referendum on EU accession.[3] Moreover, the war has revitalized the accession process for other candidate countries which were waiting at the EU's door. Consequently, European Commission President Ursula von der Leyen has hailed the prospects of an enlarged union as 'an investment in [EU] security',[4] and European Council President Charles Michel has indicated his ambition to accelerate the EU's eastward expansion, bringing Ukraine in the EU by 2030.[5]

The purpose of this chapter is to examine from an EU law and policy perspective the key steps that the EU has taken since Russia's aggression against Ukraine towards the enlargement of the EU and its reform. In particular, the chapter overviews the start of the EU accession negotiations with Ukraine and Moldova, the grant of candidate status to Georgia and Bosnia Herzegovina, and the relaunch of the enlargement process to five other countries of the Western Balkans (Albania, Kosovo, Montenegro, North Macedonia, and Serbia), which together with Turkey

---

[1] Council of the EU General Secretariat, Application of Ukraine for membership of the European Union, 4 March 2022, CM 2003/22, https://data.consilium.europa.eu/doc/document/CM-2003-2022-INIT/en/pdf.

[2] See Kyiv International Institute of Sociology press release, 'For what matters Ukraine's European Union membership, the priority of joining the EU or NATO, and the perception of Russia as part of Europe', 9 October 2023, https://www.kiis.com.ua/?lang=eng&cat=reports&id=1303&page=1.

[3] Parliament of the Republic of Moldova press release, 'Republican constitutional referendum to be held in Moldova on 20 October 2024', 16 May 2024.

[4] European Commission President Ursula von der Leyen, Statement on the 2023 Enlargement Package, 8 November 2023, STATEMENT/23/5641.

[5] European Council President Charles Michel, Speech at Bled Strategic Forum, 28 August 2023.

had already been on the waiting list to join the EU. At the same time, the chapter underlines how in the aftermath of Russia's aggression against Ukraine the EU promoted the establishment of a new organization—the European Political Community (EPC)—to cooperate with the wider Europe before the completion of the enlargement process, and deepened its partnerships with other European and transatlantic organizations like the Council of Europe (CoE) and the North Atlantic Treaty Organization (NATO), as well as with a former Member State, the United Kingdom (UK).

As the chapter argues, the EU constitution enabled the EU 'to secure the blessings of liberty',[6] as the EU responded dynamically to the war in Ukraine, opening a path to EU membership to a growing number of eastern European states, and strengthening other fora for transnational cooperation among like-minded countries. At a time when the security and independence of Ukraine and other post-Soviet states was under threat from Russia's outright military aggression, or destabilization efforts, the EU confirmed its attractiveness as a beacon of freedom and democracy and an anchor of stability and prosperity. If the very decision by Ukraine to request EU membership within days after Russia's full-scale invasion is a testament to how the EU is seen externally as a blessing for liberty, through the enlargement process the EU constitution foresees a mechanism to achieve that hopeful promise. At the same time, the EU has also promoted the establishment of a new forum—the EPC—to connect with the wider Europe before enlargement, and fostered closer partnerships with other organizations such as the CoE and NATO, which also pool sovereignty among their members, albeit with mechanisms which are different from those of the EU.

Nevertheless, as the chapter maintains, the prospect of a union with 35 or more Member States raises profound internal constitutional challenges for the EU and exposes structural shortcomings in its current design. On the one hand, the experience of prior enlargements has revealed that pre-accession conditionality has not always worked, particularly as a number of new Member States such as Hungary and Poland have increasingly experienced democratic backsliding, known as the rule of law crisis. On the other hand, future enlargements would further strain the governance structures of the EU, which depend heavily on unanimous decision-making in the Council and the European Council. In fact, if taking decisions within the EU27 has proved daunting, especially in areas related to common foreign and security policy (CFSP) and budgetary matters, increasing the number of Member States to possibly 35 will only make things worse. In this context, growing calls have been made for the EU to adjust its institutional structures to be ready for enlargement. Yet, due to national vetoes, so far the EU has failed to advance in any

---

[6] US Const, preamble.

meaningful way on the path to constitutional reform, which means it is currently ill-prepared for enlargement.

As such, this chapter is structured as follows. Section 2 examines the core steps the EU has taken in response to Russia's war of aggression to support the aspiration for freedom of Ukraine, and other countries of Eastern Europe and the Western Balkans, including the relaunch of the enlargement process, the establishment of the EPC, and the strengthening of partnership with the CoE and NATO, as well as other European states like the UK. Section 3 discusses the major consequences for the EU enlargement policy of the decision to start accession negotiations with Ukraine in reaction to Russia's war of aggression, and highlights the dynamic nature of the current European governance landscape. Section 4, however, highlights the constitutional challenges that the prospect of enlargement poses for the EU, and underlines both the limited preparation of candidate countries and of the EU itself—given the impossibility so far to agree much needed EU reforms. Section 5, finally concludes.

2 The core measures

2.1 The relaunch of the enlargement process

The war in Ukraine had major consequences for the EU enlargement process. As is well known, following Croatia's accession to the EU in 2013, the enlargement process had stalled. While several countries of the Western Balkans were formally on the path to join the EU, European Commission President Jean-Claude Juncker had clarified in 2014 that no new state would join the EU during his mandate.[7] Moreover, a major row erupted among Member States in 2019 on whether to authorize accession talks with Albania and North Macedonia.[8] In particular, France— with the backing of Denmark and the Netherlands—objected to any bureaucratic automaticity in the accession process, and called for greater political steering on decisions about enlargement.[9] In the absence of the necessary unanimity within the European Council, the issue was referred back to the European Commission, which in February 2020 put forward a new methodology for accession negotiations:[10] this confirmed a credible EU membership perspective for the Western Balkans, but also subjected the enlargement talks to further conditionality, with

---

[7] European Commission President-elect Jean-Claude Juncker, 'A New Start for Europe: My Agenda for Jobs, Growth, Fairness and Democratic Change. Political Guidelines for the Next European Commission', 15 July 2014, 12.
[8] European Council conclusions, 18 October 2019, EUCO 23/19, para 5.
[9] See French non-paper, 'Reforming the European Union Accession Process', November 2019.
[10] European Commission Communication 'Enhancing the Accession Process: A Credible EU Perspective for the Western Balkans', 5 February 2020, COM(2020) 57 final, 2–3.

negotiations on the fundamentals, including the rule of law, to be opened first and closed last, and with the possibility of suspending the accession process *tout court*. In the end, however, no real progress occurred.

Yet, the war in Ukraine profoundly changed the circumstances, and led the EU to revitalize its enlargement process. On 23–24 June 2022—just four months after the start of Russia's aggression—the European Council granted Ukraine, and Moldova, the status of EU candidate countries, while also recognizing the European perspective of Georgia.[11] Moreover, on 15 December 2022 the European Council granted candidate status to Bosnia Herzegovina.[12] At the same time, on 8 November 2023, the European Commission released a new communication on EU enlargement policy in which it hailed the benefits of enlargement for the EU, and recommended advancing accession negotiations with countries from the Western Balkans and Eastern Europe.[13] On this basis, on 14–15 December 2023 the European Council decided to open accession negotiations with Ukraine and Moldova,[14] granted candidate status to Georgia,[15] and indicated its willingness to open accession talks with Bosnia Herzegovina[16] and advance them with North Macedonia.[17] Following a positive assessment by the European Commission,[18] on 21–22 March 2024 the European Council also decided to open accession negotiations with Bosnia Herzegovina.[19]

As a result, on 25 June 2024 the EU officially started accession negotiations with Ukraine and Moldova, through a first intergovernmental conference on enlargement.[20] On the same day, the EU also published its general position, including its negotiating framework, which had been formally approved by the Council of the EU on 21 June 2024.[21] The EU general position hailed the 'historic moment … which marks a milestone in [the EU-Ukraine] relationship'[22] and emphasized how the accession of Ukraine to the EU had a particular significance in view 'of Russia's unjustified and unprovoked war of aggression'.[23] It affirmed that accession talks would be based on the Copenhagen criteria and the new accession

---

[11] European Council conclusions, 23–24 June 2022, EUCO 24/22, para 10.
[12] European Council conclusions, 15 December 2022, EUCO 34/22, para 30.
[13] European Commission Communication on 'EU Enlargement Policy', 8 November 2023, COM(2023) 690 final.
[14] European Council conclusions, 14–15 December 2023, EUCO 20/23, para 15.
[15] Ibid para 16.
[16] Ibid para 17.
[17] Ibid para 18.
[18] European Commission press release, 'Commission proposes to open EU accession negotiations with Bosnia and Herzegovina and updates on progress made by Ukraine and Moldova', 12 March 2024.
[19] European Council conclusions, 21–22 March 2024, EUCO 7/24, para 30.
[20] Council of the EU press release, 'EU opens accession negotiations with Ukraine', 25 June 2024, 577/24.
[21] See Conference on Accession to the European Union—Ukraine, General EU Position, AD 9/24, 21 June 2024.
[22] Ibid para 2.
[23] Ibid para 3.

methodology,[24] hence clarifying that progress on the fundamental cluster, relating to democracy, the rule of law, and human rights, will be opened first and closed last, and 'will determine the overall pace of the negotiations'.[25] The negotiating framework further specified the principles, procedures, and substance of the negotiations, stating that their pace 'will depend on Ukraine's progress in meeting the requirements for membership'[26] but opening up to forms of 'accelerated integration and "phasing in" to individual EU policies'.[27] The negotiating framework also made explicit that the Commission retained the power to suspend negotiations, subject to a reverse qualified majority vote in the Council, in case 'of a serious and persistent breach by Ukraine of the values on which the [EU] is founded',[28] while reaffirming the role of the Council, acting unanimously, in deciding 'on the provisional closure of'[29] each of the 32 negotiating chapters.[30]

2.2 The establishment of the European Political Community

However, beyond EU enlargement, and in the awareness that despite the best intentions this process may take years, the war in Ukraine has also led the EU to establish a new entity: the EPC. More specifically, the EPC is the brainchild of French President Emmanuel Macron, who launched the idea to create it on 9 May 2022[31]—at the concluding event of the Conference on the Future of Europe, which will also be discussed later in this chapter. According to Macron: 'This new European organization would allow democratic European nations abiding by our core set of values to find a new space for political cooperation, security, and cooperation on energy, transport, investment, infrastructure, and movement of persons, in particular our youths.'[32] From this viewpoint, the EPC would serve as a larger forum connecting both states which, like Ukraine, aimed at joining the EU—but also states, like the UK, which had just left it. As Macron stated, joining the EPC 'would not prevent future accessions to the EU as much as it would not obviously be foreclosed to those who have exited it'.[33] President Macron's idea was

---

[24] Ibid para 8.
[25] Ibid para 11.
[26] Ibid Negotiating Framework para 2.
[27] Ibid para 13.
[28] Ibid para 16.
[29] Ibid para 49.
[30] Ibid Annex II.
[31] See French President Emmanuel Macron, speech, 9 May 2022.
[32] Ibid (my translation. The original text is: 'Cette organisation européenne nouvelle permettrait aux nations européennes démocratiques adhérant à notre socle de valeurs de trouver un nouvel espace de coopération politique, de sécurité, de coopération en matière énergétique, de transport, d'investissements, d'infrastructures, de circulation des personnes et en particulier de nos jeunesses').
[33] Ibid (my translation. The original text is: 'ne préjugerait pas d'adhésions futures à l'Union européenne, forcément, comme elle ne serait pas non plus fermée à ceux qui ont quitté cette dernière').

further developed in a non-paper by the French government, which also drew on older proposals in favour of a European Confederation.[34]

The European Council quickly endorsed the EPC project on 23–24 June 2022,[35] at the same meeting which granted Ukraine candidate status for EU membership, and the EU played a lead role in organizing this new forum. The first meeting of the EPC was held in Prague, the Czech Republic—the EU Member State then holding the rotating presidency of the Council of the EU—on 6 October 2022. The second meeting of the EPC occurred in Chisinau, Moldova, on 1 June 2023. The third meeting took place in Grenada, Spain, in October 2023, again under the aegis of the rotating presidency of the Council of the EU. The fourth meeting, instead, was hosted by the UK, a former EU Member State, in July 2024. So far, 44 European states have participated to the first EPC meeting[36]—all 27 EU Member States and the leaders of the EU institutions, plus the UK, Ukraine, and 15 other countries—while 45 states attended the following ones (with Andorra and Monaco joining too, but Turkey being absent).[37] Essentially, members of the EPC match almost pari passu the members of the CoE, with minor exceptions—eg Kosovo, which is part of the EPC but not the CoE, and San Marino, which is part of the CoE but not the EPC. There is instead ambiguity with regard to Turkey, a CoE member which attended the first EPC meeting, but not the following ones.

At this stage, the EPC remains underdeveloped, and is more a forum than an organization.[38] As Bruno de Witte has perceptively pointed out, the EPC founding summit 'did not adopt any formal written document apart from press releases by various participants, nor did it create a secretariat or other organ for the EPC'.[39] From this point of view, 'the EPC is not an organization, nor a structure, nor even a process'.[40] However, the use of the term *Community* to define the EPC is not meaningless. The EU emerged out of the European Coal and Steel Community and the European Economic Community, and indeed a European Political Community was negotiated in 1952-1954 in conjunction with the European Defence Community—which ultimately did not come about. As such, while the concrete

---

[34] See 'Le project du President Macron: Retrouver le sense de la communauté au sein du continent', 16 June 2022. See also former Italian Prime Minister Enrico Letta, 'A European Confederation: A Common Political Platform for Peace', *Le Grand Continent* (25 April 2022).

[35] European Council conclusions, 23–24 June 2022, EUCO 24/22, para 1.

[36] See European Council, 'Meeting of the European Political Community', 6 October 2022, https://www.consilium.europa.eu/en/meetings/international-summit/2022/10/06/.

[37] See European Council, 'Meeting of the European Political Community', 1 June 2023, https://www.consilium.europa.eu/en/meetings/international-summit/2023/06/01/; European Council, 'Meeting of the European Political Community', 5 October 2023, https://www.consilium.europa.eu/en/meetings/international-summit/2023/10/05/

[38] See also Luigi Lonardo, 'The European Political Community: A Nebulous Answer to the Strategic Question of How to Unite Europe' (2023) 8 European Papers 755.

[39] Bruno de Witte, 'The European Political Community and the Future of the EU' (2023) (on file with author) 1.

[40] Ibid.

achievements of the EPC are so far limited, the forum holds potential. The EPC can serve not only as an ante-chamber for EU membership—which is admittedly the primary driver for this initiative, born out of the awareness that EU enlargement will take some time.[41] The EPC can also become a platform to enlarge cooperation between the EU and the wider Europe, including both a former member like the UK and a country at war like Ukraine.

2.3 The renewal of partnerships with the Council of Europe, NATO, and the United Kingdom

Finally, the war in Ukraine led the EU to strengthen its partnerships with other regional organizations, including the CoE and NATO, and to deepen bilateral cooperation with like-minded European countries, including the UK, as well as Switzerland[42] and Norway.[43]

First, the EU strengthened its partnership with the CoE. The CoE was originally established in 1949, by a treaty concluded in London, as the first post-Second World War forum for pan-European cooperation. The CoE focuses on the protection of fundamental rights and the promotion of democracy and the rule of law, and constitutes the institutional framework of the European Convention on Human Rights (ECHR) and its Court:[44] the European Court of Human Rights (ECtHR), which since the approval of Protocol 11 in 1998 acts as the court of last instance on judicial review of human rights claims raised against any of the contracting parties.[45] The CoE had become the organization with the widest membership in the European continent and, as of early 2022, it included 47 member states: all 27 EU countries, and 20 others, including Russia. Following the illegal military aggression against Ukraine, however, the CoE decided to suspend Russia,[46] which eventually withdrew from the CoE—a step that had occurred only once in the past, when Greece temporarily exited the ECHR in the 1960s, during the Colonels' dictatorship.

---

[41] See also Roman Petrov and Christophe Hillion, 'Guest editorial: Accession through War": Ukraine's Road to the EU' (2022) 59 Common Market Law Review 1289.
[42] See eg Council of the EU press release, 'EU-Switzerland: Council adopts mandate for negotiations on future relationship', 12 March 2024; and Swiss Confederation press release, 'Federal Council approves parameters for EU negotiating mandate', 21 June 2023 (calling for a reopening of negotiation with the EU for an institutional framework agreement).
[43] See eg European Union External Action Service press release, 'Security and Defence: EU and Norway sign new partnership', 28 May 2024.
[44] See Stefanie Schmahl and Marten Breuer (eds), *The Council of Europe: Its Law and Policies* (OUP 2017).
[45] See Federico Fabbrini, *Fundamental Rights in Europe: Challenges and Transformations in Comparative Perspective* (OUP 2014).
[46] Council of Europe newsroom, 'The Russian Federation is Excluded from the Council of Europe', 16 March 2022.

Given the similarities and partial overlap between the EU and the CoE, since the 1990s multiple efforts had been made to link these organizations institutionally, and also to increase the coherence of the European system of human rights protection.[47] In fact, Article 6(2) TEU, as modified by the Lisbon Treaty, which entered into force in 2009, states the EU 'shall accede to the [ECHR]', while Article 59 ECHR, as modified by Protocol No 14, and which entered into force in 2010, states that 'the [EU] may accede this Convention'. However, these attempts failed: first in 1996[48] and then, more recently, in 2013,[49] the EU Court of Justice (ECJ) invalidated a draft treaty negotiated by the EU to accede to the ECHR. In a much discussed ruling,[50] the ECJ held inter alia that the draft accession agreement negatively interfered with the preliminary reference procedure ex Article 267 TFEU. Moreover, the ECJ noted that the draft treaty empowered the ECtHR to exercise greater jurisdiction on foreign affairs than what the ECJ can on the basis of Article 24 TEU—a problematic point as noted before in Chapter 4. The ECJ ruling seemed to foreclose any door to EU accession to the ECHR. With Russia's aggression against Ukraine, however, in January 2023 the EU reaffirmed its support for 'the [CoE], the [ECtHR] and the Human Rights Convention system as the principal instruments for upholding human rights in Europe'[51] and reintensified its efforts to secure the EU's accession to the ECHR.[52]

Secondly, the EU also strengthened its cooperation with NATO. NATO was originally established in 1949, with the Washington Treaty, by the United States (US), with Canada and 10 Western European countries. As a defensive military alliance set up in the aftermath of the Second World War, NATO had progressively expanded during the Cold War, incorporating West Germany in 1955, and eventually enlarged to most of Central and Eastern Europe after the fall of the Berlin wall.[53] In fact, as also pointed out in Chapter 2, following Russia's aggression against Ukraine, Finland and Sweden—two EU Member States which had historically embraced the principle of neutrality—applied together to enter NATO in 2022 and were admitted to the alliance in 2023 and 2024, respectively.[54] The accession of Finland and Sweden is highly significant, not only because it increased NATO countries to 32, but also because it reduced the number of EU Member

---

[47] See also Federico Fabbrini and Joris Larik, 'The Past, Present and Future of the Relations between the European Court of Justice and the European Court of Human Rights' (2016) 35 Yearbook of European Law 1.
[48] Opinion 2/94 *Accession to the ECHR* ECLI:EU:C:1996:140.
[49] Opinion 2/13 *Accession to the ECHR* ECLI:EU:C:2014:2454.
[50] See Vasiliki Kosta, Nikos Skoutaris, and Vassilis Tzevelekos(eds), *The EU Accession to the ECHR* (Hart Publishing 2014).
[51] See Council of the EU, Conclusions on EU priorities for cooperation with the Council of Europe 2023–2024, 30 January 2023, 53/23, para 16.
[52] Ibid.
[53] See Wade Jacoby, *The Enlargement of the European Union and NATO: Ordering from the Menu in Central Europe* (CUP 2004).
[54] See Carl Bildt, 'NATO's Nordic Expansion', *Foreign Affairs* (26 April 2022).

States who are not in NATO to just four small Member States, namely Austria, Cyprus, Ireland, and Malta.

Building on this reality, the EU itself has upgraded its institutional partnership with NATO, which, as explicitly recognized in Article 42(7) TEU, remains 'for those States which are members of it ... the foundation for their collective defence and the forum for its application'. In particular, in January 2023 the leaders of the two organizations released a joint declaration on EU-NATO cooperation—the third ever in their history[55]—in which they reaffirmed their 'strategic partnership'[56] and committed to take it 'to the next level'[57] with cooperation on 'growing geo-strategic competition, resilience issues, protection of critical infrastructure, emerging and disruptive technologies, space, the security implications of climate change, as well as foreign information manipulation and interference'.[58] In fact, the EU is increasingly a key institutional partner to NATO on a plurality of war-related and post-conflict tasks.[59]

Thirdly, in response to the war in Ukraine, the EU also rebuilt bridges with the UK, a former Member State. As is well known, after the Brexit referendum of June 2016[60] and complex negotiations the UK withdrew from the EU in January 2020 in accordance with the terms of a withdrawal agreement (WA).[61] Subsequently, the EU and the UK negotiated a trade and cooperation agreement (TCA) regulating their new bilateral relationship, which entered into force provisionally in January 2021, and fully in May 2021.[62] At the insistence of the UK government led by Prime Minister Boris Johnson, however, the TCA established only a bare-bone free trade agreement between the parties, with limited free movement of goods, minimal cooperation in justice and home affairs, and no partnership in defence and security. Indeed, the UK pursued a sovereignty first Brexit, and its 'preoccupation with sovereignty, which dominated its discourse, demands and action, dramatically narrowed what the UK could agree to and what the EU could offer'.[63]

Following Russia's invasion of Ukraine, however, a major *rapprochement* between the EU and the UK occurred—also thanks to changes in the UK premiership. In particular, in Autmn 2022 the UK asked to join the EU's permanent structured cooperation (PESCO) project on military mobility as a third country,

---

[55] See 2016 Warsaw Joint Declaration; and 2018 Brussels Joint Declaration.
[56] See Joint Declaration on EU-NATO Cooperation, 10 January 2023, para 9.
[57] Ibid para 12.
[58] Ibid.
[59] See Paola Mariani and Davide Genini, 'EU and NATO: The Legal Foundation of an Extraordinary Partnership' (2023) 4 Eurojus Rivista 187.
[60] Federico Fabbrini (ed), *The Law & Politics of Brexit* (OUP 2017).
[61] Federico Fabbrini (ed), *The Law & Politics of Brexit. Volume II. The Withdrawal Agreement* (OUP 2020).
[62] Federico Fabbrini (ed), *The Law & Politics of Brexit. Volume V. The Trade and Cooperation Agreement* (OUP 2024).
[63] Brigid Laffan, 'Sovereignty' in Federico Fabbrini (ed), *The Law & Politics of Brexit. Volume III. The Framework of New EU-UK Relations* (OUP 2021) 240, 250.

which the Council of the EU readily accepted.[64] Moreover, in February 2023, Prime Minister Rishi Sunak brokered a deal with the EU to adjust the Protocol on Ireland/Northern Ireland (NI) attached to the WA,[65] leading to the approval of the Windsor Framework.[66] The Protocol, by establishing a border in the Irish sea, had caused much communal tension in NI.[67] Through technical changes, the Windsor Framework contributed to rebuilding trust between the EU and the UK,[68] and the dividends of a more positive EU-UK relationship quickly spilled over to areas including financial services,[69] research and space,[70] and trade.[71] Furthermore, following the landslide victory of the Labour Party in the general election held in the UK on 4 July 2024 discussions are opening to use the TCA mandated *rendez-vous* of 2026 to expand EU-UK cooperation into new sectors—eg via an ad hoc security treaty—on the understanding that democracies based on the rule of law have to partner together to face the return of war on the European continent.[72]

3 The consequences

The EU's response to the war in Ukraine in the field of enlargement and external relations reveals the dynamism of the European integration project. Most significantly, the EU reacted to Russia's aggression against Ukraine by relaunching its enlargement policy 'as a geo-strategic investment',[73] thus confirming that EU membership remains the main avenue towards peace, freedom, security, and prosperity. As such, one of the most important consequences of Russia's aggression against Ukraine has been to open the EU's doors to up to nine new countries from the Western Balkans and Eastern Europe—thus setting the stage for a much larger

---

[64] Council of the EU press release, 'PESCO: the UK will be invited to participate in Military Mobility project', 15 November 2022.
[65] Federico Fabbrini (ed), *The Law & Politics of Brexit. Volume IV. The Protocol on Ireland/Northern Ireland* (OUP 2022).
[66] Windsor Political Declaration by the European Commission and the Government of the United Kingdom, 27 February 2023.
[67] See Dagmar Schiek, 'Brexit and the implementation of the Withdrawal Agreement' in Federico Fabbrini (ed), *The Law & Politics of Brexit. Volume III. The Framework of New EU-UK Relations* (OUP 2021) 49.
[68] See also House of Lords Sub-Committee on the Protocol on Ireland/Northern Ireland report, 'The Windsor Framework', 25 July 2023, HL Paper 237.
[69] See European Commission draft Memorandum of Understanding establishing a framework for financial services regulatory cooperation between the European Union and the United Kingdom of Great Britain and Northern Ireland, 17 May 2023.
[70] See European Commission press release, 'EU-UK Relations: Commission and UK reach political agreement on UK participation in Horizon Europe and Copernicus', 7 September 2023, IP/23/4374.
[71] See European Commission press release, 'Commission proposes one-off extension of the current rules of origin for electric vehicles and batteries under the Trade and Cooperation Agreement with the UK', 6 December 2023.
[72] See also Statement by the President of the European Commission and the Prime Minister of the United Kingdom on Enhancing Strategic Cooperation, 2 October 2024.
[73] European Council Grenada Declaration, 6 October 2023.

and wider EU. In fact, as Ukraine Foreign Minister Dmytro Kuleba pointed out, 'Ukraine acted as a true European integration locomotive for Moldova, Georgia, and the Western Balkan countries, as well as a catalyst for the historic process of the European Union expanding to Europe's natural political borders'.[74] When the Brexit vote occurred in 2016, many were concerned that this would be the end of European integration, and that other Member States would follow the UK in leaving the EU. Instead, eight years later, the EU is as lively as ever and gearing towards a new eastward expansion—in many ways more significant even than the 2004 big bang enlargement in which 10 new countries joined the EU.[75]

In particular, the grant of candidate status to Ukraine in June 2022, and the official start of accession negotiations in June 2024, was a momentous historical development. Ukraine is a country at war, and there is no precedent for such a situation in any of the prior seven rounds of EU enlargement (1973, 1981, 1984, 1995, 2004, 2007, 2013). The only exception to this may be Cyprus, an island which since 1974 has been divided, with the northern part of its territory under illegal occupation by the Turkish military, and forming a state which has not been recognized internationally by any state except Turkey itself. However, the Cypriot conflict has been frozen for decades, and although in 2004 the United Nations Secretary General Kofi Annan had successfully brokered a plan to reunite the island, which was supported by residents of the Turkish Republic of Northern Cyprus, the plan was rejected by a majority in the Republic of Cyprus. As a result, Cyprus entered the EU in 2004 as a divided state, with the effects of EU law suspended for its territory over the Green Line.[76] Yet, Cyprus poses geographical and geostrategic challenges which are of a different order of magnitude than Ukraine: so the EU's decision to promise membership to Ukraine and to start accession negotiations reveals the EU institutions' ambition to leverage enlargement as a prime geopolitical tool.

At the same time, in the aftermath of Russia's aggression against Ukraine the EU's integrationist dynamic has co-existed with a phase of institutional experimentalism in the broader European governance landscape. On the one hand, the EU has promoted the establishment of a brand new organization—the EPC— designed to bring together the EU27 with the other countries of the wider Europe. And while this forum remains currently under-institutionalized, it holds the potential both to assist candidate countries during their process of accession to the EU and to reconnect the EU with other European states, including a former member like the UK. On the other hand, the EU has deepened its cooperation with other regional and transatlantic organizations such as the CoE and NATO. In

---

[74] Dmytro Kuleba, 'Ukraine's EU accession brings added value and serves historic justice', Fondation Robert Schuman, 25 June 2024.
[75] See Marise Cremona (ed), *The Enlargement of the European Union* (OUP 2003).
[76] See Nikos Skoutaris, 'The Application of the *Acquis Communautaire* in the Areas Not under the Effective Control of the Republic of Cyprus: The Green Line Regulation' (2008) 45 Common Market Law Review 727.

fact, the CoE and NATO have themselves been revitalized by the war—suggesting that Russia's illegal aggression has contributed to strengthening the bonds that tie European states together, and reminded everyone of how *l'union fait la force*.

With regard to the CoE, the jurisprudence of the ECtHR had increasingly caused a sovereigntist backlash during the 2010s, especially in the UK. As such, several diplomatic efforts had endeavoured to limit the ECtHR[77]—a process which started with the Brighton Declaration and concluded with the approval of Protocols 15 and 16 to the ECHR, enshrining the principle of subsidiarity and the margin of appreciation in the ECHR's preamble and a preliminary reference system by which national courts can request advisory opinions from the ECtHR. Yet, following Russia's aggression and such a blatant breach of international law, the members of the CoE have rallied around the organization established to promote democracy, human rights, and the rule of law. In particular, in a major summit held in Reykjavik on 16–17 May 2023 the heads of state and government of the 46 member states of the CoE reaffirmed their unity around the common values of freedom and democracy.[78] In what constituted only the fourth summit of heads of state and government since the establishment of the CoE, the contracting parties adopted a declaration expressing unwavering support for liberal-constitutional principles and 'recommitting to the convention system as the cornerstone of the Council of Europe's protection of human rights'.[79]

Similarly, with regard to NATO, its function had been increasingly questioned in recent years. NATO had played a role during the so-called war on terrorism, with its core provision Article V—which enshrines a mutual defence pledge by all members—triggered for the first time ever after 9/11. Yet, due to recurrent quarrels among its members, in 2019 French President Emmanuel Macron famously declared the alliance 'brain dead',[80] and despite diplomatic attempts to redefine its purpose,[81] its role had become less clear at a time when Russia seemed more a partner than a threat. Russia's illegal aggression in Ukraine, however, represented a turning point. Thanks also to a supportive US administration, the return of war on the European continent has revitalized NATO, which quickly became the main institutional framework to coordinate military assistance to Ukraine. Moreover, the Russian invasion, which had often been presented in the regime propaganda as an attempt to prevent a NATO encirclement, produced exactly the opposite effect with Finland and Sweden's accession to the alliance, and the commitment

---

[77] See Jonas Christoffersen and Michael Rask Madsen (eds), *The European Court of Human Rights between Law and Politics* (OUP 2011).
[78] Reykjavik Summit of the Council of Europe, Reykjavik Declaration, United around our values, 16–17 May 2023.
[79] Ibid Appendix IV.
[80] See 'Emmanuel Macron warns Europe: NATO is becoming brain-dead', *The Economist* (7 November 2019).
[81] See NATO 2023: United for a New Era, 25 November 2020.

to Ukraine's 'irreversible path to full Euro-Atlantic integration, including NATO membership'.[82]

In fact, the strengthening of transnational cooperation in Europe through multiple forums has generated interplays, for instance between NATO expansion and EU enlargement. In particular, while the EU granted Ukraine candidate status for EU membership at the NATO summit in Vilnius on 11 July 2023, NATO also promised that Ukraine's future is in the alliance—'when Allies agree and conditions are met'.[83] In the same meeting, moreover, Turkey agreed to remove its veto on Sweden's accession to NATO also thanks to political reassurances offered by European Council President Charles Michel that the EU would re-energize its ties with Turkey, whose EU membership application has been pending since 1987.[84] Consequently, in November 2023 the European Commission and the EU High Representative for Foreign Affairs and Security published a joint communication on the state of play of EU-Turkey political, economic, and trade relations, which suggested among others a pathway to upgrade the EU-Turkey customs union.[85] As such, it appears that the war in Ukraine has had profound consequences for transnational cooperation across the continent, through different forms of sovereignty sharing.

4 The challenges

Nevertheless, the prospects of European transnational cooperation generally and of EU enlargement specifically face a number of major obstacles. In fact, it cannot be downplayed how not only the entry of Sweden into NATO was unnecessarily delayed for idiosyncratic reasons by Turkey and Hungary—but even the opening of accession negotiations with Ukraine in December 2023 was the result of theatrical politicking: since Hungary opposed this decision, and technically had a right to veto it given the requirement of unanimity, the European Council could agree to open accession negotiations with Ukraine[86] only after Hungary's Prime Minister Viktor Orban conveniently left the meeting room at the time of voting, allowing the other 26 heads of state and government to greenlight the process.[87] Because, according to EU enlargement rules, progress in the negotiations of each accession chapter requires unanimity among the EU27, which must also

---

[82] NATO Washington Summit Declaration, 10 July 2024, para 16.
[83] NATO Vilnius Summit Communiqué, 11 July 2023, para 11.
[84] See Matina Stevis-Gridneff, 'Will Turkey become a member of the E.U. now?', *The New York Times* (11 July 2023).
[85] European Commission and High Representative, Joint Communication on the State of Play of EU-Turkiye political, economic and trade relations, 29 November 2023, JOIN(2023) 0050.
[86] European Council conclusions, 14–15 December 2023, EUCO 20/23, para 15.
[87] See Philippe Jacqué et al, 'Accession Talks with Ukraine: How the EU Managed to Avoid an Hungarian Veto', *Le Monde* (15 December 2023).

unanimously approve a final accession treaty, ultimately, from a political point of view, the entry of a new Member State in the EU 'is by no means certain'.[88] Furthermore, beyond questions of public support,[89] from a legal point of view, there are a number of challenges that surround enlargement, having to do with the candidate countries' preparation, the EU's preparation, and the stalemate in EU reforms.

4.1 Candidate countries' preparation

Article 49 TEU proclaims that 'Any European State which respects the values referred to in Article 2 and is committed to promoting them may apply to become a member of the [EU]'. The values indicated in Article 2 TEU are 'respect for human dignity, freedom, democracy, equality, the rule of law and respect for human rights, including the rights of persons belonging to minorities'. Since the European Council meeting of Copenhagen in 1993, accession of new Member States to the EU has been governed by four criteria—the Copenhagen criteria, which are: (i) respect for the rule of law; (ii) a functioning market economy; (iii) compliance with the EU *acquis*; as well as (iv) the EU's internal ability to absorb new Member States (which is discussed below). Specifically: 'Membership requires that the candidate country has achieved stability of institutions guaranteeing democracy, the rule of law, human rights and respect for and protection of minorities, the existence of a functioning market economy as well as the capacity to cope with competitive pressure and market forces within the Union. Membership presupposes the candidate's ability to take on the obligations of membership.'[90]

As things currently stand, leaving aside the fact that support for EU membership is low in most candidate countries, none of them meet the Copenhagen criteria and are therefore ready to join the EU.[91] Just by way of example, North Macedonia is experiencing a nationalist turn and has refused to amend its constitution to recognize the Bulgarian minority, as the EU requested;[92] Serbia has not aligned with any of the EU CFSP measures, nurturing relations with China and Russia; and Georgia has recently passed a law, inspired by Russia and opposed by the EU and the US, that requires any organization receiving foreign funding to register as a

---

[88] Sergio Fabbrini, 'From multi-speed to multi-tier: making Europe fit for herself' in Göran von Sydow and Valentin Kreilinger (eds), *Fit for 35? Reforming the Politics and Institutions of the EU for an Enlarged Union* (Swedish Institute for European Political Studies 2023) 69, 76.
[89] See also Eurobarometer, June 2023, https://europa.eu/eurobarometer/surveys/detail/3052 (reporting that 64% of respondents among European citizens agree with the EU granting candidate status as a potential member of the EU to Ukraine).
[90] European Council, Conclusion of the Presidency, Copenhagen, 21–22 June 1993, s 7, para A, iii).
[91] Dimitar Bechev, 'Can EU Enlargement Work?', Carnegie Europe, 20 June 2024.
[92] Katerina Kolozova, 'Freins nationalistes et impensés géopolitiques: le cas spécifique de la Macédonie du Nord', Fondation Robert Schuman Policy Paper no 748, 6 May 2024.

foreign agent and be subjected to pervasive governmental controls.[93] Most importantly, Ukraine faces major challenges on its preparation towards EU membership:[94] the country suffers from systemic problems of corruption, as evident by the arrest of the President of the Supreme Court for taking bribes,[95] and has only recently ratified the Rome Statute on the International Criminal Court; martial law introduced in response to Russia's war of aggression has led to the indefinite suspension of elections, the most basic form of democratic accountability;[96] and there are questions as to whether a hyper-nationalist country emerging from a life-or-death struggle can fit into the EU, a supranational organization which has been designed to tame nationalism.[97]

The EU Commission has openly acknowledged these problems. In its November 2023 communication on enlargement it duly reported the systemic problems faced by accession countries[98]—from 'political instability, tensions, the weak functioning of democratic and judicial institutions' in Montenegro,[99] arguably the most advanced candidate state, to 'the complete disagreement with the EU approach of Turkey',[100] a state with which negotiations are 'at a standstill'.[101] Nevertheless the Commission's deeds have not followed its words.[102] Despite the structural problems, the Commission has recommended advancing enlargement and opening the accession negotiations—in the case of Ukraine and Moldova with the caveat 'provided it continues its reform effort',[103] and in the case of Georgia 'on the understanding that' the country will take several further steps.[104] Yet, despite official proclamations that enlargement will be based on the candidate country's 'own merits',[105] this approach sends the wrong signal that accession is largely driven by political priorities.

Furthermore, the Commission has also weakened the internal EU mechanisms of rule of law enforcement and conditionality that could have assisted in the enlargement process. In particular, in September 2023, the Commission

---

[93] Ivan Nechepurenko, 'Georgia's Ruling Party Secures a Contentious Law on Foreign Influence', *The New York Times* (28 May 2024).
[94] Roman Petrov, 'Bumpy Road of Ukraine towards the EU Membership in Time of War: "Accession through War" v "Gradual Integration"' (2023) 8 European Papers 1057.
[95] See Daniel Victor, 'The Chief of Ukraine's Supreme Court has been detained and accused of taking a $2.7 million bribe', *The New York Times* (16 May 2023).
[96] See 'Volodymyr Zelensky's presidential term expires on May 20th', *The Economist* (16 May 2024).
[97] See Simone Attilio Bellezza, *Identità ucraina: storia del movimento nazionale dal 1800 a oggi* (Laterza 2024). See also Laszlo Bruszt and Erik Jones, 'Ukraine's Perilous Path to EU Membership: How to Expand Europe without Destabilizing It', *Foreign Affairs* (30 May 2024).
[98] European Commission Communication (n 13).
[99] Ibid 17.
[100] Ibid 22.
[101] Ibid 21.
[102] See also European Commission President Ursula von der Leyen Statement (n 4).
[103] European Commission Communication (n 13) 23, 24.
[104] Ibid 25.
[105] See eg Conference on Accession to the European Union—Ukraine, General EU Position, 21 June 2024, AD 9/24, Negotiating Framework, para 2

terminated the post-accession Cooperation and Verification Mechanism (CVM) with Romania and Bulgaria[106]—a special process of enhanced surveillance which had been put in place for the two Member States that joined the EU in 2007, and that still suffer from severe problems of internal corruption. This abrupt decision was not motivated by any real improvement by the two Member States concerned. Moreover, it was also followed in May 2024 by the decision to end the Article 7 TEU procedure against Poland,[107] which had started in 2017 following the Polish government's attack against the independence of the judiciary, also discussed in Chapter 3.[108] Yet, once again, no real legal change had occurred in Poland—save for the election in October 2023 of a pro-EU government. But the latter's effort to undo the action of its predecessor had been blocked by the Polish President and the courts. All in all, therefore, besides weakening the internal rule of law enforcement mechanisms,[109] the Commission appears to have conveniently disregarded egregious failures in the preparations of accession countries, which does not bode well either for accession negotiations or for the future of the EU.

4.2 EU preparation

Besides the preparations of candidate countries, in line with the Copenhagen criteria a fourth factor that should shape enlargement is the EU's preparation. At the time of the big-bang enlargement in 2004, the European Commission had already recognized that a critical factor in managing the accession of new Member States was the EU's 'absorption capacity, or rather integration capacity'.[110] The Commission defined this 'functional concept'[111] as the EU's capacity to 'take in new members at a given moment or in a given period, without jeopardizing the political and policy objectives established by the Treaties'.[112] From a substantive perspective, the Commission connected this absorption capacity with the functioning of the EU institutions, the delivery of EU policies, and the operation of the

---

[106] European Commission press release 'Rule of Law: Commission formally closes the Cooperation and Verification Mechanism for Bulgaria and Romania', 15 September 2023.
[107] European Commission press release, 'Commission intends to close Article 7/1) TEU procedure for Poland', 6 May 2024, IP/24/2461.
[108] European Commission reasoned proposal in accordance with Article 7(1) Treaty on European Union for a Council Decision on the determination of a clear risk of a serious breach by the Republic of Poland of the rule of law, 20 December 2017, COM(2017) 835 final.
[109] See Kim Lane Scheppele, 'The Treaties Without a Guardian: The European Commission and the Rule of Law' (2023) 29 Columbia Journal of European Law 93; and Daniel Kelemen, 'The European Union's failure to address the autocracy crisis: MacGyver, Rube Goldberg and Europe's Unused Tools' (2023) 45 Journal of European Integration 223.
[110] European Commission Communication 'Enlargement Strategy and Main Challenges 2006-2007, including annexed special report on the EU's capacity to integrate new members', 8 November 2006, COM(2006) 649 final, 17.
[111] Ibid.
[112] Ibid.

EU budget, while also emphasizing the importance of maintaining public support for the enlargement process.

By this standard, the prospect of enlargement to up to nine new Member States raises major challenges for the EU. In particular, Ukraine's potential accession poses a puzzle. On the one hand, the country is currently at war, with one-fifth of its territory under enemy occupation. On the other hand, with a prewar population of approximately 41 million people, a GDP per capita of approximately US$4,500,[113] Ukraine would become the fifth most populous EU Member State, the primary beneficiary of structural and agriculture funds, and a major game-changer for the functioning of the EU.[114] In fact, also considering the cost of post-war reconstruction, early estimates have concluded that Ukraine's accession to the EU would have significant budgetary consequences for the EU—and while some analysts have described these costs as 'manageable',[115] others have rather highlighted how adding nine new EU Member States would turn most current Member States into net contributors to the EU budget.[116]

In March 2024, the European Commission published a communication on pre-enlargement reforms and policy review, where it explored 'the implications of a larger EU in four main areas: values, policies, budget and governance'.[117] In this document, which also indicated the possibility of partial integration of candidate countries in EU policies before their accession, the Commission clearly reaffirmed the importance of safeguarding values of democracy and respect for the rule of law in the enlargement process,[118] and openly outlined the consequence of enlargement for the EU's functioning and funding. With regard to the EU budget, the Commission acknowledged that the accession of new, poorer Member States 'will put pressure on the future long-term EU budget',[119] and consequently stated that 'future EU spending programmes should be developed with future enlargement in mind'.[120] With regard to EU governance, furthermore, the Commission underlined how 'an enlarged Union of 30+ Member States triggers immediate questions on the composition of the EU institutions'[121]—and will also 'inevitably entail more work for the EU institutions in many areas'.[122]

---

[113] World Bank, 'GDP per capita (current US$): Ukraine' https://data.worldbank.org/indicator/NY.GDP.PCAP.CD?locations=UA.

[114] See Steven Blockmans, 'The Impact of Ukrainian Membership on the EU's Institutions and Internal Balance of Power', International Centre for Defence and Security, November 2023.

[115] Michael Emerson, 'The Potential Impact of Ukrainian Accession on the EU's budget—and the importance of control valves', International Centre for Defence and Security, September 2023.

[116] Lisa O'Carroll, 'Adding nine countries to EU to cost existing members more than €250 billion', *The Guardian* (4 October 2023).

[117] European Commission Communication on 'Pre-enlargement reforms and policy reviews', 20 March 2024, COM(2024) 146 final 2.

[118] Ibid 4.

[119] Ibid 18.

[120] Ibid.

[121] Ibid 20.

[122] Ibid.

Nevertheless, the Commission has been very cautious in outlining what institutional and constitutional changes would be needed to prepare the EU for enlargement.[123] This also reflect the ambiguities of the European Council: in the October 2023 Grenada Declaration—delivered on the occasion of the third EPC summit—the European Council stated that 'Looking ahead to the prospect of a further enlarged Union, both the EU and future Member States need to be ready. [... T]he Union needs to lay the necessary internal groundwork and reforms'[124]—a statement it repeated with the same words in its December 2023 conclusions.[125] However, the European Council only referred generally to the EU's 'capacity to act' without clarifying what reforms to the functioning and funding of the EU would be needed to achieve this objective; and in March 2024 it merely recalled 'that work on both tracks needs to advance in parallel to ensure that both future Member States and the EU are ready at the time of accession'.[126] Eventually, in June 2024 the Belgian Presidency of the Council of the EU published a progress report on the Future of Europe,[127] which condensed the state of the discussion on EU reforms at Member State level, and restated the objective to work on four priority areas—namely, EU values, EU policies, EU budget, and EU governance—with a tentative roadmap.

However, in its conclusions of 27 June 2024 the European Council once again largely skirted the issue of EU reforms,[128] focusing rather on the appointment of the new EU top jobs[129]—Antonio Costa as European Council President, Ursula von der Leyen as the next European Commission President, and Kaja Kallas as the new High Representative—and approving the new EU Strategic Agenda for 2024–2029,[130] which called for a free and democratic, strong, and secure, as well as prosperous and competitive Europe. In the summit, the European Council once more underlined 'the need to lay the necessary internal groundwork and reforms to fulfil the Union's long-term ambitions and address key questions related to its priorities and policies as well as its capacity to act'[131] and repeated that work on reforms 'should advance in parallel with the enlargement process'.[132] On substance, nevertheless, the European Council simply restated the four areas on which reforms should focus—once again: values, policies, budget, and governance[133]—indicating

---

[123] European Commission press release, 'Commission prepares for pre-enlargement reforms and policy reviews', 20 March 2024.
[124] European Council Grenada Declaration, 6 October 2023.
[125] European Council conclusions, 14–15 December 2023, EUCO 20/23 para 13.
[126] European Council conclusions, 21–22 March 2023, EUCO 7/24, para 29.
[127] Council of the EU, Presidency Progress Report: 'Future of Europe', 10 June 2024, Doc 10411/24.
[128] European Council conclusions, 27 June 2024, EUCO 15/24.
[129] Ibid s VI.
[130] Ibid Annex.
[131] Ibid para 48.
[132] Ibid para 49.
[133] Ibid para 50.

that 'it will review progress [in a year's time,] in June 2025 and give further guidance as needed'.[134]

Yet, this state of affairs is highly problematic. As Sylvie Goulard has argued, enlarging the EU without profoundly reforming it risks compromising the entire project of integration—as the union will grow to the point of exploding.[135] In fact, as previous chapters have pointed out, the EU constitution suffers from several substantive and institutional shortcomings which ultimately prevent it from rising to the geopolitical challenges of the moment. So, as former European Central Bank President Mario Draghi has argued, 'radical change ... is what is needed'.[136] As things are, the EU itself cannot secure the blessing of liberty to which Ukraine aspires, as it lacks the fiscal capacity and military capability to deter foreign aggression. And if Ukraine and possibly eight other countries from Eastern Europe and the Western Balkans were to join the EU à traité constant, the ability of an EU at 35 to provide security and prosperity would further decrease, given the burden of unanimous decision-making. Hence internal constitutional reforms are needed to avoid making EU membership an empty promise, and to prepare properly for enlargement.

4.3 The stagnation of constitutional reforms

The debate on EU constitutional reforms has been ongoing for several years—at least since Brexit.[137] In particular, a strong driver has been the Conference on the Future of Europe—which had been originally envisaged by French President Emmanuel Macron in March 2019[138] as a way to relaunch the project of European integration after the UK's withdrawal. The Conference took off, after delays due to the Covid-19 pandemic, on 9 May 2021, and came to a close a year later on 9 May 2022, when the war in Ukraine was already raging.[139] The Conference was organized as a citizen-focused, bottom-up exercise designed to gain input from European citizens on the key questions facing the EU. This innovative participatory process unfolded through a multilayered structure. The core of the Conference was represented by four European citizens' panels of 200 participants each, selected randomly to reflect the socio-demographic reality of the EU, which met both in person and remotely over several months. The input from the European citizens' panels—together with that resulting from analogous national processes—were

---

[134] Ibid para 51.
[135] Sylvie Goulard, *L'Europe enfla si bien qu'elle creva: De 27 à 36 Etats?* (Tallandier 2024).
[136] Mario Draghi, Speech at the High-Level Conference on the European Pillar of Social Rights, Brussels, 16 April 2024.
[137] Federico Fabbrini, *Brexit and the Future of the European Union: The Case for Constitutional Reforms* (OUP 2020).
[138] French President Emmanuel Macron, Lettre pour une Renaissance Européenne, 4 March 2019.
[139] See also Conference on the Future of Europe digital platform, https://futureu.europa.eu/.

then reported to the Plenary of the Conference on the Future of Europe, which deliberated on it. Ultimately, the Plenary endorsed 49 proposals with a list of 326 detailed recommendations, which were submitted to the executive board and released in a final report published on Europe Day 2022.[140]

The Conference on the Future of Europe's final report explicitly identified a number of shortcomings in the current EU constitutional structure and made the case for several substantive and institutional amendments to the EU treaties. The Conference, in particular, called for a strengthening of EU powers, with the expansion of EU competences among others in the fields of health, energy, digital technology, migration, and foreign affairs and security. Moreover, the Conference requested an overhaul of the EU decision-making system, with the overcoming of the unanimity rule, particularly in the field of foreign affairs and defence, and a clarification of the roles of the EU institutions. Finally, the Conference also underlined the importance of endowing the EU with the financial means to back up its actions, including by reproducing the Next Generation EU (NGEU) funding model beyond the Covid-19 pandemic. At the same time, the Conference pleaded for 'reopening the discussion about the [EU] constitution'[141] on the understanding that: 'A constitution may help to be more precise as well as involve citizens and agree on the rules of the decision-making process.'[142] All in all, therefore, the Conference called for a more sovereign federal EU.

In fact, a number of policy-makers immediately embraced the ambitious outcome of the Conference on the Future of Europe. Both French President Emmanuel Macron and then Italian Prime Minister Mario Draghi endorsed the idea of amending the EU treaties.[143] Moreover, European Commission President Ursula von der Leyen voiced support for this prospect,[144] also in the guidelines she presented in July 2024 to the European Parliament for re-election, where she stated that '[w]hile reforms were necessary before, with enlargement they become indispensable.... I believe we need Treaty change'.[145] Most importantly, the European Parliament called for a comprehensive follow-up to the Conference's outcome, including via treaty changes.[146] In fact, in a resolution approved in November 2023 the European Parliament proposed a detailed list of amendments to the EU treaties, dealing both with substantive competences and institutional mechanisms

---

[140] Conference on the Future of Europe, Report on the Final Outcome, 9 May 2022, 93.
[141] Ibid Proposal 39, recommendation 7.
[142] Ibid.
[143] Italian Prime Minister Mario Draghi, Speech at the European Parliament, 3 May 2022, official English translation available at https://www.governo.it/en/articolo/prime-minister-mario-draghi-s-address-european-parliament/19748.
[144] Commission President Ursula von der Leyen, speech, Strasbourg, 9 May 2022, SPEECH/22/2944.
[145] European Commission President-elect Ursula von der Leyen, 'Europe's Choice: Political Guidelines for the next European Commission 2024-2029', 18 July 2024, 30.
[146] European Parliament resolution of 4 May 2022 on the follow-up to the conclusions of the Conference on the Future of Europe, P9_TA(2022) 0141.

of decision-making, and called for the convening of a convention under Article 48(3) TEU to examine them.[147] Furthermore, in another resolution adopted in February 2024, the European Parliament called for a deepening of EU integration in view of future enlargements,[148] stating that 'widening and deepening the EU must go in parallel'[149] but clarifying that 'pre-enlargement reforms are needed to guarantee the efficient functioning of the enlarged EU and its capacity to absorb new members'.[150]

Nevertheless, the enthusiasm for constitutional change generated by the Conference on the Future of Europe was met with equally resolute opposition in other quarters. In a joint non-paper released on the very same day of the Conference's conclusion, in May 2022, 13 Member States from northern and eastern Europe – Bulgaria, Croatia, the Czech Republic, Denmark, Estonia, Finland, Latvia, Lithuania, Malta, Poland, Romania, Slovenia, and Sweden – clearly indicated that they did 'not support unconsidered and premature attempts to launch a process towards Treaty change'.[151] In fact, visions of the EU as a polity, which requires greater federalization, are politically and institutionally contested by competing visions of the EU as a market, or an autocracy, which push in very different directions.[152] In particular, Hungarian Prime Minister Viktor Orban—who has recently established a new European Parliament far-right parliamentary group named 'Patriots for Europe' (now the third largest faction in the European Parliament)—has skilfully exploited the opportunities of the current treaty framework, as discussed in Chapter 3.[153] As a result, the implementation of the Conference on the Future of Europe's outcome has stalled: two years after the Conference's end, its most significant proposals remain on hold, and the European Parliament's request to call a convention to revise the treaties has not even been considered by the Council.

Given the obstacles to amending the EU treaties,[154] several alternative options have recently moved to the centre of the debate on how to prepare for an enlarged EU. In particular, the use of *passerelle* clauses to change decision-making rules, notably in CFSP, has been increasingly considered.[155] *Passerelle* clauses allow for a

---

[147] European Parliament resolution of 22 November 2023 on proposals of the European Parliament for the amendment of the Treaties, P9_TA(2023) 0427.
[148] European Parliament resolution of 29 February 2024 on deepening EU integration in view of future enlargement, P9_TA(2024) 0120.
[149] Ibid para K.
[150] Ibid para U.
[151] Government of Sweden press release, 9 May 2022.
[152] Fabbrini (n 137).
[153] See Daniel Kelemen, 'The European Union's Failure to Address the Autocracy Crisis: MacGyver, Rube Goldberg and Europe's Unused Tools' (2023) 45 Journal of European Integration 223.
[154] See also Dermot Hodson and Imelda Maher, *The Transformation of EU Treaty Making* (CUP 2018).
[155] See Ramses Wessel and Viktor Szép, 'The implementation of Article 31 of the TEU and the use of qualified majority voting', study requested by the European Parliament Constitutional Affairs Committee, November 2022.

shift from unanimity to qualified majority voting (QMV) in the Council of the EU, *à traité constant*. Article 48(7) TEU foresees generally that when the EU treaties provide 'for the Council to act by unanimity in a given area or case, the European Council may adopt a decision authorising the Council to act by a qualified majority in that area or in that case'. Moreover, specific *passerelle* clauses are scattered across the treaties for specific policies.[156] Building on this, on 4 May 2023, nine Member States—Belgium, Finland, France, Germany, Italy, Luxembourg, the Netherlands, Spain, and Slovenia: all except the last from Western Europe—released a joint statement launching the group of friends of QMV in CFSP.[157] This was followed by a supportive resolution of the European Parliament on 11 July 2023, which called for using *passerelle* clauses at the earliest.[158]

Yet, the strategy to leverage the *passerelle* clauses has its hurdles. On the one hand, triggering a *passerelle* clause would still require unanimity in the European Council, which is not a given, due to the hold-out position of several Member States. Furthermore, Article 48(7) TEU empowers a single national parliament to block the use of a *passerelle* clause, even if approved by heads of state and government in the European Council, within six months. Lastly, the same provision explicitly prohibits applying the *passerelle* 'to decisions with military implications or those in the area of defence'. On the other hand, there is no escaping that the *passerelle* can achieve only so much. The EU governance structure suffers from a number of shortcomings, and enhancing the legitimacy and effectiveness of the EU requires adjustments which can only be addressed through proper treaty changes. For example, a greater role for the European Parliament in fiscal and budgetary matters is a democratic need, especially after the establishment of the NGEU, but this can be achieved only through revisions to several treaty provisions.[159]

Given these challenges, policy-makers have also increasingly looked at alternative options to advance European integration. In particular, in September 2023 a group of experts jointly appointed by the French and German governments proposed a series of recommendations to reform and enlarge the EU for the 21st century.[160] Their report outlined six options for reforms, including the approval of a supplementary reform treaty between willing Member States if there is deadlock on treaty change.[161] Indeed, there are precedents of groups

---

[156] See TFEU, art 81(3) (measures concerning family law); art 153(2) (measures concerning employment and social security); art 192(2) (measures concerning environmental policy); art 312(2) (measures related to the MFF).

[157] Joint Statement of the Foreign Ministries on the Launch of the Group of Friends on Qualified Majority Voting in EU Common Foreign and Security Policy, 4 May 2023.

[158] European Parliament resolution of 11 July 2023 on the implementation of the passerelle clauses in the EU Treaties, P9_TA(2023) 0269.

[159] Federico Fabbrini, *EU Fiscal Capacity: Legal Integration after Covid-19 and the War in Ukraine* (OUP 2022) 141.

[160] See Report of the Franco-German working group on EU institutional reform, 'Sailing on High Seas: Reforming and Enlarging the EU for the 21st Century', Paris-Berlin, 19 September 2023.

[161] Ibid 35 ff.

of vanguard Member States that have concluded separate inter se intergovernmental agreements on the side of the EU,[162] and differentiated integration has admittedly become a feature of the contemporary EU.[163] Along this line, a proposal would be to adopt a Political Compact to advance integration overcoming the veto of hostile Member States.[164] Otherwise, Article 49 TEU states that institutional adjustments to the EU and its functioning can also be achieved in the framework of new accession treaties. While this provision has traditionally been interpreted to refer only to the minimal changes to the institutions that necessarily result from the entry of a new EU Member State, a more ambitious reading of it would be to tie enlargement and wider reforms into a single agreement.[165] Yet, this avenue would delay EU reforms until enlargement happens—and it remains to be seen if this is feasible, so in this context it cannot be excluded that transnational cooperation through forums like the EPC will turn out to be the main way forward.

5 Conclusion

This chapter has examined how the war in Ukraine impacted on EU enlargement and transnational cooperation in Europe. The chapter explained how in response to Russia's aggression against Ukraine, the EU relaunched its enlargement process—notably by opening accession negotiations with Ukraine—promoted the establishment of a new EPC, and deepened its ties with other regional organizations like the CoE and NATO, and a former member like the UK. As the chapter has argued, the return of large-scale warfare on the European continent for the first time since the end of the Second World War ultimately contributed to reaffirm the role of the EU as a beacon of peace, security, freedom, and prosperity. In fact, Ukraine's request to join the EU just days after Russia's invasion showcased how EU membership is associated by third countries in the European continent with the blessings of liberty. Furthermore, beyond the EU, the war in Ukraine served as a trigger to rejuvenate organizations like the CoE and NATO, to launch a new forum such as the EPC, and indeed to strengthen the interplay between these entities—all inspired by the belief in transnational cooperation.

---

[162] See eg Treaty Establishing the European Stability Mechanism, 25 March 2011; and Treaty on Stability, Coordination and Governance in the Economic and Monetary Union, 2 March 2012.
[163] See Frank Schimmelfennig and Thomas Winzen, *Ever Looser Union? Differentiated European Integration* (OUP 2020).
[164] See further Federico Fabbrini, 'Possible Avenues towards Further Political Integration: A Political Compact for a More Democratic and Effective Union', study commissioned by the European Parliament Constitutional Affairs Committee, June 2020.
[165] See also Bruno de Witte, 'Constitutional Challenges of the Enlargement: Is Further Enlargement Feasible without Constitutional Change', study commissioned by the European Parliament Constitutional Affairs Committee, March 2019, 4.

Nevertheless, as the chapter has pointed out, a number of challenges lie ahead, both for regional integration generally and for EU enlargement specifically. With regard to the EU accession of Ukraine, and possibly eight other countries from the Western Balkans and Eastern Europe in particular, there are issues concerned both with the candidates' preparations and with the EU's own readiness: while accession countries are currently far from meeting the Copenhagen criteria—the minimal conditions necessary to join the EU—the EU itself currently lacks the capacity to absorb and integrate new members. This is a result of the stalemate in constitutional reforms, which despite being called for by multiple institutions—including the Conference on the Future of Europe and the European Parliament—have so far been blocked by a number of recalcitrant Member States. In this context, however, it remains uncertain whether the EU can really enlarge, and, if it does, whether it would survive its expansion. Alternative avenues, including the EPC, may thus emerge as necessary to advance integration in the short term—ironically also opening an opportunity for a former member like the UK to reconnect with the EU. In conclusion, if the war in Ukraine has reaffirmed the EU's blessing of liberty, and indeed the dynamism of the European project, creativeness may be needed to shape the future of Europe in times ahead.

7
Conclusion

1 Introduction

This book has examined the operation of the EU constitution in time of war. Russia's illegal aggression against Ukraine forced the EU to face—effectively for the first time—the perennial challenge of war. As an organization established to preserve internal peace, since Russia's invasion of Ukraine in February 2022 the EU had to repurpose its machinery of government to deal with external war. Indeed, the return of conventional warfare on the European continent for the first time since the end of the Second World War shattered European expectations about perpetual peace and required the EU institutions to deal with the reality of hard power. How has the EU constitution fared in wartime? This book has answered this question by advancing a nuanced, threefold argument. First, the EU constitution has proved flexible enough to enable the EU institutions to enact groundbreaking measures to support Ukraine. Secondly, however, the EU constitution has also revealed a number of substantive and institutional shortcomings: these have either prevented fast and vigorous EU action when needed, on the one hand, or failed to constrain EU action properly to protect important values such as human rights and the rule of law, on the other. For this reason, the book lastly maintains that the EU constitution needs to be reformed for good, especially in view of the prospect of enlargement and the ever more threatening geo-political environment.

2 The flexible constitution

The EU constitution has proved flexible in time of war. As argued by Alberto de Gregorio Merino, the Director of the Legal Service of the European Commission, the EU treaties have worked 'as a living constitution of the [EU] in times of crises'.[1] Indeed, as a growing body of literature has pointed out, in the past decade the EU has weathered a succession of crises[2]—the euro-crisis, the rule of law crisis, the migration crisis, Brexit, the Covid-19 pandemic, and Russia's aggression against Ukraine. Yet, in the absence of EU treaty changes, 'an evolutive reading of the

---

[1] Alberto de Gregorio Merino, 'The EU Treaties as a Living Constitution of the Union in Times of Crisis' (2024) 118 American Journal of International Law 162.

[2] See eg Francesca Bignami (ed), *EU Law in Populist Times: Crises and Prospects* (CUP 2020).

treaties [became] necessary to avoid a stasis that could compromise the very future of the EU project'.[3] In times of crises or emergency, international institutions like the EU leverage powers in ways which 'shares much in common with that of domestic institutions'[4]—and this is clearly visible following the start of the war in Ukraine. As Elena Chachko and Katerina Linos have pointed out, the EU 'built on the emergencies created by the Russian invasion along key fronts to advance unprecedented measures that inject new life into EU integration'.[5] This book has mapped this trend across five *substantive* EU policy areas, namely: (1) foreign affairs and security; (2) economic and fiscal policy; (3) justice and home affairs; (4) energy and industrial policy; and (5) enlargement and reforms.

As explained in Chapter 2, the EU responded to Russia's illegal aggression against Ukraine by adopting groundbreaking measures in the framework of Common Foreign and Security Policy (CFSP). The EU adopted a new strategic compass,[6] granted joint security guarantees to Ukraine,[7] and set up a major Military Assistance Mission (EUMAM Ukraine) to train almost 60,000 Ukraine troops on advanced weapons technology.[8] Moreover, leveraging Article 173 TFEU—the sole legal basis on industry—and Article 114 TFEU—the internal market legal basis, which was confirmed in its role 'as an effective federalization tool'[9]—the EU adopted an Act in Support of Ammunition Production (ASAP),[10] which for the first time set aside money from the EU budget to fund the joint production and procurement of weapons and missiles. Moreover, on the basis of Article 173 TFEU the EU also approved a European defence industry reinforcement through common procurement act (EDIRPA),[11] which invested in the development of the EU Defence Technological and Industrial Base (EDTIB); and proposed, on the basis of Articles 114 and 173 TFEU, the European Defence Industry Programme (EDIP),[12] designed to supranationalize EU defence industrial policy in wartime.

---

[3] See de Gregorio Merino (n 1) 162.
[4] Elena Chachko and Katerina Linos, 'Ukraine and the Emergency Powers of International Institutions' (2022) 116 American Journal of International Law 775, 778.
[5] Ibid 776.
[6] Council of the EU, 'A strategic compass for security and defence: For a European Union that protects its citizens, values and interests and contributes to international peace and security', 21 March 2022, Doc 7371/22.
[7] Joint Security Commitments between the European Union and Ukraine, 27 June 2024.
[8] Council Decision (CFSP) 2022/2245 of 14 November 2022 on an assistance measure under the European Peace Facility to support the Ukrainian Armed Forces trained by the European Union Military Assistance Mission of Ukraine with military equipment, and platforms, designed to deliver lethal force [2022] OJ L294/25.
[9] See de Gregorio Merino (n 1) 162.
[10] Regulation (EU) 2023/1525 of the European Parliament and of the Council of 20 July 2023 on supporting ammunition production (ASAP) [2023] OJ L185/7.
[11] Regulation (EU) 2023/2418 of the European Parliament and of the Council of 18 October 2023 on establishing an instrument for the reinforcement of the European defence industry through common procurement (EDIRPA) [2023] OJ L1.
[12] European Commission proposal for a regulation of the European Parliament and of the Council establishing the European Defence Industry Programme and a framework of measures to ensure the timely availability and supply of defence products, 5 March 2024, COM(2024) 150 final.

Furthermore, as argued in Chapter 3, the EU reacted to the war in Ukraine in the field of economic and fiscal affairs by building on the legacy of the Next Generation EU (NGEU) Recovery Fund created in response to the Covid-19 pandemic.[13] If the establishment of 'NGEU within the existing legal framework proves that the potential of the European treaties is far from exhausted',[14] the EU's effort to support Ukraine financially in wartime revealed a trend towards the consolidation of an EU fiscal capacity. In particular, after deploying the intergovernmental European Peace Facility (EPF),[15] and progressively expanding its budget from €5.6 billion up to €17 billion, the EU set up a Macro-Financial Assistance Instrument for Ukraine (MFA+), worth €18 billion for 2023,[16] and a Ukraine Facility (UF)[17] worth €50 billion from 2024 to 2027. Both the MFA+ and the UF, which are based on Article 212 TFEU, on economic, financial, and technical cooperation with third countries, empower the Commission to issue common EU debt on the financial markets, in combination with an amendment of the EU Multi-Annual Financial Framework (MFF) spending ceiling.

As underlined in Chapter 4, the EU also adopted major war-related measures in the field of justice and home affairs, either by activating laws such as the temporary protection directive,[18] which was on the books but dormant, or by pushing new legal boundaries. In particular, between February 2022 and June 2024, the EU resorted to Articles 29 TEU and 215 TFEU—the legal bases on restrictive measures—to adopt 14 rounds of wide-ranging sanctions against Russia, including for the first time secondary sanctions, targeting natural or legal persons who facilitated the circumvention of already-imposed sanctions. Furthermore, it added the violation of restrictive measures to the list of 'EU crimes' included in Article 83(1) TFEU.[19] At the same time, it also took steps to restore a modicum of justice towards Ukraine by deciding to forfeit the extraordinary revenues resulting from the Russian Central Bank (RCB) assets immobilized as a result of sanctions. Specifically, the Council used sanction powers to require EU-based central securities depositories (CSDs)

---

[13] Federico Fabbrini, *EU Fiscal Capacity: Legal Integration after Covid-19 and the War in Ukraine* (OUP 2022).

[14] Franz Mayer, 'NextGenerationEU and the Future of European Integration: Foreseeing the Unforeseeable' (2024) 118 American Journal of International Law 172, 174.

[15] Council Decision (CFSP) 2021/509 of 22 March 2021 establishing a European Peace Facility and repealing Decision (CFSP) 2015/528 [2021] OJ L102/14.

[16] Regulation (EU) 2022/2463 of the European Parliament and the Council of 14 December 2022 establishing an instrument for providing support to Ukraine for 2023 (macro-financial assistance +) [2022] OJ L322/1.

[17] Regulation (EU) 2024/792 of the European Parliament and the Council of 29 February 2024 establishing the Ukraine Facility [2024] OJ L1.

[18] Council Implementing Decision (EU) 2022/382 of 4 March 2022 establishing the existence of a mass influx of displaced persons from Ukraine within the meaning of Article 5 of Directive 2001/55/EC, and having the effect of introducing temporary protection [2022] OJ L71/1.

[19] Council Decision (EU) 2022/2332 of 28 November 2022 on identifying the violation of Union restrictive measures as an area of crime that meets the criteria specified in Article 83(1) of the Treaty on the Functioning of the European Union [2022] OJ L308/18.

to account separately the extraordinary cash balances accumulating on RCB frozen assets,[20] and subsequently ordered CSDs to transfer these windfall profits as a financial contribution to the EU (as of now, the EPF and UF).[21]

An expansive use of the treaty legal bases in response to the war in Ukraine has also emerged in the field of energy, as discussed in Chapter 5. In particular, to deal with skyrocketing energy prices, the EU resorted to Article 122 TFEU—a 'kind of "sleeping beauty" provision' in the EU treaties[22]—to adopt five emergency interventions in the energy markets, including a regulation on coordinated demand-reduction measures for gas;[23] a regulation on high energy prices;[24] a regulation on enhancing solidarity through better coordination of gas purchases, reliable price benchmarks, and exchange of gas across borders;[25] a regulation laying down a framework to accelerate the deployment of renewable energy;[26] and, crucially, a regulation establishing a market correction mechanism to protect EU citizens and the economy against excessively high prices.[27] Furthermore, the EU interpreted flexibly EU state aid law empowering Member States to subsidize firms and households, and leveraged powers in the field of industry and trade to develop a new European economic security strategy.[28]

Finally, as discussed in Chapter 6, the war in Ukraine also led the EU to revive the enlargement process, and connectedly, the reform debate. In this respect, Russia's war of aggression did not call for a new construction of the EU treaties' provisions—as ultimately the possibility for the EU to admit new members had always been enshrined in (what is now) Article 49 TEU. However, the war injected new political life into the process—with the EU beginning accession talks

---

[20] See Council Decision (CFSP) 2024/577 of 12 February 2024 amending Decision 2014/512/CFSP concerning restrictive measures in view of Russia's actions destabilising the situation in Ukraine [2024] OJ L and Council Regulation (EU) 2024/576 of 12 February 2024 amending Regulation (EU) No 833/2014 concerning restrictive measures in view of Russia's actions destabilising the situation in Ukraine [2024] OJ L.

[21] Council Decision (CFSP) 2024/1470 of 21 May 2024 amending Decision 2014/512/CFSP concerning restrictive measures in view of Russia's actions destabilising the situation in Ukraine [2024] OJ L, and Council Regulation (EU) 2024/1469 of 21 May 2024 amending Regulation (EU) No 833/2014 concerning restrictive measures in view of Russia's actions destabilising the situation in Ukraine [2024] OJ L.

[22] See de Gregorio Merino (n 1) 163.

[23] Council Regulation (EU) 2022/1369 of 5 August 2022 on coordinated demand-reduction measures for gas [2022] OJ L206/1.

[24] Council Regulation (EU) 2022/1854 of 6 October 2022 on an emergency intervention to address high energy prices [2022] OJ L261I/1.

[25] Council Regulation (EU) 2022/2576 of 19 December 2022 enhancing solidarity through better coordination of gas purchases, reliable price benchmarks and exchanges of gas across borders [2022] OJ L335/1.

[26] Council Regulation (EU) 2022/2577 of 22 December 2022 laying down a framework to accelerate the deployment of renewable energy [2022] OJ L335/36.

[27] Council Regulation (EU) 2022/2578 of 22 December 2022 establishing a market correction mechanism to protect Union citizens and the economy against excessively high prices [2022] OJ L335/45.

[28] European Commission and High Representative Joint Communication, European economic security strategy, 20 June 2023, JOIN(2023) 20 final.

CONCLUSION 153

with Ukraine and Moldova,[29] granting candidate status to Georgia[30] and Bosnia Herzegovina,[31] and relaunching the enlargement towards five other countries of the Western Balkans (Albania, Kosovo, Montenegro, North Macedonia, and Serbia), which together with Turkey had been on the waiting list to join the EU.[32] Furthermore, the war pushed the EU to deepen its ties with other regional organizations and neighbours—including the Council of Europe, the North Atlantic Treaty Organization (NATO), and a former Member State like the United Kingdom—and to experiment with new forms of institutional cooperation in the wider Europe, with the launch of the new European Political Community.

The EU's substantive response to Russia's aggression against Ukraine, at the same time, was facilitated by several *institutional* features of the EU constitution. Important measures in CFSP—a field where decisions have to be agreed unanimously by the 27 Member States in Council—were taken through the use of constructive abstention, a possibility foreseen by the second paragraph of Article 31(1) TEU, which hitherto had hardly been used, but which was triggered to activate the EPF and to setup the EUMAM Ukraine.[33] Similarly, in times of war the EU co-legislature—the European Parliament and the Council—managed to act at record speed to adopt key pieces of legislation, such as the ASAP and the UF, following its approval by the European Council. And while the Commission has constitutionally limited powers in foreign affairs and defence, under the leadership of its President Ursula von der Leyen this institution emerged as a centrepoint in coordinating the EU response to support Ukraine's war efforts, and a key international interlocutor in the coalition to deter Russia.[34] Indeed, while the European Council consolidated its position as a key decision-making body in the EU during the war in Ukraine,[35] 'the role of the Commission as a vector of integration and treaty evolution has been remarkable and even reinforced'.[36]

In sum, even if the EU constitution does not have a general emergency regime akin to those of other constitutional systems,[37] the EU 'does have its own body of law that can be described as emergency law'.[38] Consequently, as Bruno de Witte

---

[29] Council of the EU press release, 'EU opens accession negotiations with Ukraine', 25 June 2024, 577/24.
[30] European Council conclusions, 14–15 December 2023, EUCO 20/23, para 16.
[31] European Council conclusions, 21–22 March 2024, EUCO 7/24, para 30.
[32] European Commission Communication on 'EU Enlargement Policy', 8 November 2023, COM(2023) 690 final.
[33] Ramses Wessel and Viktor Szép, 'The Implementation of Article 31 of the Treaty on European Union and the use of Qualified Majority Voting', study commission by the European Parliament Constitutional Affairs Committee, November 2022, 60–63.
[34] See also Matina Stevis-Gridneff, 'Top E.U. Official is Becoming an Unexpected Wartime Leader', *The New York Times* (14 September 2022).
[35] See de Gregorio Merino (n 1) 164.
[36] Ibid 165.
[37] See eg Constitution of France, art 16.
[38] Bruno de Witte, 'Guest Editorial: EU Emergency Law and Its Impact on the EU Legal Order' (2022) 59 Common Market Law Review 3, 5.

has argued, in times of crises the EU can leverage powers as 'EU constitutional law is flexible enough to allow for creative interpretations, especially of those Treaty provisions that allow for purposive action by the [EU]'.[39] This state of affairs has been particularly visible in the EU's response to the war in Ukraine, as EU institutions 'managed to build on the emergency to push through ambitious policies and legal reforms that may redefine the EU's security and defence role, its energy policy', and other competences for the long term.[40] From this point of view, therefore, the war in Ukraine proved correct the insight from historians, political scientists, and sociologists that war is a powerful driver of state building and institutional change.[41]

Indeed, a comparison with the United States (US) highlights the point. Leaving aside the legal question—on which US constitutional scholars and judges are strongly divided—of whether the US Constitution should be interpreted as a living, or an originalist, document,[42] wars had a key role in US constitutional history. In the Founding period, the adoption of the Constitution in 1787[43] and the assumption by the US federal government of the states' debt in 1791[44] were largely driven by the Revolutionary war and the need to preserve the nascent nation. Subsequently, the Civil War contributed to experiment with a strong presidency and an emergency income tax.[45] Finally, building on the institutional transformations of the Progressive Era and the New Deal in the early 20th century, it was particularly the Second World War and the Cold War that led to a centralization of powers in the federal government, and a massive increase of the US federal budget.[46] Needless to say, this process was slow and incremental, but it eventually strengthened the US federal government and its fiscal and military powers. To some extent, the war in Ukraine has served a similar purpose in the EU, requiring it to upscale its capabilities step by step to face an unprecedented geopolitical threat on its doorstep.

---

[39] Ibid 17.
[40] Chachko and Linos (n 4) 785–86.
[41] See Miguel Centeno and Elaine Enriquez, *War and Society* (Polity 2016); and Charles Tilly (ed), *The Formation of National States in Western Europe* (Princeton University Press 1975) (famously arguing that 'war make states and states make war').
[42] Compare Bruce Ackerman, 'The Living Constitution' (2007) 120 Harvard Law Review 1737 and Antonin Scalia, 'Originalism: The Lesser Evil' (1988) 57 University of Cincinnati Law Review 849.
[43] See Max Edling, *A Revolution in Favor of Government: Origins of the U.S. Constitution and the Making of the American State* (OUP 2003).
[44] Tomasz Woźniakowski, *Fiscal Unions: Economic Integration in Europe and the United States* (OUP 2022).
[45] See Roger Lowenstein, *Ways and Means: Lincoln and His Cabinet and the Financing of the Civil War* (Penguin 2022).
[46] See Ira Katznelson and Martin Scheffer (eds), *Shaped by War and Trade: International Influences on American Political Development* (Princeton University Press 2002).

3 The inadequate constitution

While the EU's response to the war in Ukraine has so far surpassed realism,[47] the return of conventional warfare in Europe has exposed weaknesses in the EU's constitution. Indeed, Russia's aggression against Ukraine tested the limits of the EU's 'constitutional audacity'[48] and the suitability of EU primary law to deal with the issue of war. On the one hand, governance shortcomings and constraints on EU powers have hampered the EU's ability to react speedily and vigorously to the threat of hard power. On the other hand, however, some of the EU's responses to the war have raised questions in terms of compatibility with the EU constitution, especially its provisions enshrining respect for fundamental rights and the rule of law. Admittedly, the first problem is not new for the EU—as structural weaknesses in the EU substantive and institutional set-up had emerged in the EU's response to earlier crises. And the second problem is surely not new in comparative perspective—as governmental responses to emergencies have often led to silencing constitutional principles in other democratic regimes too. Nevertheless, these issues reveal EU constitutional inadequacies, which became evident in all five substantive policy areas discussed in this book.

As explained in Chapter 2, the EU response to Russia's illegal aggression against Ukraine in CFSP and Common Security and Defence Policy (CSDP) has suffered from both substantive and institutional hurdles. To begin with, Article 41(2) TEU states that 'expenditure arising from operations having military or defence implications' cannot be charged to the EU budget, significantly limiting the EU's power to fund CSDP operations. Moreover, pursuant to Articles 24 and 31 TEU CFSP measures have to be taken by the Council unanimously, subjecting decision-making to the agreement by all 27 Member States—a requirement which has watered down EU ambitions, as visible for instance in the underwhelming choice of the 2022 strategic compass to set up a Rapid Reaction Force of 5,000 men only, by 2025. Finally, treaty constraints—including the guarantee enshrined in the second paragraph of Article 42(2) TEU, to respect the neutrality of now four out of 27 EU Member States—has so far prevented the development of real EU military capabilities. Indeed, the war in Ukraine rather strengthened the role of NATO as the main provider of European security—a pattern visible in the decision of Finland and Sweden to join the transatlantic defence alliance.

At the same time, as underlined in Chapter 3, constitutional constraints and governance shortcomings have weakened the EU's effort to consolidate a fiscal capacity in response to the war in Ukraine. On a substantive level, Title II of Part VI of

---

[47] See Mark Gilbert, *Surpassing Realism: The Politics of European Integration after 1945* (Rowman & Littlefield 2003).
[48] See de Gregorio Merino (n 1) 162.

the TFEU, which sets the 'Financial Provisions' of the EU, lays out daunting rules regarding EU revenues and expenditure, with Article 310 TFEU, in particular, requiring the EU to run a balanced budget. Furthermore, at the institutional level, decision-making on fiscal and budgetary matters also remains subjected to the unanimity rule, as pursuant to Articles 311 and 312 TFEU the Council must unanimously approve the MFF and the Own Resource Decision (ORD), which also requires national parliamentary ratification. However, Member States' veto on budgetary decisions needed to empower the Commission to issue EU common debt, or to increase the size of the EU budget, complicated EU funding of Ukraine—as well as of other EU war-related initiatives like the ASAP, RePowerEU, or the Strategic Technologies for Europe Platform (STEP). Moreover, unanimity rules on budgetary matters offered room for Member States to obtain concessions on unrelated issues—a serious problem, given the worsening rule of law crisis. Hence, in 2022 and 2023 respectively Hungary vetoed the approval of the MFA+ and the UF in order to unblock funding which had been suspended under the rule of law conditionality regulation, thus delaying EU financial support to Ukraine.

In the area of justice and home affairs, discussed in Chapter 4, instead, the inadequacy of the EU constitution in time of war has emerged in a twofold way. On the one hand, institutional rules weakened the EU response—a pattern visible in the adoption of sanctions against Russia: given the need to obtain unanimity in the Council to adopt restrictive measures under Article 29 TEU, several packages of sanctions were delayed or diluted by national exceptions. Yet, on the other hand, EU action in the field of justice and home affairs raised issues of legality—both in terms of respect for EU fundamental rights and the rule of law, and compliance with international obligations. EU restrictive measures—including a sweeping ban on Russian media[49]—were subjected to deferential review by the EU judicature,[50] especially in the first years of the war.[51] Moreover, several other EU initiatives designed to inflict a cost on Russia for its illegal war have escaped judicial review *tout court*. In particular, the decision to seize the extraordinary revenues held by CSDs stemming from the immobilized assets of the RCB was shrouded in secrecy—with the draft legislative text never published—and poses significant international legal challenges, including compliance with rules on foreign sovereign immunity, which the EU is legally required to respect.

Issues of EU constitutional legality have also emerged in the EU's response to the energy crisis following Russia's aggression against Ukraine, discussed in Chapter 5. Indeed, several of the emergency measures adopted by the EU to tackle soaring energy prices have been challenged in court, with major undertakings in the

---

[49] Case T-125/22 *RT France v Council of the EU* ECLI:EU:T:2022:483.
[50] See also Case T-797/22 *Ordre néerlandais des avocats du barreau de Bruxelles v Council* ECLI:EU:T:2024:670 (upholding the prohibition to provide legal advice to Russian entities).
[51] But see Case T-743/22 *Mazepin v Council of the EU* ECLI:EU:T:2024:180 (annulling an individual listing).

petroleum sector bringing actions for annulment pursuant to Article 263 TFEU against the windfall contribution introduced by the Council regulation on emergency interventions to address high energy prices.[52] At the time of writing, none of these cases has yet been adjudicated by the EU courts. Nevertheless, it appears highly questionable from a constitutional viewpoint whether Article 122 TFEU—which contains two legal bases, a very generic one and a more specific one, 'for EU action in economic crisis situations'[53]—can be used to introduce a windfall contribution, which is effectively a one-off direct tax on legal persons. Furthermore, EU measures to support the green transition—and especially the Commission's decision to increase flexibility in the application of state aid law—have raised concerns for threatening the level playing field at the heart of the EU internal market, especially in the absence of EU funding to promote economic competitiveness.

Finally, as underlined in Chapter 6, constitutional problems in the current EU set-up have also impacted on the EU's ability to handle the enlargement and reform processes. Given the institutional requirement to decide matters related to accession unanimously, the historical decision to grant candidate status to war-torn Ukraine could be taken by the European Council in December 2023 only through the use of sleight of hand—with Hungarian Prime Minister Viktor Orban, who opposed the decision, leaving the meeting room at the time of voting. On the same token, given the constitutional principle enshrined in Article 48 TEU that changes to the EU treaties are taken by unanimity, no progress has so far occurred on the plan to prepare the EU to a union of possibly 35 or more countries. Despite pressures towards treaty changes coming from the Conference on the Future of Europe, the European Parliament and several EU Member States, the effort to deepen the EU has not significantly advanced. At the same time, geo-political pressures towards a fast enlargement have led the Commission to conveniently downplay the difficulties that candidate countries face in joining the EU—a path which raises extra challenges given the weakening of the EU internal rule of law enforcement toolbox.

In sum, Russia's aggression against Ukraine exposed the inadequacies of the EU constitution to deal with the challenge of war. Some of the constitutional problems that emerged in the EU since Russia's launched its large-scale invasion are well known. For example, the difficulties of EU decision-making when unanimity is the norm, and the complexities of funding the EU under the current rules had been identified and highlighted before.[54] Other problems, instead, became evident only during wartime. For instance, the prohibition to use the EU budget for defence purposes emerged as a new hurdle towards the development of military capabilities and a real EU defence union. At the same time, the war in Ukraine

---

[52] See eg Case T-803/22 *Petrogas E&P Netherlands v Council*, pending; Case T-802/22 *ExxonMobil Producing Netherlands v Council*, pending.
[53] See de Witte (n 38) 8.
[54] See eg Sergio Fabbrini, *Europe's Future: Decoupling and Reforming* (CUP 2019); and Alicia Hinarejos and Robert Schütze (eds), *EU Fiscal Federalism: Past, Present, Future* (CUP 2023).

interplayed with other constitutional crises that the EU has been weathering for a while—first and foremost the rule of law crisis.[55] And in turn, the rule of law crisis complicated even further the EU's response to Russia's aggression against Ukraine. Indeed, Hungary's opposition to the approval of CFSP sanctions against Russia, its delay of the adoption of the MFA+ and the UF, and its jockeying on the grant of candidate status to Ukraine—not to mention Prime Minister Viktor Orban's unilateral trip to Moscow in July 2024—are all part of a pattern of defiance vis-à-vis the EU, and have to be seen through the prism of the rule of law.

In the literature, the EU constitution has been variously defined as unfinished,[56] or un-resolved,[57] given both the fate of the European Constitution's project[58] and the work-in-progress nature of the European integration process.[59] Yet, the EU constitution should neither be a suicide pact[60] nor remain silent in times of war.[61] As the instrument of government for its 27 Member States, the EU treaties must enable the institutions they constitute to take effective and legitimate action when the EU faces existential security challenges. At the same time, as the basic charter of a polity founded on values of democracy, human rights, and the rule of law, the EU treaties should continue to speak also in wartime. This means taking seriously the shortcomings that have emerged in the EU institutional structure and system of conferred competences in the aftermath of Russia's aggression against Ukraine, without pretending that the EU response to the war has been faultless. At the same time, it also means thinking how human rights, democracy, and the rule of law can be enhanced in the EU in wartime, without too quickly dismissing as overblown concerns about lack of accountability and the EU illegitimately using crises to accrue power and exceed its mandate. This, after all, aligns with the prevailing perspective in the comparative literature studying constitutions in wars,[62] which this book has followed putting the EU square and centre for the first time, and with the engaged approach I embraced in my earlier scholarship.[63]

---

[55] See Carlos Closa and Dimitry Kochenov (eds), *Reinforcing Rule of Law Oversight in the European Union* (CUP 2016).

[56] See Francis Sneyder, 'The unfinished constitution of the European Union: principles, processes and culture' in Joseph H H Weiler and Marlene Wind (eds), *European Constitutionalism Beyond the State* (CUP 2009).

[57] See Niel Walker, 'The European Union's unresolved constitution' in Michel Rosenfeld and Andras Sajo, *The Oxford Handbook of Comparative Constitutional Law* (OUP 2012).

[58] See Giuliano Amato, Hervé Bribosia, and Bruno de Witte (eds), *Genesis and Destiny of the European Constitution* (Bruylant 2007).

[59] See John Erik Fossum and Augustin José Menéndez, *The Constitution's Gift: A Constitutional Theory for a Democratic European Union* (Rowman & Littlefield 2011).

[60] The statement that 'the Constitution is not a suicide pact' is usually attributed to US President Abraham Lincoln. For a more recent reappraisal see Richard Posner, *Not a Suicide Pact: The Constitution in a Time of National Emergency* (OUP 2006).

[61] The statement that 'the laws are silent in times of war' is originally by Cicero, Pro Milone, 11 ('*silent enim leges inter arma*'). For a more recent reappraisal see William Renquist, *All the Laws but One: Civil Liberties in Wartime* (Random House 1998).

[62] See Mary L Dudziak, *War Time* (OUP 2012).

[63] See Federico Fabbrini, *Economic Governance in Europe* (OUP 2016); Federico Fabbrini, *Brexit and the Future of the European Union* (OUP 2020).

4 To 'form a more perfect union'

This book has examined the EU constitution in time of war using the wording of the preamble to the US Constitution as an inspirational framework for the analysis. In words that are globally renowned, that preamble states that the US Constitution was ordained and established 'in Order to form a more perfect Union, establish Justice, insure domestic Tranquility, provide for the common defence, promote the general Welfare, and secure the Blessings of Liberty to ourselves and our Posterity'. In the previous chapters, this book has explored whether and how in wartime the EU constitution provided for the common defence; promoted the general welfare; established justice; ensured domestic tranquillity; and secured the blessing of liberty. Based on the conclusions reached in this study, however, it appears that the EU constitution should also tackle the remaining prong of the US Constitution's preamble: 'to form a more perfect Union'. While the EU constitution proved flexible in responding to Russia's aggression against Ukraine, it also revealed its inadequacies when faced—for the first time—with the challenge of war. Addressing these inadequacies requires reforming the EU constitution towards a more perfect union.

Speaking at the Harvard Kennedy School of Government in 2013, then European Central Bank (ECB) President Mario Draghi pointed out how the goal 'to form a more perfect Union' in the US Constitution's preamble resembled the commitment 'towards an ever closer union', enshrined in the EU treaties.[64] Yet, he argued, 'it is important to understand that the agenda facing Europe today is not adequately captured by the phrase 'ever closer union'. In my view, it is better encapsulated by wording borrowed from the Constitution of the United States: the establishment of a 'more perfect union'. By this, I mean that we are 'perfecting' something that has already begun'.[65] It is in that spirit that this book concludes by proposing how to reform the EU to make its constitution more perfect for a time of great power struggles. Based on the positive analysis of the EU legal responses to Russia's aggression against Ukraine, this book can advance the following normative recommendations.

First, at the substantive level, the EU should increase its military capabilities. This is necessary to provide credible security guarantees to partners such as Ukraine, and to act autonomously on the world stage, as discussed in Chapter 2. To this end, the prohibition set out in Article 41(2) TEU to use the EU budget for CSDP purposes should be removed. More fundamentally, however, the supranational dimension of EU defence policy should be scaled up, going beyond the current intergovernmental coordination of national defence policies. Following her re-election

---

[64] ECB President Mario Draghi, 'Europe's pursuit of a "more perfect union"', Lecture at Harvard Kennedy School, 9 October 2013, http://www.europeanrights.eu/public/commenti/commento_Draghi.pdf.
[65] Ibid.

as President of the European Commission in July 2024,[66] Ursula von der Leyen has announced that her college will now include a Defence Commissioner for the first time. But this risks being mere institutional window-dressing, in the absence of a shift of defence powers from the Member States to the EU. Consequently, the Commission should be vested with authority to require defence industries to prioritize productions, as was initially proposed in the ASAP, but then dropped, and as is now foreseen in the legislative proposal for the EDIP. Moreover, the treaties should empower the EU to have its autonomous defence—without depending on the capabilities provided by the Member States—and subject them to supranational, as opposed to intergovernmental, command and control.

Secondly, also at the substantive level, the EU should consolidate a fiscal capacity, This is needed externally to support partners such as Ukraine financially with measures like the MFA+ and the UF, as discussed in Chapter 3. But this is also needed internally to invest adequate amounts of resources in defence production with programmes like the ASAP and EDIRPA, as discussed in Chapter 2; and to support the energy transition, strategic resilience, and domestic industries without threatening the level playing field at the heart of the EU internal market, as discussed in Chapter 5. The European Parliament has called on the EU to increase the budget,[67] but the detailed list of amendments it proposed in its November 2023 resolution on a revisions of the EU treaties did not include changes to the EU rules governing public finances.[68] Yet, a structural overhaul is required to consolidate a fiscal capacity. The balance budget obligation enshrined in Article 310 TFEU should be abandoned. Article 113 TFEU should be changed to empower the EU to levy direct taxes—a much needed development, particularly as the EU incrementally increases the amount of common debt it will have to repay. And the procedures to authorize revenues and expenditures enshrined in Articles 311 and 312 TFEU must be reformed, in order to ease the EU's ability to mobilize resources.

Thirdly, from an institutional viewpoint, the EU must enhance the effectiveness of its decision-making process. This requires overcoming the unanimity rule and the introduction of qualified majority voting (QMV) in the Council of the EU for decisions related, among others, to foreign affairs, as discussed in Chapter 2; funding, as discussed in Chapter 3; sanctions, as discussed in Chapter 4; as well as in the choice to grant candidate status and start accession negotiations with third countries, as discussed in Chapter 6. A group of Member States defining themselves as friends of QMV in CFSP has proposed improving 'decision-making in CFSP in a pragmatic way, focussing on concrete practical steps and building on

---

[66] See European Parliament decision of 18 July 2024 on the election of the President of the Commission, P10_TA(2024) 0004.

[67] See European Parliament resolution of 15 December 2022 on upscaling the 2021-2027 multiannual financial framework: a resilient EU budget fit for new challenges, P9_TA(2022) 0450.

[68] See European Parliament resolution of 22 November 2023 on proposals of the European Parliament for the amendment of the Treaties, P9_TA(2023) 0427.

provisions already provided for in the [treaties]', via the *passerelle*.[69] Yet, ex Article 48(7) TEU *passerelle* cannot be used for 'decisions with military implications or those in the area of defence', so at its core the right to vote should be abolished outright across the treaties. Moreover, the EU should improve the coherence of its external representation This is needed to avoid diplomatic incidents, as that caused by Prime Minister Viktor Orban's visit to Moscow after Hungary took over the rotating presidency of the Council in July 2024. To this end, the overlapping roles of Presidents of the European Council and Commission, High Representative for Foreign Affairs and Security should be streamlined with the rotating presidency of the Council being banned from representing the EU overseas.

Fourthly, also from an institutional viewpoint, the EU must strengthen the legitimacy of its decision-making process. In particular, this requires increasing the role of the European Parliament—the sole EU institution directly elected by European citizens. Currently, the European Parliament finds itself largely in an inferior position to the Council and the European Council in deciding matters related to foreign and budgetary affairs. Moreover, the European Parliament is entirely excluded from the adoption of emergency measures under Article 122 TFEU. In her 2024 political guidelines President Ursula Von der Leyen acknowledged the issue, and stated: 'Many of the crises we have faced during the last mandate required exceptional responses, notably through the use of Article 122 TFEU. I have heard the European Parliament's view on this subject and will ensure that this tool is used only in exceptional circumstances. When it is used, I will ensure that the Commission will fully justify the use of Article 122 to the European Parliament.'[70] Yet, this is not sufficient. The European Parliament should have a voice equal to that of the Council under Article 122 TFEU and it should have full co-legislative powers in the fiscal domain, through an amendment of Articles 113 and 311 TFEU, in line with the old constitutional adage 'no taxation without representation'.

Finally, the EU also needs to strengthen its accountability checks. This is a precondition to ensure that EU actions always comply with the high human rights standards protected in the European multilevel constitutional order, and abide by the principles of international law, as discussed in Chapter 4. To this end, the power of judicial review of the European Court of Justice (ECJ) should be extended, removing the restrictions set out in the second paragraph of Article 24(1) TEU that exclude its jurisdiction in matters of foreign affairs, and the ECJ should confidently embrace its authority to ensure that the law is observed. Moreover, the EU also needs to strengthen its rule of law enforcement mechanisms, to make sure that rule of law backsliding Member States do not constitute a threat to the proper

---

[69] Joint Statement of the Foreign Ministries on the Launch of the Group of Friends on Qualified Majority Voting in EU Common Foreign and Security Policy, 4 May 2023.
[70] European Commission President-elect Ursula von der Leyen, 'Europe's Choice: Political Guidelines for the next European Commission 2024-2029', 18 July 2024, 30.

functioning of the EU, as highlighted especially in Chapters 3 and 4. Removing veto rights for Member States, as proposed above, will surely reduce the blackmailing power that each has. Beyond that, however, the procedures to activate Article 7 TEU and suspend voting rights for rule of law backsliding Member States should be eased and the Commission should embrace its authority to police respect for democracy at the state level with greater resolve.

The reform proposals advanced here require treaty changes. They also align with similar calls made by other institutional players. As pointed out in Chapter 6, the Conference on the Future of Europe, which concluded in May 2022, listed a package of recommendations for EU reforms, including proposals to enhance the EU's effectiveness and legitimacy.[71] The European Parliament has strongly supported steps to increase the EU's capacity to act, and requested the Council to call a convention to revise the EU treaties.[72] And a number of European leaders have indicated their openness towards treaty changes,[73] which is also backed by the French and German governments.[74] Furthermore, as explained in Chapter 5, two prominent high-level reports—authored respectively by former Italian Prime Ministers Enrico Letta[75] and Mario Draghi[76]—have called for ambitious EU action to deepen its internal market and strengthen its economic competitiveness. Both the Draghi and the Letta reports were commissioned by the EU institutions, so they are likely to influence the new EU institutional cycle, which started in June 2024 with European Parliament elections and the appointment of the European Commission President, and the European Council approval of a new strategic agenda for the period from 2024 to 2029.[77]

Nevertheless, as also explained in Chapter 6, the process of constitutional reform in the EU has been stagnating due to open opposition by several Member States. In fact, recent political developments across the EU, with the electoral rise of Eurosceptic parties, has further complicated the situation. Populist governments tend to disengage from international institutions and to deploy practices of criticism, extortion, and obstruction—short of exit.[78] At the same time, as is well

---

[71] Conference on the Future of Europe, Report on the Final Outcome, 9 May 2022.

[72] See European Parliament resolution of 19 May 2022 on the social and economic consequences for the EU of the Russian war in Ukraine—reinforcing the EU's capacity to act, P9_TA(2022) 0219; and European Parliament resolution of 4 May 2022 on the follow-up to the conclusions of the Conference on the Future of Europe, P9_TA(2022) 0141.

[73] See eg French President Emmanuel Macron, Speech, Strasbourg, 9 May 2022; and German Chancellor Olaf Scholz, Speech, Prague, 29 August 2022.

[74] See Report of the Franco-German working group on EU institutional reform, 'Sailing on High Seas: Reforming and Enlarging the EU for the 21st Century', Paris-Berlin, 19 September 2023.

[75] See Enrico Letta, Much More than a Market: Speed, Security, Solidarity, 17 April 2024.

[76] See Mario Draghi, The Future of European Competitiveness. Part A. A Competitiveness Strategy for Europe, 9 September 2024.

[77] See European Council conclusions, 27 June 2024, EUCO 15/24, Annex: 'Strategic Agenda 2024-2029'.

[78] See Agnese Pacciardi, Kilian Spandler, and Frederik Soderbaum, 'Beyond Exit: How Populist Governments Disengage from International Institutions' (2024) 100 International Affairs 2025.

known, the legal procedure to amend the EU treaties enshrined in Article 48 TEU requires the unanimous agreement by all 27 Member States—and ratification in each of them, in accordance with their constitutional requirements. However, the process to perfect the EU, and prepare its constitution for today's geopolitical challenges, cannot depend on the least integrationist Member State.[79] This is all the more so as *Pax Americana* is waning, and the benign protection offered by NATO is increasingly uncertain.[80] As such, bold new proposals have to be put forward to activate the law creatively to integrate defence in Europe, including that of reviving the European Defence Community (EDC) Treaty.[81]

5 Conclusion

In October 2024—1,000 days after Russia launched its large-scale invasion of Ukraine in February 2022—the prospect of the war remains deeply uncertain. While Russia continues merciless bombing of cities and civilian infrastructure, Ukraine has now counter-attacked by seizing some Russian territory. Yet, battlefield successes on both sides muddy the strategic assessment, and no reasonable diplomatic solution to the conflict appears in sight. In the meantime, however, the war in Ukraine remains violent, expensive, devastating—and ripe with unintended and transformational consequences. In fact, this is true for all conflicts and, beyond Ukraine, the world is experiencing many of these. Among others, more than a year since the beginning of the conflict in Israel and Gaza, war in the Middle East has escalated and now openly involves Lebanon, Yemen, and Iran, affecting also Syria; instability continues to persist in the Sahel and the Caucasus; and in the Far East, the rise of China, and its partnership with Russia, poses existential questions for Tawain, and peace in the Indo-Pacific.

For seven decades since its establishment after the Second World War, the EU could isolate itself from the nasty reality of war. Yet, the return of conventional

---

[79] See also Sergio Fabbrini, *A Federalist Alternative for European Governance: The European Union in Hard Times* (CUP 2024).

[80] See Joseph H H Weiler, 'Editorial. Sleepwalking Again: The End of Pax Americana' (2014) 25 European Journal of International Law 635.

[81] See further Federico Fabbrini, 'European Defense Integration after Trump's Re-Election: A Prosposal to Revive the European Defense Community and Its Legal Feasibility' (2024) European Law Journal. This paper sheds light on the EDC Treaty concluded by the six founding EU Member States at the heyday of the Cold War. It analyses the groundbreaking features of the EDC, which created a common European army, funded by a common budget, governed by supranational institutions, interconnected to NATO, and open to the accession of new countries. Moreover, the paper explains that from a legal viewpoint the EDC could be revived today: the treaty establishing the EDC was ratified by four out of six signatory Member States, Germany, Belgium, the Netherlands and Luxembourg, which never rescinded their ratification. As a result, it would only take the vote of two countries—France and Italy—to have it become operational today, fixing at once many of the problems that Europe faces in the defence realm. The paper kick-started a broader policy project I lead, called ALCIDE (Activating the Law Creatively to Integrate Defense in Europe): https://alcideproject.eu/.

warfare on the European continent shattered the EU's illusion of perpetual peace. This book has examined how the EU responded to Russia's aggression against Ukraine from an EU law perspective. The EU leveraged the flexibilities of its constitution to adopt groundbreaking measures in CFSP/CSDP, fiscal policy, justice and home affairs, energy and industry, and enlargement, and reform. However, the EU constitution also exposed its limits in wartime, and EU action raised multiple challenges in providing for the common defence, promoting the general welfare, establishing justice, insuring domestic tranquillity and security the blessings of liberty. As rivalry between great powers increases globally and the hegemonic role of the US as the world's superpower is ever more uncertain, the EU would be well advised to reform its constitution to establish a more perfect union for times of both war and peace.

Bibliography

Abely, Christine, *The Russia Sanctions: The Economic Response to Russia's Invasion of Ukraine* (CUP 2024)
Ackerman, Bruce, 'The Rise of World Constitutionalism' (1997) 83 Virginia Law Review 771
—— *Before the Next Attack: Preserving Civil Liberties in an Age of Terrorism* (Yale University Press 2006)
—— 'The Living Constitution' (2007) 120 Harvard Law Review 1737
Agnolucci, Irene, 'Will COVID-19 Make or Break EU State Aid Control?' (2022) 13 Journal of European Competition Law and Practice 3
Allison, George, 'UK Estimates 350,000 Russian Troops, 2600 Tanks Lost in Ukraine', *UK Defence Journal* (1 February 2024)
Amar, Akhil Reed, *America's Constitution: A Biography* (Random House 2005)
—— *The Words that Made Us: America's Constitutional Conversation, 1760-1840* (Basic Books 2021)
Amato, Giuliano, Bribosia Hervé, and de Witte Bruno (eds), *Genesis and Destiny of the European Constitution* (Bruylant 2007)
Angelos, James, 'The Eastern Front', *The New York Times Magazine* (29 January 2023) 41
Avbelij, Matej, Fontanelli, Filippo, and Martinico, Giuseppe (eds), *Kadi on Trial: A Multifaceted Analysis of the Kadi Trail* (Routledge 2014)
—— (ed), *The Future of EU Constitutionalism* (Hart Publishing 2023)
Ballester, Blanca, 'The Cost of Non-Europe in Common Security and Defence Policy', European Parliament Research Service, December 2013
Barber, Nick et al (eds), *The Rise and Fall of the European Constitution* (Hart Publishing 2019)
Barbera, Augusto (ed), *Le basi filosofiche del costituzionalismo* (Laterza 1997)
Bard, Petra and Kochenov, Dimitry, 'War as a Pretext to Wave the Rule of Law Goodbye? The Case for an EU Constitutional Awakening' (2021) 27 European Law Journal 39
Baroncelli, Stefania, 'The recovery and resilience facility' in Federico Fabbrini and Christy Ann Petit (eds), *Research Handbook on Post-Pandemic Economic Governance and NGEU Law* (Edward Elgar Publishing 2024) 110
Beaumont, Peter, 'Vast Russian Military Convoy May Be Harbinger of a Siege of Kyiv', *The Guardian* (1 March 2022)
Bechev, Dimitar, 'Can EU Enlargement Work?', *Carnegie Europe* (20 June 2024)
Bellezza, Simone Attilio, *Identità ucraina: storia del movimento nazionale dal 1800 a oggi* (Laterza 2024)
Benyon, Frank, *Direct Investment, National Champions and EU Treaty Freedoms* (Hart Publishing 2010)
Bickerton, Chris, *European Integration: From Nation States to Member States* (OUP 2012)
Bieber, Roland, 'The allocation of economic policy competences in the European Union' in Loïc Azoulai (ed), *The Question of Competence in the European Union* (OUP 2015) 86
Bignami, Francesca (ed), *EU Law in Populist Times: Crises and Prospects* (CUP 2020)
Bildt, Carl, 'NATO's Nordic Expansion', *Foreign Affairs* (26 April 2022)
Bilkova, Veronika, 'The Effects of the Conflict in Ukraine on the Human Rights Situation within the European Union' (2023) 8 European Papers 1037
Bin, Roberto, Caretti, Paolo, and Pitruzzella, Giovanni, *Profili costituzionali dell'Unione europea* (Il Mulino 2015)
Biondi, Andrea, 'The Rationale of State Aid Control: A Return to Orthodoxy' (2010) 12 Cambridge Yearbook of European Legal Studies 35

Blockmans, Steven, 'The EU's Modular Approach to Defence Integration: An Inclusive, Ambitious and Legally Binding PESCO?' (2018) 55 Common Market Law Review 1785

——, Editorial, 'The Birth of a Geopolitical EU' (2022) 27 European Foreign Affairs Review 155

—— 'The Impact of Ukrainian Membership on the EU's Institutions and Internal Balance of Power', International Centre for Defence and Security, November 2023

Blumenau, Bernhard, 'Breaking with Convention? *Zeitenwende* and the Traditional Pillars of German Foreign Policy' (2022) 98 International Affairs 1895

Bösche, Clara, 'La crise allemand du *Schuldenbremse*: un symptôme à prendre au sérieux en Europe', Fondation Robert Schuman Policy Paper n°734, 29 January 2024

Bradford, Anu, *The Brussels Effect: How the European Union Rules the World* (OUP 2020)

Brooke-Holland, Louisa, 'NATO enlargement: Ukraine', House of Commons Library research briefing, 20 July 2023

Bruszt, Laszlo and Jones, Erik, 'Ukraine's Perilous Path to EU Membership: How to Expand Europe without Destabilizing It', *Foreign Affairs* (30 May 2024)

Buchanan, Neil H and Dorf, Michael C, 'How to Choose the Least Unconstitutional Option: Lessons for the President (and Others) from the Debt Ceiling Standoff' (2012) 112 Columbia Law Review 1175

Cappelletti, Mauro, Seccombe Monica, and Weiler Joseph H.H. et al (eds), *Integration Through Law: Europe and the American Federal Experience. Vol. 1, Book 1* (de Gruyter 1986)

Caranta, Roberto, 'The EU's Role in Ammunition Procurement' (2023) 8 European Papers 1047

Cassese, Sabino, 'Che tipo di potere pubblico è l'Unione Europea?' [2002] Quaderni fiorentini per la storia del pensiero giuridico 109

Castagnoli, Adriana, 'Creare un Fondo UE per risarcire le imprese', *Il Sole 24 Ore* (1 May 2024)

Centeno, Miguel and Enriquez, Elaine, *War Society* (Polity 2016)

Chachko, Elena and Linos, Katerina, 'Ukraine and the Emergency Powers of International Institutions' (2022) 116 American Journal of International Law 775

Chamon, Merijn, 'The Use of Article 122 TFEU: Institutional Implications and Impact on Democratic Accountability', report commissioned by the European Parliament Constitutional Affairs Committee, September 2023

Charles, Jacob, 'The Debt Limit and the Constitution: How the Fourteenth Amendment Forbids Fiscal Obstructionism' (2013) 62 Duke Law Review 1227

Chemerinsky, Erwin, *No Democracy Lasts Forever: How the Constitution Threatens the United States* (Liveright 2024)

Chernohorenko, Illia, 'Seizing Russian Assets to Compensate for Human Rights Violations in Ukraine: Navigating the Legal Labyrinth' (2023) 8 European Papers 1067

Christoffersen, Jonas and Madsen, Michael Rask (eds), *The European Court of Human Rights between Law and Politics* (OUP 2011)

Claes, Monica and de Witte, Bruno, 'Competences' in Steven Blockmans and Adam Lazowski (eds), *Research Handbook of EU Institutional Law* (Edward Elgar Publishing 2016) 9

Closa, Carlos and Kochenov, Dimitry (eds), *Reinforcing Rule of Law Oversight in the European Union* (CUP 2016)

Cole, David and Dempsey, James, *Terrorism and the Constitution* (The New Press 2002)

——, Fabbrini, Federico, and Vedaschi, Arianna (eds), *Secrecy, National Security and the Vindication of Constitutional Law* (Edward Elgar Publishing 2013)

Cooper, Helene et al, 'Troop Deaths and Injuries in Ukraine War Near 500,000, U.S. Officials Say', *The New York Times* (18 August 2023)

Cooper, Ian, 'Support to mitigate unemployment risk in an emergency: SURE' in Federico Fabbrini and Christy Ann Petit (eds), *Research Handbook on Post-Pandemic Economic Governance and NGEU Law* (Edward Elgar Publishing 2024) 80

Craig, Paul, *The Lisbon Treaty: Law, Politics, and Treaty Reform* (OUP 2010)

Cremona, Marise (ed), *The Enlargement of the European Union* (OUP 2003)

—— 'The EU as a Global Actor: Roles, Models and Identity' (2004) 41 Common Market Law Review 553

De Baere, Geert, *Constitutional Principles of EU External Relations Law* (OUP 2008)

de Gregorio Merino, Alberto, 'The EU Treaties as a Living Constitution of the Union in Times of Crisis' (2024) 118 American Journal of International Law 162

De Vergottini, Giuseppe, *Guerra e costituzione* (Il Mulino 2004)

de Witte, Bruno, 'The European Union as an international legal experiment' in Gráinne de Búrca and Joseph H.H. Weiler (eds), *The Worlds of European Constitutionalism* (CUP 2012) 19

—— 'Constitutional Challenges of the Enlargement: Is Further Enlargement Feasible without Constitutional Change', study commissioned by the European Parliament Constitutional Affairs Committee, March 2019

—— 'The European Union's Covid-19 Recovery Plan: The Legal Engineering of an Economic Policy Shift' (2021) 58 Common Market Law Review 635

—— 'Guest Editorial: EU Emergency Law and Its Impact on the EU Legal Order' (2022) 59 Common Market Law Review 3

—— 'Legal Methods for the Study of EU Institutional Practice' (2022) 18 European Constitutional Law Review 637

—— 'The European Political Community and the Future of the EU' (2023) (on file with author)

Dermine, Paul, *The New Economic Governance of the Eurozone: A Rule of Law Analysis* (CUP 2022)

Dijkstra, Hylke and van Elsuwege, Peter, 'Representing the EU in the area of CFSP: Legal and political dynamics' in Steven Blockmans and Panos Koutrakos (eds), *Research Handbook on the EU's Common Foreign and Security Policy* (Edward Elgar Publishing 2018) 44

Dominion, Goran and Esty, Dan, 'Designing Effective Border-Carbon Adjustment Mechanisms: Aligning the Global Trade and Climate Change Regimes' (2023) 65 Arizona Law Review 1

Donnelly, Shawn, 'Clocks, Caps, Compartments and Carve-Outs: Creating Federal Fiscal Capacity Despite Strong Veto Powers' (2023) 11 Politics & Governance 92

Dopfer, Kurt, 'Toward a Theory of Economic Institutions: Synergies and Path Dependency' (1991) 25 Journal of Economic Issues 535

Draghi, Mario, 'Europe's pursuit of a "more perfect union"', Lecture at Harvard Kennedy School, 9 October 2013, http://www.europeanrights.eu/public/commenti/commento_Draghi.pdf

—— Speech at the European Parliament, 3 May 2022

—— Speech at the High-Level Conference on the European Pillar of Social Rights, Brussels, 16 April 2024

—— The Future of European Competitiveness. Part A. A Competitiveness Strategy for Europe, 9 September 2024

Dubois, Laura, 'Frozen Russian assets yielded €4.4bn in 2023, says Euroclear', *The Financial Times* (1 February 2024)

Dubout, Edouard, *Droit constitutionnel de l'Union europeénne* (Bruylant 2023)

Dudziak, Mary L, *War Time* (OUP 2012)

Duke, Simon, 'Capabilities and CSDP: resourcing political will or paper armies' in Steven Blockmans and Panos Koutrakos (eds), *Research Handbook on the EU's Common Foreign and Security Policy* (Edward Elgar Publishing 2018) 154

Eckes, Christina, *EU Counter-Terrorist Policies and Fundamental Rights: The Case of Individual Sanctions* (OUP 2009)

Editorial Comments, 'Keeping Europeanism at Bay? Strategic Autonomy as a Constitutional Problem' (2022) 59 Common Market Law Review 313

—— 'Paying for the EU's Industry Policy' (2023) 60 Common Market Law Review 617

—— 'A European Industrial Policy and the EU's Turning Point' (2024) 49 European Law Review 317

Editorial, 'The Pitfalls of Seizing Russian Assets to Fund Ukraine', *The Financial Times* (22 December 2023)

—— 'It's Time to Seize Russia's Reserves', *The Wall Street Journal* (21 February 2024)

Edling, Max, *A Revolution in Favor of Government: Origins of the U.S. Constitution and the Making of the American State* (OUP 2003)

Edmonson, Catie, 'Congress Passed an $858 Billion Military Bill. Here is what's in it', *The New York Times* (16 December 2022)

Eeckhout, Piet, *EU External Relations Law* (OUP 2012)

Eilstrup-Sangiovanni, Mette and Verdier, Daniel, 'European Integration as a Solution to War' (2005) 11 European Journal of International Relations 99
Eleftheriadis, Pavlos, *A Union of Peoples* (OUP 2020)
Emerson, Michael, 'The Potential Impact of Ukrainian Accession on the EU's budget—and the importance of control valves', International Centre for Defence and Security, September 2023
Engelbrekt, Kjell, 'Beyond Burden-sharing and European Strategic Autonomy: Rebuilding Transatlantic Security after the Ukraine War' (2022) 27 European Foreign Affairs Review 383
Erlanger, Steven, 'Ukraine Needs Shells, and Arms Makers Want Money. Enter the E.U.', *The New York Times* (8 March 2023)
Eurobarometer, May 2022, https://europa.eu/eurobarometer/surveys/detail/2772
—— June 2023, https://europa.eu/eurobarometer/surveys/detail/3052
—— May 2024, https://europa.eu/eurobarometer/surveys/detail/3216
Fabbrini, Federico 'The Role of the Judiciary in Times of Emergency: Judicial Review of Counter-Terrorism Measures in the US Supreme Court and the European Court of Justice' (2010) 28 Oxford Yearbook of European Law 664
—— *Fundamental Rights in Europe: Challenges and Transformations in Comparative Perspective* (OUP 2014)
—— *Economic Governance in Europe: Comparative Paradoxes and Constitutional Challenges* (OUP 2016)
—— and Jackson, Vicki (eds), *Constitutionalism Across Borders in the Struggle Against Terrorism* (Edward Elgar Publishing 2016)
—— and Larik, Joris, 'The Past, Present and Future of the Relations between the European Court of Justice and the European Court of Human Rights' (2016) 35 Yearbook of European Law 1
—— (ed), *The Law & Politics of Brexit* (OUP 2017)
—— 'Do NATO Obligations Trump European Budgetary Constraints?' (2018) 9 Harvard National Security Journal 12
—— *Brexit and the Future of the European Union: The Case for Constitutional Reforms* (OUP 2020)
—— 'Possible Avenues towards Further Political Integration: A Political Compact for a More Democratic and Effective Union', study commissioned by the European Parliament Constitutional Affairs Committee, June 2020
—— (ed), *The Law & Politics of Brexit. Volume II. The Withdrawal Agreement* (OUP 2020)
—— 'The Conference on the Future of Europe: Process and Prospects' (2020) 26 European Law Journal 401
——, Celeste Edoardo, and Quinn John (eds), *Data Protection beyond Borders: Transatlantic Perspective on Extraterritoriality and Sovereignty* (Hart Publishing 2021)
—— *EU Fiscal Capacity: Legal Integration after Covid-19 and the War in Ukraine* (OUP 2022)
—— (ed), *The Law & Politics of Brexit. Volume IV. The Protocol on Ireland/Northern Ireland* (OUP 2022)
—— (ed), *The Law & Politics of Brexit. Volume V. The Trade and Cooperation Agreement* (OUP 2024)
—— 'The Recovery and Resilience Facility as a New Legal Technology of European Governance' (2024) 46 Journal of European Integration 1
—— 'European Defense Integration after Trump's Re-Election: A Prosposal to Revive the European Defense Community and Its Legal Feasibility' (2024) European Law Journal
—— 'Covid-19, Human Rights and Judicial Review in Transatlantic Perspectives' (2025) 31 Columbia Journal of European Law
Fabbrini, Sergio, *Compound Democracies: Why the United States and Europe Are Becoming Similar* (OUP 2008)
—— 'Intergovernmentalism and Its Limits' (2013) 46 Comparative Political Studies 1003
—— *Which European Union? Europe after the Euro Crisis* (CUP 2015)
—— *Europe's Future: Decoupling and Reforming* (CUP 2019)

—— 'From multi-speed to multi-tier: Making Europe fit for herself' in Göran von Sydow and Valentin Kreilinger (eds), *Fit for 35? Reforming the Politics and Institutions of the EU for an Enlarged Union* (Swedish Institute for European Political Studies 2023) 69
—— *A Federalist Alternative for European Governance: The European Union in Hard Times* (CUP 2024)
Fabrichnaya, Elena and Faulconbridge, Guy, 'What and where are Russia's $300 billion in reserves frozen in the West', *Reuters* (28 December 2023)
Famà, Rosalba, 'RePowerEU' in Federico Fabbrini and Christy Ann Petit (eds), *Research Handbook on Post-Pandemic Economic Governance and NGEU Law* (Edward Elgar Publishing 2024) 128
Farrell, Henry and Newmann, Abraham, *Underground Empire: How America Weaponized the World Economy* (Random House 2023)
Favuzza, Federica, 'How does Belligerent Occupation End? Some Reflections on the Future of the Territories Occupied in the Russia-Ukraine Conflict' (2023) 8 European Papers 803
Fazio, Federica, 'Collective defence in NATO: A legal and strategic analysis of Article 5 in light of the war in Ukraine' Dublin European Law Institute working paper 2/2024.
Fisher, Louis, *The Constitution and 9/11: Recurring Threats to America's Freedoms* (University of Kansas Press 2008)
Fisk, Catherine and Chemerinsky, Erwin, 'The Filibuster' (1997) 49 Stanford Law Review 181
Fossum, John Erik and Menéndez, Augustin José, *The Constitution's Gift: A Constitutional Theory for a Democratic European Union* (Rowman & Littlefield 2011)
Frosini, Justin, 'Constitutional Preambles: More than Just a Narration of History' (2017) 2 University of Illinois Law Review 603
Fukuyama, Francis, *The End of History and the Last Man* (Free Press 1992)
Ganster, Ronja et al, 'Designing Ukraine's Recovery in the Spirit of the Marshall Plan', German Marshall Fund, September 2022
Ganty, Sarah, Kochenov, Dimitry, and Roy, Suryapratim, 'Unlawful Nationality Based Bans from the Schengen Zone' (2023) 48 Yale Journal of International Law Online 1
Genschel, Philipp and Jachtenfuchs, Markus (eds), *Beyond the Regulatory Polity?: The European Integration of Core State Powers* (OUP 2014)
Gentiloni, Paolo and Breton, Thierry, 'I 200 miliardi della Germania sulle bollette: serve una risposta europea comune e solidale', Op-ed, *Il Corriere della Sera* (3 October 2022)
German, Tracey and Tyushka, Andriy, 'Ukraine's 10-point peace plan and the Kyiv Security Compact: An assessment', study commissioned by the European Parliament Foreign Affairs and Trade Committee, January 2024
Gilbert, Mark, *Surpassing Realism: The Politics of European Integration after 1945* (Rowman & Littlefield 2003)
Gordon, Brady, *The Constitutional Boundaries of European Fiscal Federalism* (CUP 2022)
Goulard, Sylvie, *L'Europe enfla si bien qu'elle creva: De 27 à 36 Etats?* (Tallandier 2024)
Grand, Camille, 'Defending Europe with Less America', European Council on Foreign Relations Policy Brief, 3 July 2024
Gross, Oren and Ní Aoláin, Fionnuala, *Law in Times of Crises: Emergency Powers in Theory and Practice* (CUP 2006)
Hancher, Leigh, 'EU Energy Market Regulation after the 2022 Energy Crisis: the reforms so far and the challenges ahead', SIEPS European Policy Analysis, January 2024
Helwig, Niklas, 'EU Strategic Autonomy after the Russian Invasion of Ukraine: Europe's Capacity to Act in Times of War' (2023) 61 Journal of Common Market Studies 1
Higgins, Andrew, 'How Hungary Undermined Europe's Bid to Aid Ukraine', *The New York Times* (17 December 2023)
Hill, Christopher, 'The Capabiliy-Expectations Gap, or Conceptualizing Europe's International Role' (1993) 31 Journal of Common Market Studies 305
Hinarejos, Alicia and Schütze, Robert (eds), *EU Fiscal Federalism: Past, Present, Future* (CUP 2023)
——, 'Legacy and Limits of NGEU' (2024) 118 American Journal of International Law 157

Hodson, Dermot and Maher, Imelda, The Transformation of EU Treaty Making (CUP 2018)
Hoffmeister, Frank, 'Strategic Autonomy in the European Union's External Relations Law' (2023) 60 Common Market Law Review 667
Hughes, Siobhan, 'Republicans Block Ukraine Aid Bill, Putting New Pressure on Border Talks', The Wall Street Journal (6 December 2023)
Huhta, Kaisa and Reins, Leonie, 'Solidarity in European Union Law and Its Application in the Energy Sector' (2022) 72 International & Comparative Law Quarterly 733
Human Rights Watch, 'Delivering Justice for Human Rights in Ukraine', 23 May 2023, https://www.hrw.org/news/2023/05/23/delivering-justice-war-crimes-ukraine
'Hungary Welcomes Russia Crude Supply Deal after Ukraine Halts Lukoil Transit', The Moscow Times (10 September 2024)
Ikenberry, G John, After Victory: Institutions, Strategic Restraint and the Rebuilding of Order after Major Wars (Princeton University Press 2001)
Jacoby, Wade, The Enlargement of the European Union and NATO: Ordering from the Menu in Central Europe (CUP 2004)
Jacqué, Philippe et al, 'Accession Talks with Ukraine: How the EU Managed to Avoid an Hungarian Veto', Le Monde (15 December 2023)
James, Harold, 'The new globalization and the economic consequences of Brexit' in Federico Fabbrini (ed), The Law & Politics of Brexit. Volume V. The Trade & Cooperation Agreement (OUP 2024) 29
Kagan, Robert, Of Paradise and Power: America and Europe in the New World Order (Knopf 2003)
Katznelson, Ira and Scheffer, Martin (eds), Shaped by War and Trade: International Influences on American Political Development (Princeton University Press 2002)
Kelemen, Daniel, Eurolegalism (Harvard University Press 2011)
—— 'The European Union's failure to address the autocracy crisis: MacGyver, Rube Goldberg and Europe's Unused Tools' (2023) 45 Journal of European Integration 223
—— and Pavone, Tommaso, 'Where have the Guardians Gone? Law Enforcement and the Politics of Supranational Forbearance in the European Union' (2023) 75 World Politics 779
Kempf, Elena and Linos, Katerina, Shaming the Court: The German Constitutional Court's NGEU Reversal(2024) (on file with author)
Khaliq, Urfan, 'The European Union's foreign policies: An external examination of the capabilities-expectations gap' in Steven Blockmans and Panos Koutrakos (eds), Research Handbook on the EU's Common Foreign and Security Policy (Edward Elgar Publishing 2018) 459
Kirst, Niels, 'Rule of law conditionality' in Federico Fabbrini and Christy Ann Petit (eds), Research Handbook on Post-Pandemic Economic Governance and NGEU Law (Edward Elgar Publishing 2024) 195
Kolozova, Katerina, 'Freins nationalistes et impensés géopolitiques: le cas spécifique de la Macédoine du Nord', Fondation Robert Schuman Policy Paper no 748, 6 May 2024
Kosta, Vasiliki, Skoutaris, Nikos, and Tzevelekos ,Vassilis (eds), The EU Accession to the ECHR (Hart Publishing 2014)
Koutrakos, Panos, The EU Common Security and Defence Policy (OUP 2013) 252
Krotz, Ulrich and Wright, Katerina, 'CSDP military operations' in Hugo Meijer and Marco Wyss (eds), The Handbook of European Defence Policies and Armed Forces (OUP 2018) 870
Kuleba, Dmytro, 'Ukraine's EU accession brings added value and serves historic justice', Fondation Robert Schuman, 25 June 2024
Laffan, Brigid, 'Sovereignty' in Federico Fabbrini (ed), The Law & Politics of Brexit. Volume III. The Framework of New EU-UK Relations (OUP 2021) 240
Larik, Joris, Foreign Policy Objectives in European Constitutional Law (OUP 2016)
Larsen, Signe Rehling, The Constitutional Theory of the Federation and the European Union (OUP 2021)
Laughlin, Martin, Against Constitutionalism (Harvard University Press 2023)
Lefebvre, Maxime, 'L'Union européenne face à la guerre en Ukraine', Fondation Robert Schuman Policy Paper no 651, 9 January 2023

Lenaerts Koen, 'Constitutionalism and the Many Faces of Federalism' (1990) 38 American Journal of Comparative Law 205
—— and Van Nuffel, Piet, *Constitutional Law of the European Union* (Sweet & Maxwell 1999)
—— and Gutiérrez-Fons, José, 'Epilogue. High Hopes: Autonomy and the Identity of the EU' (2023) 8 European Papers 1495
Lendvai, Gergely Ferenc, 'Media in War: An Overview of the European Restrictions on Russian Media' (2023) 8 European Papers 1235
Letta, Enrico, 'A European Confederation: A Common Political Platform for Peace', *Le Grand Continent* (25 April 2022)
——, Much More than a Market: Speed, Security, Solidarity, 17 April 2024
Levitsky, Steven and Ziblatt, Daniel, *Tyranny of the Minority* (Crown Publishing 2023)
Lobina, Benedetta, 'Between a Rock and a Hard Place: The Impact of the Rule of Law Backsliding on the EU's Response to the Russo-Ukrainian War' (2023) 8 European Papers 1143
Lonardo, Luigi, 'The European Political Community: A Nebulous Answer to the Strategic Question of How to Unite Europe' (2023) 8 European Papers 755
Lowenstein, Roger, *Ways and Means: Lincoln and His Cabinet and the Financing of the Civil War* (Penguin 2022)
Macho Perez, Ana Belen, 'The Own Resource Decision (ORD) and EU public finances' in Federico Fabbrini and Christy Ann Petit (eds), *Research Handbook on Post-Pandemic Economic Governance and NGEU Law* (Edward Elgar Publishing 2024) 255
Macron, Emmanuel, Lettre pour une Renaissance Européenne, 4 March 2019 https://www.elysee.fr/emmanuel-macron/2019/03/04/pour-une-renaissance-europeenne
—— Speech, Strasbourg, 9 May 2022
Maduro, Miguel, *We the Court: the European Court of Justice and the European Economic Constitution* (Hart Publishing 1998)
Mancini, Giuseppe Federico, *Democrazia e costituzionalismo nell'Unione europea* (Il Mulino 2004)
Mariani, Paola and Genini, Davide, 'EU and NATO: The Legal Foundation of an Extraordinary Partnership' (2023) 4 Eurojus Rivista 187
Markakis, Menelaos, *Accountability in Economic and Monetary Union* (OUP 2020)
Matheson, Scott, *Presidential Constitutionalism in Perilous Times* (Harvard University Press 2009)
Mayer, Franz, 'NextGenerationEU and the Future of European Integration: Foreseeing the Unforeseeable' (2024) 118 American Journal of International Law 172
McIver, Alastair, 'Accountability: European Parliament' in Federico Fabbrini and Christy Ann Petit (eds), *Research Handbook on Post-Pandemic Economic Governance and NGEU Law* (Edward Elgar Publishing 2024) 225
McMillan, Margaret, *War: How Conflict Shaped Us* (Profile Books 2020)
Meheut, Constant, 'Thousands Wait at Ukraine Border after Polish Truckers Blockade It', *The New York Times* (10 November 2023)
Menon, Rajan and Rumer, Eugene, *Conflict in Ukraine: The Unwinding of the Post-Cold War Order* (MIT Press 2015)
Meunier, Sophie and Nicolaïdis, Kalypso, 'Who Speaks for Europe? The Delegation of Trade Authority in the EU' (1999) 37 Journal of Common Market Studies 477
Meyer, Christoph O, Van Osch, Ton, and Reykers, Y F 'From EU Battlegroups to Rapid Deployment Capacity: Learning the Right Lessons?' (2024) 100 International Affairs 181
Miller, Russel, 'Germany's Basic Law and the Use of Force' (2010) 17 Indiana Journal of Global Legal Studies 197
Mills, Claire, 'Military Assistance to Ukraine since the Russian Invasion', House of Commons Library research briefing, 30 March 2023
—— 'Military Assistance to Ukraine since the Russian Invasion', House of Commons Library research briefing, 24 September 2024
Moiseinko, Anton, 'Legal: The Freezing of the Russian Central Bank's Assets' (2023) 34 European Journal of International Law 1007

Monar, Jörg, 'Justice and home affairs' in Erik Jones, Anand Menon, and Stephen Weatherill (eds), *The Oxford Handbook of the European Union* (OUP 2012) 613

Monciunskaite, Beatrice, 'To Live and to Learn: The EU's Commission Failure to Recognize Rule of Law Deficiencies in Lithuania' (2022) 14 Hague Journal of the Rule of Law 49

Moran, Niall, 'Milestones and targets' in Federico Fabbrini and Christy Ann Petit (eds), *Research Handbook on Post-Pandemic Economic Governance and NGEU Law* (Edward Elgar Publishing 2024) 179

Moro, Domenico, *Verso la difesa europea* (Il Mulino 2018)

Müller, Jan-Werner, 'Militant democracy' in Michel Rosenfeld and Andras Sajo (eds), *Oxford Handbook of Comparative Constitutional Law* (OUP 2012) 1253

Münchmeyer, Max, 'The Principle of Energy Solidarity: *Germany v. Poland*' (2022) 59 Common Market Law Review 915

Myers, Steven Lee and Crowley, Michael, 'U.S. Accuses Russian TV Network of Conducting Cover Intelligence Acts', *The New York Times* (13 September 2024)

Nardelli, Alberto and Drozdiak, Natalia, 'EU Prepares Plan to Give Ukraine Lasting Security Commitments', *Bloomberg* (21 November 2023), https://www.bloomberg.com/news/articles/2023-11-21/eu-prepares-plan-to-give-ukraine-lasting-security-commitments

Nechepurenko, Ivan 'Georgia's Ruling Party Secures a Contentious Law on Foreign Influence', *The New York Times* (28 May 2024)

Nic Shuibhne, Niamh, *Regulating the Internal Market* (Edward Elgar Publishing 2006)

Nicolaïdis, Kalypso and Howse, Robert (eds), *The Federal Vision: Legitimacy and Levels of Governance in the United States and the European Union* (OUP 2001)

O'Brien, Carl 'Head of Defence Forces elected first Irish chair of the EU's highest military body', *The Irish Times* (15 May 2024)

O'Carroll, Lisa, 'Adding nine countries to EU to cost existing members more than €250 billion', *The Guardian* (4 October 2023)

Oberg, Jacob, 'The Definition of Criminal Sanctions in the EU' [2013] EU Criminal Law Review 273

Orenstein, Mitchel A (guest ed), 'Special Issue: Transformation of Europe after Russia's Attack on Ukraine' (2023) 45 Journal of European Integration 333

Pacciardi, Agnese, Spandler, Kilian, and Soderbaum, Frederik, 'Beyond Exit: How Populist Governments Disengage from International Institutions' (2024) 100 International Affairs 2025

Pancevski, Bojan, 'One Million are Now Dead or Injured in the Russia-Ukraine War', *The Wall Street Journal* (17 September 2024)

Patrin, Maria, *Collegiality in the European Commission: Legal Substance and Institutional Practice* (OUP 2023) 115

Pech, Laurent and Scheppele, Kim Lane, 'Illiberalism Within: Rule of Law Backsliding in the EU' (2017) 19 Cambridge Yearbook of European Legal Studies 3

Petit, Christy Ann, 'Covid-19 and financial union' in Federico Fabbrini and —— (eds), *Research Handbook on Post-Pandemic Economic Governance and NGEU Law* (Edward Elgar Publishing 2024) 43

Petrangeli, Federico, 'Il riassetto dei poteri dell'Unione europea in tempo di guerra' [2004] Osservatorio Costituzionale 39

Petrov, Roman, 'Bumpy Road of Ukraine towards the EU Membership in Time of War: "Accession through War" v "Gradual Integration"' (2023) 8 European Papers 1057

——and Hillion, Christophe, 'Guest editorial: "Accession through War": Ukraine's Road to the EU' (2022) 59 Common Market Law Review 1289

Pew Research Centre, 'Growing Partisan Divisions over NATO and Ukraine', May 2024

Piernas Lopez, Juan Jorge, 'The Transformation of EU State Aid Law … and Its Discontents' (2023) 60 Common Market Law Review 1623

——, 'State aid' in Federico Fabbrini and Christy Ann Petit (eds), *Research Handbook on Post-Pandemic Economic Governance and NGEU Law* (Edward Elgar Publishing 2024) 93

Plokhy, Serhii, *The Russo-Ukranian War: The Return of History* (Norton 2023)

Posner, Richard, *Not a Suicide Pact: The Constitution in a Time of National Emergency* (OUP 2006)
Ragonnaud, Guillaume and Mileusnic, Marin, 'Strategic Technologies for Europe Platform', European Parliament Research Service, February 2024
Rappeport, Alan, '$50 Billion in Aid to Ukraine Stalls over Legal Questions', *The New York Times* (17 September 2020)
Rasi, Aurora, 'Providing Weapons to Ukraine: The First Exercise of Collective Self-Defence by the European Union?' (2024) 9 European Papers 397
Renquist, William, *All the Laws But One: Civil Liberties in Wartime* (Random House 1998)
Riehle, Cornelia, '20 Years of Joint Investigation Teams in the EU' (2023) 24 ERA Forum 163
Rodrigues, Stéphane, 'Financing European Defence: The End of Budgetary Taboos' (2023) 8 European Papers 1155
Rogge, Ebbe, 'The European Energy Crisis, the Dutch TTF, and the Market Correction Mechanism: A Financial Markets Perspective' (2024) 17 Journal of World Energy Law and Business 184
Rosas, Allan 'From Freezing to Confiscating Russian Assets?' (2023) 48 European Law Review 337
——, and Armati, Lorna, *EU Constitutional Law: An Introduction* (Hart Publishing 2012)
Rosenthal, Lawrence, *Empire of Resentment* (New Press 2020)
Rutigliano, Stefania, 'Ukraine Conflict's Impact on European Defence and Permanent Structured Cooperation' (2023) 8 European Papers 765
Sadurski, Wojciech, *Poland's Constitutional Breakdown* (OUP 2019)
Sajo, Andras, *Ruling by Cheating: Governance in Illiberal Democracy* (CUP 2021)
Sargent, Thomas, 'Nobel Lecture: United States Then, Europe Now' (2012) 120 Journal of Political Economy 1
Sasse, Gwendolyn, *Russia's War Against Ukraine* (Polity 2023)
Scalia, Antonin, 'Originalism: The Lesser Evil' (1988) 57 University of Cincinnati Law Review 849
Scheppele, Kim Lane, 'The Treaties Without a Guardian: The European Commission and the Rule of Law' (2023) 29 Columbia Journal of European Law 93
Schick, Allen, *The Federal Budget: Politics, Policy, Process* (Brookings Institution Press 2007)
Schiek, Dagmar, 'Brexit and the Implementation of the Withdrawal Agreement' in Federico Fabbrini (ed), *The Law & Politics of Brexit. Volume III. The Framework of New EU-UK Relations* (OUP 2021) 49
Schilde, Kaja, 'European Military Capabilities: Enablers and Constraints on EU Power?' (2017) 55 Journal of Common Market Studies 37
Schimmelfennig, Frank and Winzen, Thomas, *Ever Looser Union? Differentiated European Integration* (OUP 2020)
Schmahl, Stefanie and Breuer, Marten (eds), *The Council of Europe: Its Law and Policies* (OUP 2017)
Schmidt, Vivien, 'Discursive Institutionalism: The Explanatory Power of Ideas and Discourse' (2008) 11 Annual Review of Political Science 303
Scholz, Olaf, Speech, Prague 29 August 2022
Schütze, Robert, *From Dual to Cooperative Federalism: The Changing Structure of European Law* (OUP 2009)
—— *European Constitutional Law* (OUP 2012)
—— *Foreign Affairs and the EU Constitution: Selected Essays* (OUP 2014)
Scott, Antonella, 'Caso Ariston, da Mosca un ricatto in vista del G7 sulle sanzioni', *Il Sole 24 Ore* (28 April 2024)
Seidman, Louis, *From Parchment to Dust: The Case for Constitutional Skepticism* (Beacon 2021)
Silga, Janine, 'Differentiation in the EU Migration Policy: The "Fractured Values" of the EU' (2022) 7 European Papers 909
Simon, Luis, 'The "Third" Offset Strategy and Europe's "Anti-Access" Challenge' (2016) 39 Journal of Strategic Studies 417

Skoutaris, Nikos, 'The Application of the *Acquis Communautaire* in the Areas Not under the Effective Control of the Republic of Cyprus: The Green Line Regulation' (2008) 45 Common Market Law Review 727

Slaughter, Anne-Marie, 'War and Law in the 21st Century: Adapting to the Changing Face of Conflict' [2011] Europe's World 32

Sneyder, Francis, 'The unfinished constitution of the European Union: principles, processes and culture' in Joseph HH Weiler and Marlene Wind (eds), *European Constitutionalism Beyond the State* (CUP 2009)

Snyder, Timothy, *The Road to Unfreedom: Russia, Europe, America* (Crown Publishing 2018)

Steinbach, Armin, 'The EU's Turn to "Strategic Autonomy": Leeway for Policy Action and Points of Conflict' (2023) 34 European Journal of International Law 973

Steiner, Nils et al, 'Rallying around the EU Flag: Russia's Invasion of Ukraine and Attitudes towards European Integration' (2022) 61 Journal of Common Market Studies 283

Stephen, Paul, 'Giving Russian Assets to Ukraine: Freezing Is not Seizing', *Lawfare* (26 April 2022)

—— 'Seizing Russian Assets' (2022) 17 Capital Markets Law Journal 13

Stevis-Gridneff, Matina, 'Top E.U. Official Is Becoming an Unexpected Wartime Leader', *The New York Times* (14 September 2022)

——, 'Will Turkey become a member of the E.U. now?', *The New York Times* (11 July 2023)

Sullivan, Gavin, *The Law of the List: UN Counterterrorism Sanctions and the Politics of Global Security Law* (CUP 2020)

Szep, Viktor and Wessel, Ramses, 'Balancing Restrictive Measures and Media Freedom: RT France v. Council' (2023) 60 Common Market Law Review 1384

The Economist, 'Emmanuel Macron warns Europe: NATO is becoming brain-dead' (7 November 2019)

——, 'Don't Seize: Capitalize' (2 March 2024) 10

——, 'Volodymyr Zelensky's presidential term expires on May 20th' (16 May 2024)

Thiéry, Sylvain, 'La protection temporaire de l'Union européenne en faveur des ressortissants ukrainiens: Perspectives d'avenir après un an d'application' (2023) 8 European Papers 779

Thym, Daniel, 'The Intergovernmental Constitution of the EU's Foreign, Security and Defence Executive' (2011) 7 European Constitutional Law Review 466

Tilly, Charles (ed), *The Formation of National States in Western Europe* (Princeton University Press 1975)

Torres Pérez, Aida, *Conflicts of Rights in the European Union* (OUP 2009)

Tribe, Laurence H and Lewin, Jeremy, '$100 Billion. Russia's Treasure in the U.S. Should be Turned Against Putin', Op-Ed, *The New York Times* (15 April 2022)

Tridimas, Takis, 'Competence after Lisbon: The elusive search for bright lines' in Diamond Ashiagbor et al (eds), *The European Union after the Lisbon Treaty* (CUP 2012) 47

Troianovski, Anton et al, 'Ukraine-Russia Peace Is as Elusive as Ever: But in 2022 They Were Talking', *The New York Times* (15 June 2024)

Trybus, Martin, 'The new European Defence Agency: A contribution to a common European security and defence policy or a challenge to the Community acquis?' (2006) 43 Common Market Law Review 667

Uitz, Renata, 'The Perils of Defending Rule of Law through Dialogue' (2019) 15 European Constitutional Law Review 1

Vance, J D, 'The Math on Ukraine Doesn't Add Up', Op-Ed, *The New York Times* (12 April 2024)

van der Horst, Ron, 'Illegal, Unless: Freezing the Assets of Russia's Central Bank' (2023) 34 European Journal of International Law 1021

van Gerven, Walter, *The European Union: A Polity of States and People* (Hart Publishing 2005)

Vedaschi, Arianna, *À la guerre comme à la guerre? La disciplina della guerra nel diritto costituzionale comparato* (Giappichelli 2007)

Verellen, Thomas and Hofer, Alexandra, 'The Unilateral Turn in EU Trade and Investment Policy' (2023) 28 European Foreign Affairs Review 1

Victor, Daniel, 'The Chief of Ukraine's Supreme Court has been detained and accused of taking a $2.7 million bribe', *The New York Times* (16 May 2023)

Villani-Lubelli, Ubaldo and Zamparini, Luca (eds), *Features and Challenges of the EU Budget* (Edward Elgar Publishing 2019)

von Sydow, Göran and Kreilinger, Valentin (eds), *Fit for 35? Reforming the Politics and Institutions of the EU for an Enlarged Union* (Swedish Institute for European Political Studies 2023)

Walker, Neil, 'Big "C" or Small "c"?' (2006) 12 European Law Journal 12

—— 'The European Union's Unresolved Constitution' in Michel Rosenfeld and Andras Sajo (eds), *The Oxford Handbook of Comparative Constitutional Law* (OUP 2012)

Walzer, Michael, *Just and Unjust Wars: A Moral Argument with Historical Illustrations* (Basic Books 1997)

Weiler, Joseph H H, 'Federalism without a constitution' in Kalypso Nicolaïdis and Robert Howse (eds), *The Federal Vision* (OUP 2002)

——, 'Editorial. Sleepwalking Again: The End of Pax Americana' (2014) 25 European Journal of International Law 635

Wessel, Ramses and Szép, Viktor, 'Common Foreign, Security and Defence Policy' in Ramses Wessel — and Joris Larik (eds), *EU External Relations Law* (Hart Publishing 2020)

—— 'The Implementation of Article 31 of the Treaty on European Union and the use of Qualified Majority Voting', study commission by the European Parliament Constitutional Affairs Committee, November 2022

Wood, Gordon, *The Creation of the American Republic, 1776-1787* (University of North Carolina Press 1969)

Woźniakowski, Tomasz, *Fiscal Unions: Economic Integration in Europe and the United States* (OUP 2022)

Yang, Suhong and Tan, Yudan, 'The Joint Investigation Team in Ukraine: Challenges and Opportunities for the International Criminal Court' (2023) 8 European Papers 1121

Yellen, Janet, 'American Economic Aid to Ukraine Is Vital', Op-Ed, *The New York Times* (28 February 2023)

Yoo, John, *The Powers of War and Peace: The Constitution and Foreign Affairs after 9/11* (University of Chicago Press 2005)

Zelger, Bernadette, 'EU Competition Law and Extraterritorial Jurisdiction: A Critical Analysis of the ECJ's Judgment in Intel' (2020) 16 European Competition Journal 613

Zelikow, Philip and Johnson, Sumon, 'How Ukraine Can Build Back Better', *Foreign Affairs* (19 April 2022)

Zoller, Elisabeth, 'The War Powers in French Constitutional Law' (1996) 90 Proceedings of the Annual Meeting (American Society of International Law) 46